BECOMING

YOUR OWN

PARENT

ALSO BY DENNIS WHOLEY

The Courage to Change: Personal Conversations About Alcoholism

Are You Happy? Some Answers to the Most Important Question In Your Life (released in paperback as *Discovering Happiness: How to Get the Most Out of Life*)

BECOMING

YOUR OWN

PARENT

THE SOLUTION FOR ADULT CHILDREN OF ALCOHOLIC AND OTHER DYSFUNCTIONAL FAMILIES

DENNIS WHOLEY

A
BANTAM
TRADE
PAPERBACK

BANTAM BOOKS
NEW YORK · TORONTO · LONDON · SYDNEY · AUCKLAND

*This edition contains the complete text
of the original hardcover edition.*
NOT ONE WORD HAS BEEN OMITTED.

BECOMING YOUR OWN PARENT
A Bantam Book/published by arrangement with Doubleday

PRINTING HISTORY
Doubleday edition published October 1988
Bantam edition/January 1990

Library of Congress Cataloging-in-Publication Data
Becoming your own parent: the solution for adult children of alcoholic
and other dysfunctional families/[edited by] Dennis Wholey.
    p.   cm.
Originally published: New York: Doubleday, 1988.
ISBN 0-553-34788-8
    1. Adult children of alcoholics—Psychology. 2. Problem families—
Psychological aspects.   I. Wholey, Dennis, 1937-
[HV5132.B43   1990]
362.29′23—dc20   89-1486
                                                                        CIP

Published simultaneously in the United States and Canada

*Bantam Books are published by Bantam Books, a division of Bantam Doubleday Dell
Publishing Group, Inc. Its trademark, consisting of the words "Bantam Books" and
the portrayal of a rooster, is Registered in U.S. Patent and Trademark Office and in
other countries. Marca Registrada. Bantam Books, 666 Fifth Avenue, New York, New
York 10103.*

PRINTED IN THE UNITED STATES OF AMERICA

0 9 8 7 6 5 4 3 2 1

CW

This book is for—
David and Gayle, Michael, Scott,
Chuck, Debbie, Rich, Richie,
Michelle, Paul, Philip, Ed,
Joan, Steve, Ann, Tony,
Robin, Bill, Richard, Arthur,
Nonie, Dottie, Steve, Margie,
—and my dear mother.

ALICE·AUDREY·BETH·BRIAN·DICK

HARRY·JAN·JEFF·JIM·KAREN

LYNN·MANOLITO·MARY·MICHAEL

CLAUDIA BLACK, PH.D.

JOHN BRADSHAW

CATHLEEN BROOKS

STEPHANIE BROWN, PH.D.

TIMMEN L. CERMAK, M.D.

TERENCE T. GORSKI, M.A.

EARNIE LARSEN

ROKELLE LERNER

JOAN PHENEY, M.S.W.

ROBERT SUBBY, M.A.

SHARON WEGSCHEIDER·CRUSE

CHARLES L. WHITFIELD, M.D.

ACKNOWLEDGMENTS

My sincere thanks go to all of the contributors to *Becoming Your Own Parent*. It is their book as well—a collective effort.

I am especially grateful to my good friend and researcher David Dodd. We have traveled a lot of miles together—through three books now and a lot of living. David's encouragement and support make my work easier and my life happier. He is an excellent writer and reporter and a very special person.

I cannot begin to express my appreciation for my typist, Robin (Stawowczyk) Thompson. Her work is the very finest. Robin and I have also done three books together, and this one turned out to be the most complex. Robin has spent hundreds of hours transcribing, typing, and retyping transcripts, edited material, and the final manuscript. She has done a wonderful job. Robin received a very important assist at a crucial time in our work from Sandy Forsyth. This is Sandy's second time as a member of the team, and I thank her for her fine work too.

My friend and former coworker at WTVS Greg Fuhrman handled all of the audio engineering duties at our group meetings. He is a wonder both professionally and personally. On our audio setups we were assisted by Lynwood Gardner, Mike Gardner, and Mark Pilarchio. My thanks also to Julie Scott and the staff at the Radisson Hotel in Southfield, Michigan—the site of our group meetings.

I also thank Jan, Denise, Kathleen, Don, Dina, Denise, Gloria, Bobbie, and Barbara for their assistance in settng up the meetings with the experts.

Of the many people at Doubleday I wish to express my appreciation first of all to my editor, Paul Bresnick, not only for his belief in my past work but, most important, for his commitment to this book. His assistance and counsel have been invaluable. Also at Doubleday I want to thank: Keith Dawson for his editorial assistance with the manuscript; copy editor Leland Lowther for making the words flow on these pages; Alex Gotfryd for an inspired jacket design; Peter Kruzan and his staff for clear and tasteful book designing; Jackie Deval, Lisa Dunkley, and the energetic folks in the Publicity Department; Nancy Stauffer and everyone else in Subsidiary Rights; Dick Heffernan, Jackie Everly, Michael Carter, and the entire sales and marketing team. Thanks also to Mark Garofalo and Amy Strassler.

If there is one person who can make me believe in myself when it comes to writing books, it is my agent and friend, Richard Pine. He is terrific. Richard and his father, Arthur—both excellent literary agents—are two people with incredible enthusiasm and integrity; we can all learn from them. They were ably assisted by Lori Andiman and Mimi Mork as this book was coming together.

I also want to express my gratitude to two major figures in the publishing world—Austin Olney, who gave me my first opportunity to write books, and Tom Congdon, who encouraged me on this project way back when I needed to focus my ideas.

On a very personal note I want to thank Paul Kasper, Jerry Stanecki, and Rev. Ed Pritchard for keeping me headed in the right direction; and Rev. Vaughan Quinn, O.M.I., has a fond spot in my heart, always. Sharon Kraft once again helped me out at a crucial time on this book and I appreciate her support always.

Three very close friends died before seeing this book, but the friends and families of Rev. Morty Fox, Rocco Radice, and Joe Carmitchell should continue to know about their importance in my life.

Last I want to thank my close friends and family for their support, friendship, and love during the preparation of this book and during my life. To my dear mother and my brothers and sisters, I will add that what is presented on these pages is the very personal experience of my own youth and its impact on my life. Your experience and recall may be different. If this book causes you any hurt, I hope you know it was not my intent. I love you too much for that.

CONTENTS

PART III
THE SOLUTION

BECOMING YOUR OWN PARENT

NAME	AGE	FAMILY BACKGROUND
Alice	Mid-30s	Alcoholism
Audrey	Late 40s	Alcoholism, Sexual Abuse, Abandonment
Beth	Late 20s	Workaholism
Brian	Early 40s	Physical and Sexual Abuse, Alcoholism
Dick	Late 50s	Compulsive Gambling
Harry	Early 40s	Workaholism, Depression, Suicide
Jan	Early 50s	Alcoholism
Jeff	Early 30s	Workaholism, Eating Disorder, Physical Abuse
Jim	Late 50s	Alcoholism
Karen	Early 30s	Prescription Drug Addiction
Lynn	Late 30s	Foster Homes, Adoption
Manolito	30	Alcoholism, Eating Disorder
Mary	Mid-20s	Alcoholism, Workaholism
Michael	Early 40s	Divorce

MARITAL STATUS	OCCUPATION	COMPULSIONS OR ADDICTIONS
Married, One Child	Teacher	Food
Married, Two Children	Teacher	Co-dependency, Worry
Single	Television Producer	Relationships with Emotionally Unavailable Men
Married, Two Children	Publicist	Work, Food, Money
Married	Retired Salesman	Gambling, Alcohol
Married	Therapist	Cocaine, Alcohol
Separated, Four Children	Condominium Saleswoman	Alcohol
Married, Three Children	Collections Supervisor	Alcohol, Work
Married, Five Children	Auto Line Inspector	Alcohol
Divorced	Marketing Executive	Co-dependency, Emotionally Abusive Relationships
Divorced, One Child	Social Service Caseworker	Marijuana
Single	Free-lance Copywriter, Scriptwriter	Alcohol, Work, Food, Drugs
Single	Photographer	Food, Alcohol, Drugs
Twice Divorced, Two Children	Lawyer	Alcohol

PART

I

THE

GROUP

1

THE
FIRST
STEP

This is a book about pain. It is about the emotional pain of millions of American adults who were severely damaged by their childhood.

These people are not lying on a bed in a mental institution, nor are they the abuse victims we read about in the newspaper. They are not the criminals and the suicides who act out their frustration and hopelessness.

These Americans go to work, pay their bills, vote, and often raise families. However, they also get involved in unhealthy relationships, fall into compulsive behaviors, and have little or no self-esteem. They react to life as victims, live in a world of denial, and try to control the actions of others. They feel "different," struggle to survive, and are often depressed.

These people are the "adult children" of dysfunctional homes. These millions of America's walking wounded are our friends, neighbors, and family members. They are us. "They" may be you. If you grew up in a dysfunctional home and made it through to adulthood, you are an "adult child."

While the experts may debate an acceptable definition of the term "dysfunctional," they are quick to agree that dysfunctional homes are the families of alcoholism, physical and sexual abuse, physical neglect, compulsive gambling and eating disorders, workaholism, incest, legal and illegal drug addiction, and emotional abandonment.

We are who we are, because of our past. Our past is real and often very ugly. This is a book about breaking through the denial of family secrets and real problems that were not talked about openly and frequently never acknowledged. This is not a book about blaming parents; it is an honest examination of facts. It is a look at the "whats" of people's lives rather than the "whys."

You are about to meet an incredible group of people who have been fortunate enough to discover not only what was wrong with their lives but also the way to make it right. If the group's members have a common denominator that caused them to seek help, it is pain.

Becoming Your Own Parent is a book about hope. These "adult children" are trying to find out who they really are. They are heroic in their search, truthful in their self-evaluation, open with their feelings, and willing to do what is necessary to bring about change. Every one of them is a remarkable human being. These are not weak people. They have dignity and courage. Learning from each other's pain, they have discovered that the protective patterns of behavior developed by a child in a dysfunctional home have damaging consequences when that child becomes an adult. The fourteen people you will get to know demonstrate the beauty of human beings as survivors.

You are now in a hallway. The sign on the open door reads, "ACA" or "COA" or "ACOA" or "ACDF." The sign translates the same way: Adult Children of Alcoholics; Children of Alcoholics; or Adult Children of Dysfunctional Families.

There are fifteen chairs around a large table. You are the newcomer. You are welcome. This will be like no meeting you have ever attended. It will be different from a meeting at work, a family gathering around the dinner table, or a group of friends at a local restaurant.

The group members will speak one at a time. There will be no interruptions or cross-talk. They will concentrate and listen hard. What they say will be amazingly honest. This meeting is about life and death.

Around the table sit a lawyer, a therapist, a television producer, a social worker, a collections supervisor, a real estate saleswoman, two schoolteachers, a public relations executive, an auto line inspector, a marketing consultant, a free-lance advertising copywriter, a former salesman, and a photographer. There are seven men and seven women. Half of the group grew up in alcoholic homes; the rest come from other types of dysfunctional homes.

This meeting and all the other meetings in subsequent chapters have been put together especially for you. Keep an open mind. If you can identify with the stories and understand the pain, you are in the right place. You probably belong here.

These could be the most important meetings of your life. This book of meetings can change your life forever—if you need it and if you let it.

Karen is a marketing executive for one of the "big three" auto companies. Born and raised in Indiana, Karen is divorced and in her early thirties.

KAREN ► Hi, I'm Karen. I'm an adult child of a prescription drug addict. I came into the ACA program through the grace of God, and my life's never been the same since then. My mother is the addict in my family. She is addicted to tranquilizers and has been for many years.

To the outside world we looked like a typical American family, but inside things were really crazy. As a small child I can remember doctors coming to our house and giving her shots to calm her down. We lived next door to a veterinarian, and in later years he would get my mother Miltowns in a quart mayonnaise jar. Those came in handy when she would attempt suicide.

I had a lot of years of unhappiness as a child. I went away to college and separated myself geographically from the family. As I got older I entered into one relationship after another that was just like my parents' in so many ways. The women in my family —both of my grandmothers and my mother—were the strong, domineering type, and the men were always weak and passive. I tended to choose that kind of man in my relationships as well. I was always taught that you manipulate people to get what you want; you never ask directly for it. I was shown how to do that very well.

When my own marriage to an alcoholic ended a few years ago, I realized my life was really unmanageable. I was desperately unhappy and suicidal. Outwardly I had the trappings of success: a good education, a good job, and a nice home. I had repeated my family's pattern very well.

I hit bottom about three years ago and started to climb out. My life is going so well now; there's no comparison. I guess I had to live through all of it to get to where I am now. It was very crazy.

Alice is a special education teacher who works with learning disabled and handicapped students. She is in her mid-thirties. Raised in Michigan, Alice is married to a recovering alcoholic and is the mother of a daughter two and a half years old.

A L I C E ▸ I'm Alice. I'm the adult child of an alcoholic. My mother had some fairly serious illnesses. She had cluster headaches with each pregnancy. When I was nine months old, she got pregnant with her second child and just checked out.

I spent a lot of my early childhood in my bedroom, where my mother placed me. I like to believe it was to protect me from the anger that was caused when I made noises in the house. I think she felt she would abuse me. My grandmother talks still about the tremendous fear she had when my mother would call her up and say, "Come and get these kids. I'm going to kill them." My grandmother would drive very rapidly over very poor country roads to save us because she did believe that my mother *was* going to kill us. My mother was very depressed, and her depression was acted out in the homicidal rage that she felt. She had five pregnancies in six years, so during my early years she was sick all the time.

Although my dad was quiet, he was there for me and I worshipped him. I'm not sure that my dad's alcoholism really got rolling until I was in elementary school, but my mother was so deathly ill that I kind of raised myself. I was at my grandmother's house a lot. Through therapy, I've been able to go back and figure out I was sexually abused while I was at my grandmother's house by one of my uncles, who was an adolescent at the time.

I was a good girl. I was a little bit like a piece of woodwork: I didn't attract a lot of attention and I did not rock the boat in any way. But the humiliation of dad's drinking and my mother's lack of nurturing were pervasive. It's something I walked away with, and it has ruled my life in lots of ways.

Jeff is a collections supervisor for a Fortune 500 company. He was raised in Michigan and is in his early thirties. He has been married for eleven years and is the father of three children. His wife is a recovering alcoholic.

JEFF ► My name is Jeff. My father and mother are not alcoholic. My father owns his own shoe-repair shop and makes shoes by hand. When I was growing up, my mother usually worked outside the home.

As a kid, I spent a lot of time working in the family business. It was required in our family that when we reached an age where we could show some responsibility, we would work on a regular basis. I put in my first forty-hour work week when I was eight. I was a master-craftsman shoemaker at fourteen, opened up my own store at fifteen, and at sixteen had my own ulcer and nearly died.

My father was overweight and had diabetes and undiagnosed high blood pressure for a number of years. He was very forceful with us children and quite frequently went into rages and beat us when we didn't perform exactly as he expected us to. He really verbally and physically abused me when it came to discipline.

I have three children now. I've been married eleven years. A lot of the negative behaviors that I experienced with my father while I was growing up repeated themselves in me in the way I dealt with my children. I did not like that at all. I didn't want to carry on with my children in the rageful fashion I was exhibiting toward them.

There's a lot of pain there in the way that my childhood went, but there's hope there, too, because of choices I've made in my life and a real willingness to let things get better for me. There's so much of me that is my father, but the ACA program has helped me to be aware of these things. If there need to be changes made, then I can work toward those changes.

Mary recently graduated from college and is a professional photographer. She was raised in New York and New Jersey. Mary is single and is in her mid-twenties.

MARY ▸ Hi, my name's Mary. I come from a family where both parents are still abusing alcohol. My father is both an alcoholic and a workaholic.

I grew up in a big house in New Jersey and a penthouse on Fifth Avenue. I went to boarding school. I've flown on the Concorde, traveled around the world twice with my father, and have a family house on Cape Cod.

My parents' marriage was never a good one. They always fought and I always thought it was my fault. I have these childhood memories that at night the goblins would come out and craziness would happen. The sun went down and my parents went at it. One night my mother had a knife in her hand and went after my father, who was one of the most well respected men on Wall Street at that time. But when the sun came up, my father said, "No, no, your mother didn't do that; everything's fine." I started to become more and more crazy, thinking, "Oh my God, I'm not seeing these things," but I was seeing them. I just didn't trust myself. For years I was told, "No, no, no, no, you didn't see that." You don't make up that your mom had a knife in her hand going after your dad. Kids don't do that.

I come from a family of a lot of money, and the denial of reality can be covered with money.

I was sent away to boarding school at fifteen, which was probably the kindest thing my parents could have ever done for me. When you get sent away to an all-girl boarding school, there's not a whole hell of a lot to do. That's where my addiction with food started. It was the obsession to be the perfect person. I knew things in my house were falling apart, but I thought as long as I looked good and looked like I had my shit together, it would be okay. In an all-girl WASP boarding school, having a perfect figure was something a lot of us knew how to do. Of course, I drank too, and my drug abuse started in college.

I am where I am today because of how I was raised. It's really amazing—the power our parents can have over us as children and how we can carry those ghosts with us.

Brian is a public relations executive in his early forties and has a six-figure income. He was raised in Ohio, is married, and has two children, a son age fifteen and a daughter age seventeen. His wife is a recovering alcoholic.

BRIAN ► I'm Brian. I'm an adult child of two adult children, which is an insight I've only had in the last couple of years.

My dad was an abused child. At least he made it. Of four brothers, two died, one very mysteriously. No one ever found out how that boy died, but the stories were that he was stuffed to death with food. Because of that, my granddad, who was an alcoholic, went out to shoot himself, but didn't. My mother's father also is an alcoholic. I didn't realize any of this until this period of recovery began. I still fight the belief that I had a wonderful childhood. Each time I talk about it, that breaks down the denial.

My mother talked about how much her dad hated her, picked on her, called her names, and ridiculed her. All of that was passed on. When I was a kid, my dad when he'd been drinking would say that I was a bad kid, I was a son of a bitch, I was going straight to hell. When he'd come home and I'd misbehaved, he'd rip me out of my bed, throw me in the closet, lock the door, and leave me there. I was beaten. He broke paddles over me, and he'd hit me with a thick rubber hose.

I was sexually abused by my mother. Most of this I've learned through regression therapy, where you go back to a very early age and reexperience early events firsthand. This is where I reexperienced the closet, the beatings, and my dad trying to choke me to death, which was another of his favorite tricks.

As a kid, I took out on animals the abuse I got. I killed a pet turtle, and I killed a pet cat that belonged to the neighbors. I was called "cat killer" as a kid. I was constantly teased for being too fat, too tall, and not coordinated. I also went through a period when I was sure I was so bad that I'd been castrated. It was a classic victim role. So I was a great one for pleasing my parents. Love was always a very conditional thing. Perform, get good grades, be a star student. I certainly couldn't be a star athlete; I was too hung up to do that.

I spent years as a workaholic and ended up feeling grossly inadequate and a failure. By most standards, I was "successful" —a large house, three new cars, a swimming pool in the backyard, a wife and two kids. I achieved the absolutely perfect American dream shit and I was miserable.

Manolito was born and raised in San Juan, Puerto Rico. He is thirty years old, single, and currently works as a free-lance scriptwriter, copywriter, and publicist.

MANOLITO ► My name is Manolito. I'm the son of an alcoholic. My mother is the alcoholic in my family, and she continues to be a daily drinker.

My mother was an undisciplined disciplinarian. My father was pretty harsh too. I was punished with a belt a lot. I don't remember the things that I did which would have made me deserve being hit eleven or twelve times with a belt. I would have scars after being belted. I remember begging for compassion like a slave or a prisoner. Those beatings would make me feel I wasn't worth anything. In addition to physical punishment, I also received a lot of emotional abuse from my mother. She was always talking about suicide and about her resentments against my grandmother and her mother-in-law. There was a whole lot of negativity. If I look at a soap opera today on the television, I say, "This is soft." Where's the trauma, where's the drama, where's the conflict?"

What kind of outlook could I expect in life if I was presented daily with the bleakest, loudest, most abusive, and painful kind of drama to deal with at the age of two, three, or four? I never knew when the storm was going to start.

By the time I finished college, I was a drug addict and alcoholic. I hadn't had a real relationship throughout my entire life. I'm gay, but gay people do have relationships. I didn't have a problem with my sexual preference. My parents had more problems than I did accepting it.

I began to go to ACOA meetings in Miami. There I began to deal with the issues of being an adult child of an alcoholic.

Beth is a television producer. She was raised in Massachusetts and New Jersey, is single and in her late twenties.

BETH ▸ I'm Beth. On both sides of my family there is a lot of alcoholism; however, my own parents are not alcoholics. I have uncles, aunts, and cousins who are alcoholics. My father was a workaholic. He came from an alcoholic family, and I didn't know until about a year or two ago that the effects of his not being emotionally available damaged all of the children in our family.

My father always worked at a regular job. He also took on civic activities and was elected to political office. He would come home every night at six-thirty and dinner would be on the table at six-thirty-five. He would be home for about an hour, and then he, or both of my parents, would go out to meetings. So from seven-thirty on, it was baby-sitters five nights a week from when I was about six until I was old enough to baby-sit myself.

I think the biggest effect on my life of having an emotionally unavailable father is that I get myself into relationships with emotionally unavailable men. Most of the guys I've gone out with, and I've been engaged to two of them, were alcoholic. One out of five long-term relationships hasn't been an alcoholic, although I saw him lately and he might be headed that way, unfortunately.

I have a sister who married an alcoholic and a sister who had some problems with alcohol herself. My own problems have mostly been in relationships. As the girlfriend of alcoholics, I'd go out with them and drink and listen. They'd tell a lot of stories, but when it came time for them to talk about what they wanted out of life, or what their goals and aspirations were, they really had nothing to say.

It's been hard finding intimacy in my relationships. I'm in group therapy now, and I've been in private counseling for about ten months. I'm searching.

> Lynn is a social worker and is in her late thirties. She was born and raised in Michigan; she is divorced from her husband of eleven years and is the mother of a five-year-old daughter.

LYNN ▸ Hi, I'm Lynn. I was placed in a social-service foster home for about a month immediately after I was born. I was a "failure to thrive baby" during that month, and the agency people didn't know whether it was because I wasn't getting the proper care in this home or the consequence of being pulled away from my natural mother. After about a month, they put me in another foster home, where I stayed for about six months. I seemed to do a lot better in that second home. However, foster mothers did not have the option of adopting back then, so I was put up for adoption and came to my family when I was about seven months old.

My mother is very businesslike, very cold and distant. She never laughs and doesn't smile a whole lot. She isn't a very warm, feeling person at all. Whenever I came to her with concerns as a child, she would go in her bedroom, shut the door, and wait till my dad got home. She never dealt with me head-on about anything, and my perception is, as a kid, I made her very anxious. Being an adopted child, my fear all along was that if I made a wrong move, they'd take me back to wherever I came from and get me a new set of parents. Like the kid in *Oliver*, I had these fantasies that if I didn't keep my mouth shut, I was going to be back at the orphanage and I'd be with all the other orphans eating gruel. I understand now that most adopted children have this fear.

My father's very sensitive. He's just a wonderful man. It was always, "Whatever you're going to do I'm behind you." He has never criticized me and he's sixty-seven years old. I'm his "shining light." Thank God for him, because he compensated really well for my mother. I'd always try to win my father away from my mother because I liked my father and never liked my mother. I would tell my father, "I don't like her. I don't know why you married her."

I was sexually abused by an older cousin for about two years, and I never told my parents, because I felt like they really couldn't handle that and I'd be out on the street. From my perspective, I had a real difficult childhood. I was very unhappy.

I met my ex-husband in graduate school. He turned out to be an alcoholic, and after eleven years of marriage, I packed my bags and left with my two-year-old daughter. We were divorced two years ago. I used to say I left because of my daughter, but I've finally come to realize I left because of me.

In a way, leaving my husband was the best thing I could do for me as well as for him. I'm carving out my own identity now for the first time. I'm not someone's wife or someone's kid. I'm a mother myself. I'm doing well professionally. This is the second half of my life. I feel pretty positive now.

Jim, a line inspector for one of the major auto companies, was born and raised in Kentucky. And is in his late fifties. Twice previously married, Jim is the father of five daughters. His present wife is a recovering alcoholic and adult child.

JIM ▸ Hi, I'm Jim. I come from a family where my father drank. In my case, my father was much more generous and pleasant when he drank than when he didn't. Mother was very protective of his needs.

Dad was very insecure, afraid, and angry, and he had a poor self-image. Something in his childhood spilled over into my childhood because I grew up afraid. We got used to his strong personality changes. He was a Jekyll/Hyde. He was fun and generous when he drank. He was an angry, mean father when he was sober because he was so insecure. He would yell and be very impatient if we weren't doing exactly what he thought we should be doing. He used to pull the hairs on the back of my neck or slap me in the back of the head when he was angry. His abuse was verbal as well as physical.

My true identity in high school as a success story came from being six foot four, looking older, and having false ID. I was able to go buy beer when no one else could buy it. They needed me, I felt needed, and the beer was free. All I had to do was go get it, and I couldn't afford it anyway.

In the service I used my ability to drink not to buy. I could consume a lot. I became very famous for my ability to drink almost anyone in the outfit under the table.

I'm an alcoholic, and the reason I came into the adult children program is because I want quality sobriety. The only way I can get quality sobriety is to deal with those issues I experienced as a child.

Audrey is a junior high school remedial-reading teacher in her late forties. Audrey, who was raised in Kentucky, Alabama, and Mississippi, is married and the mother of two children, a son twenty-one and a daughter twenty-five.

A U D R E Y ▸ Hi, I'm Audrey. I was born in the South in the late 1930s. My father was a coal miner and struggled to take care of us four children. Something happened when I was about age five. There was a lot of commotion in the house, a lot of arguing, fighting, and screaming. I had no idea what was going on, but I remember very vividly my father making it known the next day that he was going to leave the family. The day he left there was a lot of commotion and crying. I remember sitting in the backyard on a stump. I cried all day, and I thought that if I cried and pleaded enough, he would not go. But he went into town and came back with a cardboard suitcase. He literally tore the house apart packing his things to go. I don't remember my mother coming out to console me, even though I was crying. I do remember him coming out with that suitcase. He said something to me and he walked right down the railroad track. At that time, we lived at the end of the railroad track. Some kids wonder where the railroad tracks end. I knew where they ended; they ended with our house.

When I was about six or seven, my mother's grandfather passed away in Mississippi, and she went there for the funeral. While she was attending the funeral that day, her mother had a stroke and died right there in the church. So she stayed there in Mississippi to bury her mother also. She came back and packed us up, and we went off to Mississippi to live in her mother's home.

I was always hungry. Sometimes during the school day I would not have the quarter for lunch. I would hope that my mother would show up to bring my lunch money. If she didn't, I would walk home. There was no food there, but at least the other kids didn't know that I was not having lunch. I recall once going home and there was absolutely nothing there except a bottle of ketchup. I put that in a bowl, added water, stirred it and that was lunch. It was during this time I became aware of what was happening to my body and to my teeth. I was very aware of the bones sticking out of my elbows and knees.

I have always been afraid of success and afraid of failing. I have become super-responsible, a real high achiever. I was told by my high school teachers who cared for me the most to always be the best. They always said that because you're black, you're going to have to be much, much better than the white person in order to compete. So I grew up with "It's never good enough." I have to do more and more and have to be a super-educator, a supermother, a superwife.

Now I want off that merry-go-round. I just want to be me. I don't want all of the struggling and striving; I just want the peace. I no longer want to be a victim of my situation.

Dick was raised in Michigan. He is retired from a career in sales and currently takes care of family business for his mother and aunt, who are both legally blind. In his late fifties, Dick and his wife, who is a recovering alcoholic, have been married for twenty-one years.

D ICK ▸ My name's Dick. I'm an alcoholic and a compulsive gambler. My childhood was very strange. There was no love in my family whatsoever. I never heard the words "I love you" spoken by either my mother or my dad to each other or to any of us children. I was brought into this world and that was that.

My father was a compulsive gambler. Neither of my parents had a drinking problem, but they both had emotional problems.

I never wanted my father around when I was with friends. I never had any kids over to the house, because I never knew when he was going to act up. I didn't want to be embarrassed by him. I didn't want him at school either, because I was afraid that somebody would recognize he was a con artist. I didn't want my mother to be around anybody either because of her big-shotitis. She would carry on a conversation like she knew everything. She put on an image of a loving mother and a very religious person, but I knew she was nothing but a phony.

My father hated his father because his father was a compulsive gambler. My mother hated her mother because my grandmother had taken an opportunity for some education away from my mother and given it to another daughter. There wasn't any love in them and that was passed on to us children. To be brought up in a home like that was difficult—very difficult.

Michael, an attorney in private practice, was born in Houston, Texas. He is in his early forties and has been married and divorced twice. He is the father of a son, six, and a daughter, twelve.

M ICHAEL ▸ Hi, my name is Michael and I'm the adult child of a dysfunctional home.

The only thing unique about my childhood was the structure of the family. It was not a home with a typical mother, father, and children. My folks were separated when I was eighteen months old, and my mother took me and returned to her parents' home.

There was no dad, and yet, there were three dads in that house. There were two uncles and my grandfather. I think I had two mothers as well—my own and my grandmother. I was raised by a committee.

I've heard about beatings, abject poverty, violent drunkenness, knives being raised by Mom against Dad. I can relate to none of those things.

As a child I had people telling me how good I was, people reminding me that God makes only perfect things and that I was made in His image and likeness. I had people who did everything to make sure that I had what I needed. Although I cannot identify with the horror stories of incest, physical abuse, and alcoholism, the fact is, I have a lot in common with people who were raised in those environments.

When I finished my two college degrees and did my stint in the Marine Corps, I promptly hit the civilian world and came to a rip-roaring halt, and I have had a problem getting on with my own life in a creative, productive, fulfilling way since then. For fifteen years I have felt unable, unentitled, and unwilling to do that, flogging myself all along the way because, after all, I had this perfect upbringing.

What I have come to understand about the dynamics of my family is that there was an oppressive tension in the house, a sense of walking on eggshells that neither I nor anybody else in my family ever understood and nobody ever admitted to. But I certainly felt it. Each of us knew in our own way that there was something not quite right. Each of us wanted to fix it. Each of us was unable to talk about it. Each of us cared very much about the others, and nobody had any goddamn idea how you go about clearing the fog.

There was a house full of people. None of them knew what normal was. None of them was comfortable talking about their feelings. None of them was comfortable with anger or confronting another human being, especially a family member about anything that might raise any feelings except warm, sweet love. What was created out of that was a tremendous denial and avoidance system. What they did with little Michael was throw lots of nice-sounding words and toys his way and tell him how good he had it.

Early on, I began living my life terrified to make a wrong move, fearing that something god-awful, horrible would happen and that it would be completely my fault. Recently I have begun to experience the recapturing of the person that I was born to be. Without the support groups, I don't think any of that would have happened. I'm grateful to be gradually getting away from the self-judgment and accepting the kid in me.

Jan, a sales person for a condominium contractor, was born and raised in California. She is now in her early fifties. Recently separated from her husband after a thirty-two-year marriage, she is the mother of four children ranging in age from twenty-three to thirty-one.

JAN ▸ Hi, I'm Jan. My eighty-six-year-old father is a practicing alcoholic, and all four of my grandparents were alcoholic. I'd like to tell you I didn't repeat the same life-style myself and the same life pattern bringing up my own kids, but I can't tell you that. I'm an alcoholic and three of my four kids are chemically dependent; two of them are recovering.

My mother was not an alcoholic. Her way of dealing with my father's alcoholism was to be very busy and stay out of the house as much as possible. She was a teacher and took on all kinds of outside projects. Kids growing up with a teacher for a mother usually have her a lot of the time because of the school schedule, but my mother was never there.

I always felt as a child that I had to be perfect. I thought if I were better, my father would not drink again. I can remember coming home in high school with a straight-A report card and a B in chemistry and my mother saying to me, "And why is the B there?" My father didn't do that; he didn't say much about anything. He never missed a day of work, went to mass every Sunday, and went on his merry way.

My husband and I were married several years before I started to drink. We entertained a lot, and he said to me one time, "You know I can't drink." He is physically allergic to alcohol. "We're making people uncomfortable when we have them over so you better learn to drink." Boy, did I learn. It worked for me for a lot of years. It covered over a lot of the feelings I didn't want to deal with, especially the fact that after a few years I knew I shouldn't be married to this man. A couple of years ago I got a national award for selling millions of dollars of real estate for the builder I worked for. I thought, "God, this is a hell of a long way from drunk on the couch." I showed the award to my husband and he said, "Maybe next year you'll sell more." He was so like my mother it was incredible. It was like all the A's and the one B. I think it's amazing the way so many of us go out and pick a mate who's so similar to one of our parents. My daughter married an alcoholic. It just goes on and on.

The issues and feelings I grew up with certainly have influenced the way I've lived my life and the way I brought up my kids.

Harry is a therapist in private and group practice. He was raised in Pennsylvania and North Dakota, and recently he returned to school to study for a master's degree. Harry, who is in his early forties, has been twice divorced. His wife is a recovering alcoholic, and they are expecting their first child.

HARRY ▸ My name's Harry. My father is a workaholic. My dad's hooked on his profession; he's a surgeon. His job provides an external sense of selfhood. He always said the only thing relevant was his career.

The secrets that nobody knows in a family are the things that are encoded in everybody's life and get played out again and again and again—because they're secret. You're not allowed to be aware of them, so you act them out. In our family those secrets run back generations.

When my mother was a little girl, she was sent away to an aunt who could afford to parent her. After my mother's death, when one of her suicide attempts was finally successful, I got a chance to see some letters she had written as a child. They begin being dictated to this aunt because the little girl couldn't write yet: "Please let me come home, I'll be good. I won't eat a lot, I won't take a lot, I don't cost very much." When the little girl learned how to write in a childish scrawl, she began to articulate her pain and her depression. Later she was brought back to her family and grew up. Years later, my parents met and I was born.

I was the oldest of eight kids. One of the ways my father dealt with my mother's need to have somebody around was to offer more and more kids as he got more and more involved in his career. The sense that I always had growing up was that I'd better behave or they'd send me home, and I was home. Sometime into my recovery I saw the list of characteristics of the adult child, which I thought were normal. As I moved on through childhood things got much more "normal."

I am a recovering cross-addicted alcoholic, and like most recovering alcoholics and cocaine addicts, I went to meetings. As I did, pieces of me began to hook up. I began going to ACOA meetings, and I've been in therapy for several years now.

I'm married for the third time, and in the last couple of years I've become aware that I really do want to become a father. When life happens differently in a family with my last name is when this madness and pain will end. It will take another generation to find out; but I want the bullshit to stop.

2

ADULT
CHILDREN

America is a nation of emotional orphans. These adult children grew up without effective parents. Tens of millions of our friends, neighbors, spouses, and lovers had childhoods where their parents were not *emotionally there* for them. Their parents were involved with their own compulsions, obsessions, addictions, and dependency on each other.

Whether the focus of their lives was drugs, alcohol, food,

sex, gambling, or success, the focus was *not* on being healthy partners and loving parents. These parents were so emotionally handicapped, they couldn't be role models, love-givers, or teachers of self-esteem. Their children were raised without these emotional benefits; and deprived of a normal upbringing, they grew up to become today's walking wounded. Actually they are twice wounded. Not only did they suffer from lack of normal parenting, but they were also subject to sick and psychologically damaging influences.

The most traumatic effects of growing up in an emotionally bankrupt home are the tendency to fall into addictive or compulsive behavior as an adult and the relationship response of codependency—the obsession with another person. Equally devastating as a result of this kind of childhood is a personality profile that encompasses a variety of mental and emotional characteristics, such as horribly low self-worth, the inability to have fun, being super-responsible or super-irresponsible, and becoming a dependent personality terrified of abandonment.

The tragic consequence for tens of millions of adult children from unhappy homes is that they don't know who they are, what they are doing, or how to do it. They guess at what normal is, don't know how to take care of their own needs and feel good about themselves, and don't enjoy intimacy. These millions get involved in disastrous relationships, act impulsively, judge themselves without mercy, and constantly seek approval and security.

After listening to the emotional pain and horror stories of some adult children one night, I created the following fantasy radio or television public-service announcement:

If you are addicted to alcohol or other drugs, physically or sexually abuse a child, compulsively overeat or overwork, or emotionally neglect your family, your actions today will be the cause of your child's life of loneliness, frustration, and hurt for many years to come.

Your alcoholism or other compulsive behavior will be a deciding factor in your child's marrying an alcoholic, becoming an alcoholic, or getting involved in some kind of compulsive behavior. Because your child's low self-worth is being learned from you, he or she will not be able to live a happy life or raise a healthy family. Your child will not know how to have fun, enjoy friendships, or even take care of his or her own basic needs.

Your child deserves your love and attention. Your behavior is affecting the lives of your spouse and children, and it may take them an entire lifetime to reverse the incalculable damage you are doing now.

You may have the right to wreck your own life, but do you really have the right to wreck the lives of others? You can kill your pain with alcohol or other kinds of addictive behavior. How will they handle theirs?

When former First Lady Betty Ford stepped forward to talk about her own addictions to alcohol and prescription drugs, a train of awareness and education started moving through America. What has happened in the last ten years in this country is astounding. Not long ago the focus was solely on the alcoholic. Then treating the spouses of alcoholics began. Now alcoholism is recognized as a family disease. According to a Gallup poll, one out of three families has been affected by alcoholism. Almost thirty million Americans have (or had) at least one alcoholic parent.

Only recently has it been discovered that adult children of alcoholics have similar behavioral characteristics and develop many stress-related medical problems. According to the charter statement of the National Association for Children of Alcoholics, "COA children often adapt to the chaos and inconsistency of an alcoholic home by developing an inability to trust, an extreme need to control, excessive sense of responsibility and denial of feelings—all of which result in low self-esteem, depression, isolation, guilt, and difficulty in maintaining satisfying relationships. These and other problems persist throughout adulthood."

While Adult Children of Alcoholics (ACA, ACOA, or COA) has become the fastest-growing self-help movement in the country, today something even more surprising is happening: adult children from other types of homes in which alcohol did not play a central role have found their way to ACA and ACOA meetings. These people from varied painful childhoods are meeting and sharing their experiences with adult children of alcoholics. They are identifying the core issues of their present-day unhappiness and know that when it comes to the consequences on a child, it doesn't matter what form his or her parent's dysfunctional behavior took, the impact on the children is largely the same.

One organization that welcomes all comers is Adult Children of Addictive Family Systems. This organization's material states, "This is a generic meeting for adult children of alcoholics, drug addicts, compulsive overeaters, workaholics, nicotine addicts, relationship addicts, compulsive gamblers, and codependents. Many of us suffer from one or more of these addictions as well. The focus of our meetings is not our particular addiction, but what we have in common growing up in an addictive system."

The therapist Terence T. Gorski, who appears later in this book, says, "Fifteen percent of the American population is actively addicted to alcohol, illegal or legally prescribed drugs. This 15 percent affects a minimum of three other family members. This brings the total of family members affected by alcoholism and drug addiction to 45 percent. The 15 percent who are addicted and the 45 percent who are affected total 60 percent. By expanding addictive disease to also encompass addictive behaviors such as workaholism, gambling, compulsive overeating and other eating disorders, the number of people in families of origin using or affected by either chemical dependency or other addictive behavior is raised to 80–90 percent of the population." (Homes of physical and sexual abuse, and homes of physical or emotional neglect or abandonment, must be included in any list of dysfunctional family systems; often they overlap.)

The emotional devastation is enormous. The cycles of behavior and response continue from generation to generation. Children raised in emotionally handicapped homes develop serious emotional problems and fall into addictive behavior patterns themselves as adults.

I grew up in such a home. I am an adult child. My father had the disease of alcoholism. My mother was the daughter of an alcoholic. I was an "accident waiting to happen."

It's not normal to grow up in a house where bureau drawers are thrown down the staircase in anger. It's not normal to live in a house where no one comes to visit except relatives. It's not normal to get thrown out of your own house by your own father at two o'clock in the afternoon because he can't sleep. When my father slept, we either whispered or didn't talk.

At supper my father would drunkenly tell the same stories over and over again, year after year. After eating, we'd help him upstairs to bed. Sometimes in the evening the rest of the family would gather in the living room to watch a favorite television program with the doors to the hallway shut. Halfway through the show my father would shout from his room upstairs for us to "turn that thing off."

As a child, I'd lie in my bed late at night and listen to my father yelling at my mother. He'd order her out of bed, and she would go downstairs to sleep on the couch. A half hour later, when it was finally quiet, he'd be hollering again, "Come up here *now.*" His ritual of ordering my mother in and out of bed would last for hours.

My mother was often understandably tired, tense, and depressed from struggling to keep a family together that, in retrospect, might have been better off apart. Whether she developed co-dependency in her own childhood as the daughter of an alcoholic or learned her co-dependent behavior from many years living with my father, my mother was often critical and negative. She probably struggled with her own self-esteem issues. My mother's sacrifice, suffering in silence, and taking care of my father were distorted lessons about relationships that have been passed along to me. My father's role-modeling of dependency, egomania, and alcoholism came my way as well.

My father was preoccupied with work, making ends meet, and drinking. He had had polio as a child, and I never saw him exercise, although at one time he had been an excellent golfer and even won a couple of club championships.

I can only remember my father playing with me twice. Once we had a game of catch in the driveway. It didn't last long, because every time he missed one of my throws, I'd have to chase the ball. He was unable to move around because of his weak legs. Another time, he watched me hit a couple of golf balls at the driving range, hit a couple of balls himself, and then got back in the car to read his book. Although he was very stern at report-card time, he never studied with me, and I cannot recall one thing he ever showed me how to do. While my mother did encourage me with my hobbies and read to us when we were young, she always seemed to be busy doing household chores, catering to my father's whims, and following his orders.

I cannot remember experiencing much warmth, love, or support from either of my parents. As a child, I was very sensitive about being "skinny." To improve myself I sent away for a Charles Atlas course on muscle building. I remember vividly when it arrived, my mother laughed at me and made me send it back.

Our house was a house where everyone hid behind a book reading, being very quiet, or trying to escape somewhere either indoors, outdoors, or away. It was not a house of closeness. It was not a house of happiness and laughter. It was a house of chaos, disappointment, tears, frustration, anger, and an overwhelming sense of sadness. Unhappy homes produce unhappy children who become unhappy adults.

I was a sad, scared, and lonely child and I turned out to be a sad, scared, and lonely adult. As a child, I didn't learn much about self-esteem, self-reliance, self-pride, and self-development. I did learn about self-pity and self-destruction.

I discovered alcohol when I was sixteen, and in a way it saved my life during my teenage and early adult years. Alcohol allowed me to release my pent-up feelings and frustrations, become connected to other people, take some risks, and gain a sense of security and confidence. During those years, I traveled through the use and abuse stages of drinking. Alcohol turned finally on me at thirty, and I crossed "the invisible line" and became addicted. Once drinking controlled me, my life was a steady downward spiral into hopelessness and despair. Fortunately, some years later I sought help and quit drinking with the aid of others.

Occasionally I contemplate the question, Where would you be today if you had kept drinking? The answer I keep coming up with for myself is, You'd probably be living in Florida or Puerto Rico unconnected to family and friends, working at a job for two hundred a week, and drinking yourself to death.

All alcoholics quit drinking. Some of us are fortunate to quit while we are still alive.

I know my mother and father loved me, and I am grateful for the many good things they gave me. I am letting go of the past. My father died a dozen years ago. My mother is alive and well. I consider her my oldest friend. I have struggled, but I am proud of what I've done with my life and my parents have my appreciation and love. A lot of the good things about me have come from my parents and I am now able to see that clearly.

It is important for me to remember my mother and father loved each other very much. People liked my father and he did many wonderful things for many people. My mother is a very unselfish and amazing woman. She has changed a lot over the years. I respect and love her a lot.

I have enjoyed success personally and professionally since I quit drinking. I can attest to the fact there is life after alcohol (and Valium). In recent years I have hosted a nationally broadcast television series, written two best-selling books, attained financial security for the first time in my life, and developed a strong circle of friends.

A couple of years ago, despite my recovery from alcoholism, I felt I had some major unfinished business to examine. There is a saying among recovering alcoholics: You can sober up a drunken horse thief, but you'll still have a horse thief. While I was not a "horse thief," I was a sober alcoholic who still had lots of problems. I realized I was still unhappy. It wasn't enough to stop drinking. I found out I had to take a look at my past, examine the lessons of my childhood, understand how they were affecting me, and make some changes in my behavior.

On a regular basis for the past two years I have been involved in one-on-one therapy and have been attending meetings with other adult children. They are some of the most wonderful people I have ever known. As it happens, they aren't all children of alcoholics. The meetings I attend also attract the adult sons and daughters of spouse- and child-abusers, some who grew up with mental illness in the family, and many from backgrounds of incest, compulsive gambling, sexual addiction, workaholism, drug abuse, and emotional neglect. The common bond among us is that each of us grew up in some kind of a dysfunctional home and arrived at adulthood without the benefit of really having parents in the true sense of the word.

My difficult childhood, like that of other adult children, has had a profound impact on my adult life.

I have tried to win approval, acceptance, and security.

Since I never learned I was good and lovable, I searched for others to tell me I was. If people didn't love me, I manipulated and tried to control them. I became a dependent person, often looking to others to make me happy, take care of me, and solve my problems, and I gravitated toward others who were also emotionally damaged. I have experienced difficulty with closeness and entered into many friendships and relationships with both men and women that were doomed to fail from the start. Isolation, guilt feelings, overreacting, hypersensitivity, excitement-seeking, and taking myself too seriously are just a few of the emotional and destructive behaviors I have experienced since childhood. Certainly my own alcoholism was the direct result—genetically and environmentally—of growing up in an addictive home.

Those of us who grew up in dysfunctional homes are, to one degree or another, all the same. A child deserves love and attention from his or her parents as a birthright. Through interaction with normal healthy parents, children learn to feel good about themselves, the world, and life. Children learn they are lovable by being treated with specialness. The uniqueness of a child must be celebrated, and the child must internalize that "self-love" message. Adult children never learn to love themselves, and as grown-ups, they are confused, hopeless, and despairing. Adult children do not get positive messages in childhood and often spend a lifetime searching for affirmation and validation as adults. Adult children pay a devastating price for the lack of warmth, love, care, and attention.

We prostitute our own needs and dreams to hold on to physically or emotionally abusive relationships. We give away our souls and our bodies to others to feel good about ourselves. We reach for greater heights to accomplish more-spectacular things, to be noticed and loved. We become addicted to substances and behaviors to kill the loneliness. We pray, "God deliver us from the pain of longing; take away this empty heart; I can struggle no longer."

Adult children of alcoholic or dysfunctional homes have a choice today: they can continue to suffer or they can do something about it. They can become their own parents. And that is what many of these people are doing through the country—in private and group therapy, workshops, and support-group meetings. They are identifying their problems and unhealthy patterns of behavior, and they are making remarkable and positive changes in their lives.

Because dysfunctional problems affect so many, the number of self-help groups for adult children is growing at an astounding rate throughout the United States.

Adult children's groups are opening their doors to the victims of dysfunctional homes of every sort. Together these unparented grown-ups are learning how to become their own parents.

This is how it works: New members meet other adult children and realize they are not alone. Immediately the sense of isolation and loneliness is lifted. In a way, the adult child has a new family—a group of people who really care. The new family listens to the newcomer's story with compassion. The newcomer senses the members' empathy and support. This is a wonderful experience for someone who has felt uncared for all of his or her life.

Newcomers learn that they were surrounded in their childhoods, and often in their adult lives, by parents, siblings, and others who were, or are, selfish, critical, negative, undependable, and often sick. They recognize they are living their lives seeking security and fearing abandonment. They begin to comprehend that at the root of their people-pleasing, self-sacrificing, fear-of-being-rejected behavior is a horrendous lack of self-worth.

The group is the family, and new members follow as children. The group members are trusted as parents. Ultimately, new group members learn to see their childhood as a tragic time when they did not receive the basic message that they were good, lovable, important, special, unique, and gifted. Through the process of recovery, they accept responsibility for their own lives today and become their own parent.

This is a book of meetings of adult children for adult children. The group of people you met in the first chapter have come together specifically to share their stories, feelings, and insights with you. They see themselves in each other, understand each other's pain, recognize the unique negative behavior they fall into as a result of their upbringings, and support each other's growth. As this book progresses you will get to know these remarkable people well. Though their behavior may appear different on the surface, there are similarities on a very basic, human level that make it possible for them to help each other.

In addition to the fourteen group members, twelve nationally recognized experts—all prominent leaders in the field of alcoholic and dysfunctional-home issues—appear on these pages to share their wisdom with you. As in my previous books, I have interviewed all of the experts and group members individually and then deleted my questions. Their powerful words need no intrusion from me. With one exception, all of the members of the group came together for many hours of meetings. A few specifics have been changed, but the alterations are of no consequence. To speak out as an adult child requires incredible courage. In some sections of this book, specific questions are addressed to specific group members; however, the dynamics of these meetings are based on the principle of equals talking with equals. These group meetings were a powerful experience for all of us.

Our parents never intended to hurt us. To the contrary; regardless of the nature of our dysfunctional homes, they did love us. Adult children must accept responsibility for their own lives today. They can no longer be slaves to childhood reactions and restrictions.

As you read this book you may see your own martyrdom, caretaking, fears, perfectionism, struggle, and obsession for everything from cigarettes to nail-biting, from work to booze, from controlling people to sex. You will see the truth about your own relationships and the truth about yourself.

The purpose of life is to know yourself, accept yourself, love yourself, and forget about yourself so you can love others unconditionally and be of service to them.

The challenge of self-discovery is to break through denial, discard delusions, unlock feelings, raise self-esteem, make the body healthy, select caring friends, set aside time for play, love and praise yourself, accept life as it is, admit powerlessness, live life to its fullest, and experience true intimacy and real happiness.

You deserve happiness. You are special.

3

CHILDHOOD

At the first adult children meeting I attended, a woman compared her childhood to "living in the middle of World War III." I identified with those words then and I still do.

Recently I saw the British film *Hope and Glory*. It's the story of a family's survival of the World War II bombings of England. The effect of the warning wail of the siren that caused the family to take cover from the impending bombing assault in the film was similar to the effect of the horn of my father's car arriving in the driveway, causing me to run to take emotional cover as a kid.

Psychologists and psychiatrists use the term post–traumatic-stress disorder to describe not only the symptoms and behavior of many Vietnam combat veterans but also the emotional legacy of many adult children of alcoholic and dysfunctional homes. Like the war veteran, I lived through long-term stress; I reexperienced the trauma, my feelings have been numbed, and often, in recovery, I experience the survivor's guilt for being disloyal to my family.

As you read the group members' personal, in-depth stories, you may reexperience the pain, shock, and trauma of these childhoods and your own.

Charles L. Whitfield, M.D., has been treating adult children of dysfunctional families for many years. He is the medical director of the Resource Group in Baltimore, Maryland, a private outpatient program that specializes in treating professionals. The Resource Group is one of the oldest and most comprehensive family and adult-child treatment programs in the country. A founding board member of the National Association for Children of Alcoholics, Dr. Whitfield lectures and conducts workshops throughout the country and is the author of two books, *Healing the Child Within: Discovery and Recovery for Adult Children of Dysfunctional Families* and *Alcoholism, Attachments and Spirituality.*

CHARLES L. WHITFIELD, M.D. ▸ A dysfunctional family is one that doesn't work. It doesn't support the psychospiritual growth of each individual in the family. The psychological aspect of that support and growth has to do with feelings, needs, working through conflict, sharing, and accepting. The spiritual side is all of that, plus forgiveness, compassion, creativity, the ability to love others, and unconditional love for self. If somebody could have parents and a family like that, they'd be totally free to live a successful, joyful, and cre-

ative life. It would be an unusual gift to a child to be born into a
family where there was that much evolution and freedom.

The alcoholism recovery movement, the adult children
movement, other self-help movements, and the whole human-
potential movement are all coming together now and have all
contributed to people getting healthier and healthier. People
are getting to know themselves better, and in that way they're
getting more and more functional. When you get more and
more functional individuals together, you can have more functional families.

Today more than 50 percent of families are dysfunctional.
Some experts use much higher figures. The degree of dysfunction can range from mild to severe.

A severely dysfunctional family is in constant chaos. No one
ever has any peace. It is a rare time that anybody is able to catch
his or her breath. They are stuck down at the survival and safety
level. A starving family in Africa or a very violent family where
parents beat the kids every day would qualify as a severely cha-
otic and dysfunctional family. They're just trying to survive.

A typical moderately dysfunctional family has an active alcoholic and a co-dependent as parents. Co-dependence is any
suffering or dysfunction associated with focusing on the needs
or behaviors of another. In this case the spouse is "co-dependent" on—or toward—the drinking alcoholic. While this family
is more functional than the severely dysfunctional family, the
parents are not there for one another and they're not there for
the kids. They are caught up in these two active diseases of
alcoholism and co-alcoholism (or co-dependence). In this case,
kids may go to any lengths not to have any of their friends walk
in their house. This might happen if the kids bring home a
friend and find their mother passed out on the floor and then
see her get up, slur a few words, and fall back into her vomit.
These children would be so embarrassed that they would never
want to bring a playmate home again. At the time of the incident, somebody, of course, cleaned the mother up, put her to
bed, and everything would be nice for a few days. But the kids
never knew when it was going to happen again.

Another example of a moderately dysfunctional home is
the violent home. Violence does not have to include physical
violence. The father in this case is a rage-aholic and has very

low self-esteem. His parents were dysfunctional when he was growing up, and he learned to handle his conflicts by lashing out, manipulating people, trying to control people, and putting people down. So any time he doesn't get his own way now as a husband and father, he rages, slams doors, screams at people, cusses people, calls his wife a whore and a slut in front of the kids, and runs out of the house. He's gone for hours or maybe even the day. There is very little difference between this kind of family and an active alcoholic family.

An example of a mildly dysfunctional family is a family with a father-husband who is gone most of the time. Whenever there is any conflict or tension, the husband just leaves. The wife is stuck with nobody but the kids with whom to interact. There is an intimacy vacuum between the husband and wife. The mother wants somebody to talk to and relate to; she wants a husband and she doesn't have one, except part-time. He provides the money and the home, pays his taxes, never loses a job, but is not very much interested in being a husband or a father. The children develop low self-esteem. The mother nags the father and his answer is to leave, and so she gets angry with the kids. Then the kids act out trying to bring the parents back together and trying to do something to fix the family.

Families of alcoholism; physical, emotional, or sexual abuse; mental or physical illness; perfectionism and rigidity; or co-dependence can fit into the dysfunctional spectrum, depending upon the severity. Each family has its own personality. However, one characteristic of a dysfunctional family that is pretty much consistent and universal is that it is shame-based, with low self-esteem.

The price a child pays for growing up in a dysfunctional home is alienation from his true self in adulthood. He cannot know and be his true self, his child within, his real self. Such a person is a pretend self, a false self, or a co-dependent self. The price is self-alienation, chronic unhappiness, confusion, difficulty with relationships, and basically an unsuccessful life.

About a third of the people whom I see in therapy and who go to the adult children of alcoholics self-help meetings did not come from alcoholic homes. Many of these groups no longer call themselves Adult Children of Alcoholics but, rather, Adult

Children Anonymous or Adult Children of Dysfunctional Families.

The needs of a child are survival, safety, security, touching, attention, mirroring, guidance, listening, participating, accepting, the support to grieve, growing, loyalty, trust, accomplishment, fun, play, sexuality, freedom, nurturing, and unconditional love.

Children need to do their own grieving whenever they have a loss, a hurt, or a trauma. If they don't grieve, the need goes unsatisfied. But if it's put on the back burner, it will come up again and again in later life. This is called repetition compulsion. Adult children of dysfunctional families have many losses in childhood. When ungrieved, unfinished business is present, it keeps trying to express itself so as to complete the business. If the environment or the self doesn't support that, then a person will get into compulsions or addictions to try to finish the business. Adult children of dysfunctional homes do a lot of acting out. Recovery is the process of working out. What we don't work out, we don't talk about. What we don't work out, we act out.

If youngsters grew up in homes where there was rage, physical abuse, sexual abuse, or drunken behavior and if they have never worked that out—have never been able to talk about it—they will think there's something wrong with themselves deep down inside and they'll want to cover that up in the ways they relate to other people and to themselves. The tension of the unfinished business of childhood, combined with current unfinished business of adulthood, produces such tension that it has to come out. There are two common ways it comes out: through compulsions or addictions such as food, alcohol, gambling, sex, abuse, or work, or as mental illness, such as depression, psychosis, personality disorder, or overt criminal behavior.

All these conditions are shame-based. "I'm bad, so I don't deserve any better." It's also habit. "This is what I'm used to doing." The payoff for attachments, compulsions, and addictions is that through them we get a glimpse of the true self. We get to feel again, to feel alive again, to feel excited, to feel some connection with ourselves or others. We get some semblance of what's really real. The reward is a glimpse of the true self and the punishment is the shame that comes from the compulsive behavior. Shame is about *"I'm* bad" and guilt is about "What I *did* (or didn't do) is bad." We don't want to deal with it, we put a lid on it, we don't share it with anybody. We hold it in, walking around feeling miserable for days, weeks, months or years, until the tension builds up. Because the self wants to come out and the unfinished business wants to be finished, it explodes again. *We want to be ourselves and we want to know ourselves.*

Some of the core issues of recovery are self-esteem, which is closely related to shame, all-or-none thinking and behaving, control, trust, dependence, getting needs met, and fear of abandonment. The basic issue is abandonment. If the parent has abandoned the child's needs, the child thinks it's because he or she is unworthy, bad, defective, imperfect, not good enough, inadequate, incomplete, rotten, undesirable, and repulsive. That means "I'm bad," and that's shame. The conclusion: "I'm bad, and if I were good enough, somebody would help me with my needs."

The truth is that the parents were just as wounded as the child is going to be. Shame also develops because parents, brothers and sisters, and society project shame onto others. So the parents feel inadequate, bad, and unfulfilled. The parents feel shameful. The parents feel they are bad before the child is even born because of their own unfinished business, their own woundedness. In an attempt to get goodness and fulfillment, they reach outside themselves. Unskilled and inexperienced in doing anything healthy, they project their badness onto someone else whenever there's conflict, differences, problems. Rather than work it out in a healthy way, they project their own shame onto others; their spouse, family, parents, co-workers, and especially their kids.

There are two major ways to get shame: one is watching your own needs being neglected, and the second is having badness projected onto you through parental shame. It's projected family shame. It's inherited. It's multigenerational shame; it has come down from generation to generation. The parents' negative rules and messages are the projections of their own shame. The parents feel inadequate, bad, and unfulfilled, so they look for others to fulfill them and make them all right. That includes having a spouse and having children.

Co-dependence is looking outside ourselves for something

we feel is deficient inside. That's the basis of all attachments, compulsions, and addictions. The addiction is looking elsewhere, trying to find an answer outside ourselves in what some of the self-help programs call "people, places, and things." Until they work all this out, adult children will carry those scars and that baggage with them. That's why the self-help movements and the therapy movements of today are so important and effective. They are bringing about results.

Mary, the daughter of a prominent Wall Street workaholic, was raised in an environment where "the denial of reality can be covered with money." Both her mother and father are alcoholics. She says, "We looked great on the outside, but inside our family was crumbling." Mary, a professional photographer, says her addictive and compulsive behaviors with alcohol, drugs, and food were a "reaction" to being raised by parents who were "sick themselves."

MARY ▸ As a child I always went to private schools. I had my own pony. I would fox hunt on the weekends, and for spring vacations we'd go to someplace like Trinidad. I had it all materially, but there was something missing. It was the alcoholism that made life really quite ugly.

My older sister was a rebel and got into trouble a lot. My middle sister was a disaster academically. She kept getting kicked out of boarding schools. She's now an investment banker in London, and she's my father's little dream girl, because she doesn't talk about his alcoholic problem.

My mother's really a beautiful person. I don't mean only physically; I mean on the inside too. She came from a very wealthy family herself. She married my father when she was twenty-two and basically went from her father's arms into my father's arms. She fell in love with this real controlling man, and my mother lost herself. My father is the main figure in our family, and what he says goes. Part of her went into the bottle when my mother started to drink.

When I was growing up, I'd have to leave every night around seven o'clock and go upstairs. I hated that time because my mother would be drunk by then. My favorite show was

"The Brady Bunch," the all-perfect family. I would be watching the show, and my father's car would arrive. I remember my mother just freaking out, "Your father's home, your father's home! Turn off the TV, turn off the TV! Brush your hair! Come downstairs!" All of us had to come down because the Ayatollah had come home. He'd always be in a foul mood. He'd pat us on the head, our job was done, and all of us would go isolate. Our house was set up for isolation. It was the perfect place for a dysfunctional family.

After my homework I'd always have to come down and say goodnight. By that time they both were looped. They would always be fighting. I thought I was going crazy. I thought, "What did I do wrong?" That's when I started becoming the clown of the family. I would do anything to stop the fighting. Of course, when the sun came up in the morning, "nothing happened." "What are you talking about, Mary? There was no fight." This was a pattern which happened throughout my entire life.

My home sucked. My mom and I never communicated; we never knew each other. There was no mother-daughter relationship. I was brought up by a French nanny. I thought this was normal. I was shipped off to boarding school, and when parents came to visit, mine never came. That's when my lying started, making excuses why they didn't come. I didn't understand back then that it was the alcoholism that kept them from coming.

My sisters and I became distant from one another. My older sister stopped saying anything that would cause trouble. My middle sister said, "Nothing's wrong, nothing's wrong." I was always the one who said, "Something's wrong," so I became a very unpopular child rather quickly.

At the time I was in boarding school, my mother's drinking got out of hand. I remember once when I came home for a weekend and went in to kiss her goodnight, she was out cold with a suicide note near a bottle of pills.

As my father's success on Wall Street grew, the family grew sicker. He bought a two-bedroom apartment on Park Avenue for himself and Mom. The ironic thing about it was my mother never had keys to the apartment, and my father only came home on the weekends. It did come out of the closet that my father had a girlfriend and my mother knew this. She was drinking every night. She was paralyzed. She didn't know what to do. When I was home and not away at school, I had to take care of Mom. I had to put her in bed at night. Sometimes I wouldn't go to bed until two or three o'clock in the morning because Mom would get out of bed and I was afraid she was going to hurt herself. A couple of nights she got in the car and drove off, but the next day: "Nothing happened." Our family should get an Academy Award. Like a lot of alcoholic families, we really fooled a lot of people for a long time. Not anymore. The cat is out of the bag.

In a dysfunctional family you're dealing with parents who are sick themselves and have never received help. They became adults and decided to have children, yet they never grew up themselves. Their parenting was abusive, but they didn't know they were being abusive. In the same way, if I had a child today, I would probably be a dysfunctional mother because I don't have my shit together either. It's like constructing a bridge where the main structures are made out of plastic instead of steel. The bridge is going to crack because of plastic. The foundation is not there. So the bridge decays until somebody decides to replace the plastic supports with steel supports. In life, this means recovery.

My bridge started to crack in high school. I knew my mother was an alcoholic. In high school I remember saying, "God, drinking is terrible," but I used to get stoned every night with my friends. Of course, I wasn't "drinking." My compulsion for food started then too. When I graduated, more pressure was added. My father sat me down and said, "Harvard, Yale, Michigan, or Dartmouth?" I said, "Parsons," and it was the first time I ever stood up to my father. I said, "I want to be an artist." I had gotten accepted to Parsons on a full scholarship because I lied about my finances. My father just said, "Absolutely not."

I remember the summer of my senior year I saved up $2,400 and bought a Volkswagen bug. I drove out to Michigan, and my grandmother, my mother's mother, took me in. My grandmother's a rebel, and that's why I respect her. Granny does what Granny believes in. She listened to me, noticed my talents, and knew I was different. I ended up going to Hillsdale College for a year.

I don't know why I chose Hillsdale, but it's a good thing I left there because they would have kicked me out sooner or later. It's just so conservative, and that's where everything got completely out of hand. I started hanging around with the real burn-outs of that school. We were angry kids who came from a lot of money, blowing our minds out every night. I was doing drugs and the campus was full of males. I decided I was fat; I wasn't fat but I thought I was fat, so my bulimia started. I ate food compulsively, and then, feeling incredibly guilty, I'd throw it up and then repeat the same behavior. A lot of kids were doing this kind of thing, so it helped foster my belief that I didn't have a problem.

I remember going home on vacation for Christmas and purposely not eating in front of my father. It was, "Look, I'm killing myself. Will you give me attention? Will you love me? Will you stop putting all this pressure on me?" I got a real high off that. Once the anorexia stopped, the bulimia came back into play.

When I finally decided I was in trouble with both alcohol and food, I went to my parents. We sat and talked about it for an hour. Afterward my mother asked, "You really don't do that, do you?" I said, "Mom, why would I fly all the way into New York to tell you this is my behavior if it isn't what I'm doing?" My family hears what they want to hear and they see what they want to see. In my own relationships I'm finding out that I also see what I want to see and I hear what I want to hear. But I'm learning, I'm growing up.

It's scary to break the family mobile, but that's what I'm doing. It's a neat feeling. It's better than any high. I feel I saw too much at too young an age. A friend of mine calls me "wise fool" all the time, and he says, "You've got a forty-year-old soul in your body." Well, damn, I was my mother's mother. I put her to bed. She never put me to bed. I had to grow up really quickly, which is too bad. I never had a childhood. I didn't have time for it. I had to be an adult and I have a lot of anger about that. Two of my professors have said, "You're different, Mary. You've seen a lot, but yet you're so naive still."

About five years ago my father and mother got divorced. All I wanted was to be loved. If it meant cutting off my right arm, I would have done it. My whole life has been a reaction to my parents. That's where the food, alcohol, and drugs came in. I was always running from pain; but the pain wasn't as bad as the abusive behavior. Pain hurts, but the other stuff hurts so much more. There was a big price to pay. I was throwing away my health, my sanity, and myself.

Michael, an attorney and recovering alcoholic, must constantly remind himself that he identifies with the list of characteristics of people who grew up in a dysfunctional home. Even though he was an only child from a broken home, he thought he had a "very perfect upbringing." So severe, however, was his sense of negative self-judgment, insecurity, and guilt that when reading about adult children of alcoholism, he got the sense that "somebody was reading my mail."

MICHAEL ▸ When I was eighteen months old, my parents divorced. My mother left my father in Houston, Texas, got on a train with me, and returned to her parent's home in Michigan. At eighteen months I went from a mother-father family structure to an extended family of me, my mother, two uncles (my mother's brothers), and my grandparents. I never saw my father again till I was about twelve or thirteen.

Back in the fifties and early sixties I would have been described, with some pity in people's voices, as an only child from a broken home. I jokingly say now that that's become the nuclear family. That's a very caustic joke, but a lot of kids now are being raised more like I was raised, as far as family structure goes.

Until the last year or so, I was convinced that I had no issues with my father. What I have found out is that much of the way I've lived my life has been in denial of the fact that I missed my father and I wanted a Mom-Dad situation. I've been told in therapy that a trauma at eighteen months can have a very significant impact on a person's life.

During the time I grew up, my grandparents never once slept in the same room. Never once was there a display of affection from my grandmother toward my grandfather. A few times he would try to get affectionate toward her, but she was very put off. She found his advances for a hug very distasteful. I don't know why to this day. My mother, their oldest child, has said, "I don't know why Grandma and Grandpa got married." She didn't tell me this when I was real small, but as I got up into the later teen years and into adulthood she would talk about them occasionally and would say such things as, "You're so lucky you missed it all. You don't know what it was like. It was just awful."

I don't understand what happened before I got there. I only know what I lived with. There was an aura of tension about that house that I never understood.

About four years ago, after a fourteen-year marriage, I got a divorce, remarried, and found myself desperately trying to re-create the same kind of dependent situation I'd had with my first wife, realizing it wouldn't work, and hating myself for do-ing it. It was as if the whole thing was on the rails. I could not stop falling into the same pit. I could see what I was doing; I could see it wouldn't work and I couldn't stop it.

One of the things that I've had problems with throughout my entire life was feelings of tremendous insecurity and a driv-ing sense of self-judgment. There is no abusive father, no abu-sive boss, no abusive dictator that could impose upon me the expectations and sense of guilt that I impose on myself.

My second wife and I separated, and about four months later I found myself thinking a lot of suicidal thoughts but pass-ing them off as intellectual fantasies. Then one day at work while I was sitting around morosely contemplating my second separated situation, it occurred to me that I really should com-mit suicide. I wrote a very serious suicide note and experienced a sense of relief for having made the decision. I went on about the day, and it was the most productive day I'd had in months. I was actually beginning to plan the thing a couple of ways. That afternoon, as I was walking across the office, I stopped dead in my tracks and something said to me, "Holy shit, I've decided to commit suicide and it's real. I have made the decision." Click, click, click. "That means I'm sick."

I called the Lawyers and Judges Counseling Program and ended up in Alcoholics Anonymous. I decided I was going to whip this alcoholism stuff by learning about it. In the first two months, I bought probably three feet of shelf space worth of books. I breezed through them all. Running low on reading

material, I went to another bookstore, and next to the alcohol section, there was Claudia Black's book *It Will Never Happen to Me.* I was quizzical about that phrase, "It will never happen to me." Something registered at a deep level. I picked up the book and opened it up to the table of contents. It was obvious this was a book about people who grew up with alcoholism. I was convinced that it would have nothing to do with me. But in the table of contents there was a title of one chapter, "Don't Talk, Don't Trust, Don't Feel." My brow furrowed. It wasn't so much the "Don't Trust"; it was the "Don't Talk" and "Don't Feel" that hit me.

I opened the book to that chapter and read a couple of sentences. I bought that book and another book next to it, *Adult Children of Alcoholics,* feeling guilty for buying them, because there was an implied indictment of my family in there. I went home, read them, and went looking for ACA meetings.

About a year ago I experienced something that was very important in the growth I've gone through. It's called, I found out, "spontaneous age regression in an autohypnotic state." A psychiatrist told me that after I reported what happened.

I had some folks over for dinner one Saturday night, and they left about ten-thirty. I lived alone then and physically and mentally I was bushed. I sort of let everything go to get to sleep, but I didn't go to sleep. What happened was that I lay there in my bed, a forty-three-year-old adult with my eyes closed, and I realized I was in the same position I used to be in as a little kid. I thought about that and just sort of let my mind wander back to the room I grew up in and, Boom, I was there—smell, touch, sight, sound, everything. I could have told you the books that were on the bookshelves. At the same time, I was still oriented to being a forty-three-year-old male. During the hour and a half it lasted, I was a child at various stages, as far back as two and as old as nine.

Until I was about five, six, or seven, I slept, in effect, in my mother's room. My mother's room had a little alcove reading room off of it separated by an archway but no door. I slept in the alcove area. The sequence began with me there, my mother thinking I was asleep, and me watching her undress. I was probably five. My mother was an actress and was a very attractive woman with a nice figure. As I was experiencing that in this age regression, the adult me got aroused, had an erection, and felt very guilty. What happened was the kid got up and left the room. He walked around the house and then went through various scenes, playing with friends, riding his bike, and being in a hospital when he was two years old. I was in that crib, smelled that hospital, and saw the fat nurse with the white outfit. When I rode my bike down the street, I felt the wind on a fall day. My subconscious just opened up. In the course of that age regression, among other things, I walked around the house, and everything was normal. My grandmother was downstairs watching television, my mother was knitting, my two uncles were there briefly, and my grandfather was as usual in the back room out of sight. He lived in his bedroom, had a TV in there and would drink beer, smoke cigarettes, and watch sports. I had to go by that room to get to the bathroom, and in this age regression I walked by the room with a certain degree of fear or a little anxiety. It was very clear to me I had to be very, very quiet.

The experience ends with an episode of the elementary school bully threatening to cut my dick off. He had me cornered. He was a sixth-grader and I was probably a third- or fourth-grader. That was a very scary thing that happened to me, but that's how the whole thing ended, and I fell asleep.

Now when I told this episode to the therapist, she said, "Stop right there. You've just relived the classic Oedipal story: you desire your mother, you feel guilty, you leave the room and end up recalling an incident about castration." She asked, "Do you understand what was missing in there? You had no identification with a man that was ever adequately completed." There simply never was a single male figure, and it was something I had craved.

When my therapist also indicated to me that I was in fact an abandoned child, I almost got up and left. I said, "Abandoned? My God, I had five adults in my family. I was showered with gifts and praise. How in the hell can you say I was abandoned?" Over the last year, I have realized that in fact all of us in that house emotionally abandoned each other.

The real deep therapy work I have done gets to those kinds of basic issues of male identity and the fact that I emotionally married my mother. There was never any overt sex abuse with me at all. But as the therapist said to me when I told her I had slept in my mother's room till I was five or six or seven, "My God, Michael, I didn't realize your mother was so seductive with you."

My grandmother and my mother were pretty heavily into Christian Science and I grew up being told repeatedly that I was —and saw myself basically as—a child of God and a spiritual creature by nature. What I didn't get was the fact there are other parts that we've got to deal with, like our bodies. I've been blessed with a pretty healthy one, but it has feelings, it is sexual, it has needs, it has emotions. Other people have emotions too. I didn't learn a damn thing about dealing with any of that because I was taught you don't deal with it, that "it's not real," that we are "spiritual by nature."

I think I got stuck with a couple of very loving women, my mother and my grandmother, who were off on a very metaphysical trip because of their religion, and in an effort to please them I became too much that way myself without developing normally as a kid.

Photographs of me before I was a year and a half old show spontaneity, aliveness, and brightness. When I look at the photographs taken after eighteen months, there's a pasted-on smile on my face and a compliant sort of kid. As a baby, you blame yourself when someone leaves. I'm sure I did. From that point on, I was pretty obedient. As a child I felt very much that I was the cause of any anger, dissatisfaction, or sadness going on around me. My mother's chief disciplining tactic was simply to turn from me with a look that said, "I don't understand what you're talking about. You're crazy." She wouldn't say it, but that was what I took the look to mean.

Around age fifteen or sixteen I recall feeling tremendous frustration. I remember being down in the basement of the house all alone, pacing back and forth, back and forth, fists clenched, mouth clenched, pacing, pacing, pacing, trying to hold it in. I thought I was going to explode. My mother and grandmother were upstairs, and I was going nuts. I think it had to do with the possibility that I'd be stuck living there taking care of those women all my life, and I felt angry and guilty about it. I finally resolved it when I made a decision that I lived by for a good many years. I concluded what you have to do in this life is please people. This was a conscious thought at the foot of those basement stairs. I decided as my life's mission, I would be the guy who never upset anybody. "That's it, that's the answer," I thought. I relaxed, the tension left me, I went upstairs with a smile, and I did my damndest to try to make that work for the next twenty years.

Jeff, a collections supervisor, was physically and verbally abused by his workaholic father. According to Jeff, "There is so much of me that is my father." He fell into the behavior of workaholism himself and sought help because of the way he was disciplining his own children. Jeff is determined: "I didn't want to carry on with my children in the rageful fashion I was exhibiting toward them."

JEFF ► My father was a shoemaker, and everything he did revolved around his business. He was a real heavy smoker as we were growing up. He smoked four packs of Pall Malls a day and quit cold turkey in 1963. I never could quite understand how he could do that. I still smoke myself.

My mother was a theater manager most of my growing years. She was there when we got up in the morning, but she was gone by the time we got home from school and we didn't see her again until the next morning. We lived over the store about 80 percent of my childhood. My dad oversaw the meals being cooked and the house being cleaned. There were six children in my family; I was the second-oldest, but I was the one that was relied upon. I never was able to be a child and play. From the time I was nine years old, my dad could go out of town and I'd run the store.

Dad was a compulsive eater and overweight when he quit smoking, and he got even more overweight after he had quit. He had quit because he was diagnosed with high blood pressure.

When Dad got upset, he would blow up and have a tantrum. He would also isolate himself and indulge in eating large amounts of food that wasn't on his diet. Mom would try to get him to stay on his diet, but he would have us kids popping popcorn at night while she was away at work.

Mom was always trying to get Dad to lose some weight and feel better. Dad would fight her, saying she was denying him enjoyment and that eating was important to him. They had a lot of arguments over that kind of thing. I remember one time he pushed my mother and I stepped in between them. He turned a whole dish cupboard over on top of me. I had to pick up the cupboard and wash every dish, at least the ones that weren't broken.

My dad would discipline us by spanking us with a belt. If he got real upset, he would turn it around and use the buckle end of it. I know there were times when my dad would get driven up on the high of an adrenaline buzz when he was disciplining us. I don't know if I've quite forgiven him for those times. The verbal abuse was continuous, and he was physically abusive a couple of times a week.

There were times when he was going to beat one of my sisters and I would step in the way. He would beat the hell out of me, and then he'd be too tired to hurt them. I remember my dad beating me because I splashed some water on my sister while she was washing dishes. He tore off my shirt and started beating me with the buckle end of his belt. I wouldn't cry. I remember him jumping up and down, all three hundred and twenty-five pounds of him, beating me with the buckle end of the belt. I was huddled on the floor, trying to cover up my head, and he was screaming, "Let's kill him. Let's kill him." I didn't give a shit at the moment if I died. I felt that would be better than where I was.

I was angry at Mom, too, for letting it go on that way, for not stepping in more often when she could see we were being physically abused. She condoned it, saying, "You know better than to cross your father." I didn't have to do anything to cross my father a lot of the time. It was the insanity created by the sugar, lack of insulin, and high blood pressure. All those things together made him as crazy as he was at times. In the midst of all that uncertainty, I didn't expect there was any way that things could get any better or change.

The first time my dad ever told me he loved me was about a year and a half ago, after he had a heart attack; I had to tell him first. As a kid, there wasn't nurturing between my father and me. My mother would hug me and kiss me and tell me I was a good boy, but my dad would always try to push me to be better, to do better, to work harder, to be a lot of things that he wanted me to become.

If my dad didn't like the way things were, he would blame it on us kids: "If it wasn't for you dirty, rotten kids, I wouldn't have this situation that I'm stuck in now. I'd be driving a Cadillac."

I wanted my father to be proud of me, and I tried everything in the world that I could to get him to pay attention to me and be warm with me. I was an honor-roll student and I worked hard in the family business.

Dad made me drop out of football when I was a freshman in high school because it was conflicting with my work schedule. He did let me involve myself in theater arts during high school because the rehearsals were at night after the store closed.

Looking back on my family background, I felt very different from other children. None of the other kids I knew had to come home and work in their family business every day after school and all summer long. I remember going over to dinner at a friend's house. They sat down to a dinner and carried on a normal conversation about things that happened during their day. I thought how different that was from my home, where conversation at dinner always centered around the business and what duties needed to be done.

Dad's mellowed out over the past couple of years. He was a sick person. Our family was a difficult family to grow up in. My dad is now very ill with congestive heart failure. He's been given about a year and a half to live. He has diabetes, high blood pressure, and emphysema. He got a lot of that from the glue we used in the shoe-repair trade and from heavy tobacco use.

The dysfunctional part of our family had to do with my dad's illness with diabetes and hypertension and my reaction to it. I don't put myself either at fault or at blame for this. It's the way it was, and my part in all this is, How can I move on from there? How do I get better?

I have three children. My daughter is nine, one son is eight, and another son is six. They're active, happy, healthy kids most of the time. Sometimes when they get really boisterous and I've had a day that's been rather taxing, I'll get upset with my kids. I find myself acting a lot like my dad acted toward me, not allowing them to be kids. If I'm getting too upset, I let my wife handle them for a while. I go for a walk, calm down, cool out, come back, and explain to the kids that I love them and it wasn't them that I was mad at but their behavior. It certainly wasn't pointed out to me that way growing up.

I feel a lot of pity for my brothers and sisters. They went through what I went through, but any attempts I've made with them to discuss it fall on deaf ears. My family and I are not real close. A lot of the time, I avoid my family because I don't want to get too involved in their problems. A lot of my family are still comfortable in their uncomfortability, and they haven't made a choice to try to make things different in their lives.

I've been an introverted extrovert all my life. I try real hard to be out among people, making jokes and having people like the me I can present to them; but it's hard for me to get down to the real me and share that with anybody. A lot of my extrovertedness is holding inside what is really me. I am afraid of sharing it. I'm afraid of letting other people know I can be less than adequate, have fears, and can fly into a rage.

I don't want my children to grow up knowing a dad like I knew. I can see my father in me when I'm disciplining my children. It's a rememberance of my own childhood I carry around with me.

Karen, a marketing executive, is the daughter of a prescription-tranquilizer addict. Repeating the relationship pattern her parents modeled for her as a child, Karen has had many relationships with emotionally unavailable men. These relationships, including some with married men and her own marriage to an alcoholic husband, left her feeling "worthless." She says, "I get sad when I think of how little I valued myself."

KAREN ▸ My mother was eighteen and my father was twenty or twenty-one when they were married. She was pregnant with me; they had to get married. I always felt somewhat responsible for that, and this feeling was reinforced a lot: "If it hadn't been for you, this wouldn't have happened." They were both, and still are, so emotionally immature.

I was shuffled from one set of grandparents to the other frequently, because my parents were having problems. In old family movies, I was always the performer. It was "Twirl around, Karen, blow us a kiss, and give your grandfather a hug." I was always rewarded for that type of thing. I was loved when I was on. If I was having a down day, then nobody loved me. Because of that I learned to be a pretty good actress and manipulate.

A few years ago I met a woman who used to baby-sit for us, and she said to me, "My memory of you is of a very small child running around trying to make everything okay and keep everybody happy." I got rewarded by both sets of my grandparents for being strong, keeping things on track, and for getting dinner on the table at the right time. Those grandparents almost became my parents. As sick as they were in their own way, they were less sick than my own parents. The love that I got really came from my grandparents.

I'm not sure when my mother really started with the tranquilizers. I can remember doctors coming to our house when I was a child and giving her shots to settle her down when she would go into one of her tirades and go berserk. There really wasn't a lot of physical violence. In fact, it was very confusing because when she did punish me, ten minutes later she would bring me cookies and juice and say, "Oh, I'm sorry." I didn't know what kind of behavior was okay and what wasn't. One minute I was getting slugged for something and the next minute I was getting rewarded.

When a younger brother and sisters came along, I was really thrust into the role of the little mother. I took care of them, cooked for them, rocked the carriage, and walked them. My brother is a diabetic, so I had to cook special meals for him and make sure he took his insulin. As a result, I never got to be a child and play. I never got to do a lot of the carefree things I saw my friends doing. I grew up really fast. My brother and I were extremely aggressive toward each other. He'd hit me over the head with a hammer, and I'd knock him off of his bicycle and break his arm. We've talked about it since then, and we understand now that we were really angry at our parents. Since it wasn't okay to show our anger upward, we showed it toward each other.

My father, who was a car salesman, was never there. I recall very little interaction with him at all, and when he was there, I remember being criticized by him. I don't remember ever being stroked or held or being told "I love you." I can remember trying to please him a lot and doing lots of things to try to get attention.

My mother re-created in her own marriage the same type of relationship that she had with her father. She was constantly frustrated with my father because he wouldn't talk and he wouldn't feel. Those were the same things her father didn't do. She kept trying to change my father, but he never would. The more frustrated she got with him, the more she turned to drugs.

I can remember at night hearing my parents screaming and yelling and fighting. I can remember getting up in the night saying, "What's wrong," and my parents would say to me, "Nothing's wrong." So I'd go back to my room thinking, "I hear anger, but they're saying everything's fine, so there must be something wrong with me."

When I was thirteen, my mother and father divorced. My mother had an affair with the minister at a local church, and my father moved in with his parents and didn't talk to any of us.

After my parents were divorced, we moved about a half hour north of Indianapolis, and it was quite a culture shock. From a huge home, we moved into an apartment, and my mother went to work.

The minister she'd been having the affair with broke it off and was moved to New York. Things began to really go downhill for her then and she became suicidal. We'd only see my dad every other weekend. He remarried very quickly to a woman who babied him, buttered his rolls, and put his socks on his feet in the morning. My mother was never really that way; she was far too wrapped up in herself to be able to relate to anybody else.

My body started to develop very early, so I always looked a lot older than I was, and I acted a lot older, too, because of the way I was raised. All of a sudden I was in an apartment complex with a swimming pool. I was with boys, and I had never been exposed to that sort of thing before in my life. My mother sensed some of this and decided it would be good for me to have an older man, like a father role model, to talk to. There was a history teacher at my school who happened to live in the same apartment complex, so she would send me over there for talks. He molested me. He never went as far as having intercourse with me, but he did some pretty bizarre things that were terribly frightening. Yet, I thought because my mother told me I should go there and be with him, there was something wrong with me. To this day, I've never told my mother about that.

My mother became involved with a man in her business whom she subsequently ended up marrying. It turned out he had spent twenty-one years on death row in Pennsylvania. He happens to be a wonderful man, and I love him dearly to this day, but my mother hasn't been married to him for fifteen years.

Since I went to college and moved away, my mother met an attorney, to whom she's now married, and lives in New York. He's very well established and is very powerful. That was very attractive to my mother because she felt she was very powerless. In reality, he's extremely weak and is very much manipulated by her.

In my own life, I have done exactly the same things my mother did after telling myself I did not want to be like her. When I was twenty-six years old, I looked around and started thinking, "Oh my gosh, I'm starting to get a little older here and I'm not married." So I married somebody who is very much like my father, very much unable to feel, talk, or communicate. He gave me strokes for the way I looked and the way I acted. At the time I met him, I was heavy and he told me, "If you lose thirty pounds and let your nails grow, I'll marry you." I did, and he did.

I put on this wonderful wedding. I wore my great-great-grandmother's wedding dress, had harp music, and got married in an old mansion. It was beautiful. The papers all raved about it. I can remember looking out in the parking lot and watching my husband take a swig out of a bottle. He was loaded. I didn't know at the time that he was an alcoholic, but I know he is now. For a long time he would blow-dry my hair and lay out my clothes like I was a Barbie Doll. I thought at first it was great, but I began to see that it was sick and I rebelled against it totally. I adopted the arrogance and the superiority that people with low self-esteem often do. I began acquiring a lot of things. I had a beautifully landscaped home with a pool in the backyard, expensive cars, and lots of clothes, and became unhappier by the minute.

A man I had an affair with before I was married reentered my life about the time that things were really getting bad in my marriage. We started up again, and I thought he would save me. The exact same thing happened to me, however, that happened to my mother when she left her marriage to go with the minister. This guy ended up saying to me, "Gee, I can't do this."

What makes me the saddest when I look back is how I was always turning to people who were not capable of giving me love for love. I think I turned to them because I thought I could change them. I was never in a relationship with anybody that I didn't try to change. All that did was allow me not to look at myself and only got me deeper and deeper into my own despair.

About three years ago, I turned thirty, got divorced, and found myself totally alone. I became suicidal. I denied my responsibility for any of my problems. I put on my victim hat and tried to continue my life. On the outside it looked like everything was great. I did a good job isolating myself and freezing my feelings and nobody ever worried about me. Nobody got close enough to know any differently. I also kept entering into relationships with people who were abusive in one way or another. Looking back, I've picked a whole string of people who were either alcoholics or had drug problems.

My growing up affected me in personal relationships and at work. On the surface I appeared very arrogant; deep inside I was terribly insecure. I had a horrible fear of both failure and success. I sabotaged myself all the time. I was a horrible procrastinator. I get sad when I think of how little I valued myself.

I now realize that I wasn't given the most critical thing in life—a positive feeling about myself. I was always given the message that I was bad or I wasn't good enough. I played that back to myself; and because of that, I didn't have any confidence. I had a neon sign on my forehead saying, "Stomp all over me. I'm a victim, victim, victim." I wasn't an unwilling victim. I went along with the scenario. Even when I knew I was a freight train heading for the wall at a very high speed, I couldn't stop my behavior.

Today I know I deserve a lot more. That gives me a lot of

hope, because I can attract even healthier people into my life now.

I totally abandoned me. I have never treated anyone else in my life as badly as I've treated myself. I realize that now, and now I'm trying to make up for it and be a lot nicer to me.

Harry is a recovering cocaine addict and alcoholic. A therapist himself, Harry analyzes his past destructive life-style of addictions, skydiving, and use of women as his adult way of surviving the emotional and sexual abuse of his mother and the failure to stop that abuse by his workaholic surgeon father.

HARRY ▸ As a little girl, my mother was sent away to live with relatives. Something happened in her family, so they could "no longer keep her." My mother's depression had started long before I was born. It's that depression, that inability to tolerate a separation, and that abandonment that I've struggled with all my life. Everybody in my family struggles with it in his or her own way. For my mother it culminated in her suicide.

My mother had been a very intelligent high school student and had won a scholarship to the university. When my parents got married, she dropped out of school. That was another kind of loss in her life, and the bitterness about that stayed alive in her right up until the end.

When I was born, I was powerless over my parents. My life was unmanageable at the very beginning; I think all children are born that way. However many kids can look at that time and feel a sense of safety and nurturance. For a long time in my life, when I moved back deep inside myself, I would find nothing.

When I was two and a half, my mother had a daughter who was born dead and clearly experienced that loss as a repetition of the loss of her own parents, and she turned on me. By the time I was three, because of my mother's depression and my father's movement more and more deeply into medical school, a bunch of things happened to make me "responsible."

At a very young age, I became accountable to manage my mother's sense of self—esteem, respect, and coherence. I remember more and more clearly meeting that demand to take care of her, in order to have a mother for myself, and my fa-

ther's inability to deal with her. My mother's depression because of my father's long absences with his career turned her
toward me to meet her needs. Her use of me to undo his abandonment also became an abuse. She began to use me to regulate
her moods. When I tried to get my father's help, he became
angry, and I assumed that the anger was because of what I had
done. So my father, in his anger, and I, in my own rage, moved
further and further apart. He was available to me only as an
abstract, perfectionistic, demanding image that I struggled to
live up to. My mother was in command verbally. My father was
mute, aloof, unresponsive, and yet not criticizable, because of
the idealized function as a doctor he carried on outside.

My parents' interactions were a war. It was always a battle-
field. Within the dynamics of their marriage, one of the things
my father did was to offer my mother eight children to feed her
neediness.

My father saw my mother using me, fondling me, playing
with me, exploring me, finding out how to explore a man by
using her own child. I experienced it in my life as sexual abuse.
My father's still a fearful figure for me. Even now, as I begin to
experience him as an old man who's harmless, another part of
me still sees him as that young father, confused and terrified at
what his wife was doing to his son, standing enraged in a doorway and turning away. My terror was that I thought it was
because of me. I didn't know—as children never know—that his
anger was because of what she was doing with me.

My mother used a lot of pills, and my father would bring
them home because they're offered to doctors. My mother's
heavy smoking—four and a half packs of unfiltered cigarettes a
day—and her constant complaints about hay fever were the reasons given for the medication she took. I had been some years
into recovery when an insight about this first appeared. I was
sitting in a meeting and I wondered, "How come we could
never wake up Mom before eleven-thirty in the morning?" I
heard my father's voice say, "Don't you dare ask that about
your mother." I was terrified. My heart was pounding. I broke
out in a sweat. I know now there were two things I was uncovering. One was that my mother's chronic use of the pills and the
medications was the reason we couldn't wake her up in the
morning; therefore, we couldn't get fed by her and we had to

take care of her. The other thing involved a very young father who, when I needed him but couldn't say, "Help me with this woman; she's doing something to me; she's using me, she's abusing me, she's having sex with me," stood angrily in the doorway and responded with a look that said, "Don't you dare say that about your mother," and left me forever.

As I moved into life I needed to keep the only connections I had to both her and my dad, which meant that I've had a war going on with myself all my life. Only in the last two years has a cease-fire been put in place.

I spent my senior year of high school with a family in Germany and experienced two things. I saw a family that could function completely differently from my own and I was introduced to alcohol. What emerged was the ability to construct a self that would work and would be admired. I came back to the United States and I went away to college.

Those were the years when the Vietnam War was getting hot and the atrocities were building. Morally I knew that I couldn't participate in that war and in 1967 I was indicted for failing to keep the draft board notified of my whereabouts. First I left the country; then I snuck back across the border and hid out. At one point, the FBI was twenty minutes behind me and I had to flee. For six years I lived underground. During that time I didn't make any contact with my family at all.

I played in a band, and somebody gave me some amphetamines, and I liked what they did. I tried a lot of other drugs but became addicted to speed. Being addicted was a way of staying in touch with my mother. Being addicted is a way of putting something inside of you that meets all your needs but abuses the hell out of you. When I first used that drug it didn't abuse me, it made me feel good. The first time I was put in my mother's arms she didn't abuse me either; she made me feel good.

At the end of the time I was hiding out from the government, I was real crazy. I was isolated and the pain of living was more than I could bear. I went to see a psychotherapist. After a couple sessions he said, "You need to do something." I made contact with my family for the first time in those six years. I called and I was welcomed back. I had to go out to North Dakota to deal with the legal matters and my father helped me.

I took the physical exam but refused to cooperate. I'd invested six years in fighting the draft and wasn't about to give up. When that happened, they said that I was unfit for military service and dropped the charges.

So I went back to college and got a job as a waiter in a big rock 'n' roll bar. I met somebody who had just made her first skydive, and I became totally involved in jumping. I'd kicked the speed and I was drug-free, but I began to drink at the time I got started jumping.

Skydiving is instantly gratifying. All you have to do is step out of the door. It's involving mentally, physically, and emotionally, and becomes a social sport when you jump with other people. It's also a way to combat something that I think is endemic to my family—a lack of pleasure. I was also able to risk and save myself constantly. I made more than two thousand jumps in nine or ten years. I've only made a couple of jumps since I got sober.

My alcoholism and skydiving career began at about the same time, and the symptoms of the one addiction fed into the symptoms of the other. By the time I was thirty, I was fully hooked on both. The sport was making a transition then between the macho types and the people who were more involved in the drug culture and were into free-fall formations. I became very involved and got real good at it too. When a list was made of twenty-eight people from the United States to try some jumps that had never been tried, I was invited. I was in some world-record jumps. In the late seventies cocaine came into the sport as well.

From the very first, cocaine was a very powerful drug for me for two reasons: I'd already been addicted to speed and cocaine's a powerfully erotic drug. In a very frightening, crazy way, cocaine is the most addictive drug there is on the street. If you gave me Ronald Reagan, Prince Charles, and two needles, I'd hand you back two cocaine addicts in eight hours.

I began to use cocaine in short runs; it's usually called a run rather than a binge. I would use a needle too. It was a way of being in touch with my physician father. I would defend that to myself by saying it was more efficient that way. Alcohol was constant: I drank every day. Early on in my drinking, I lost a marriage to a woman who was aware that I was alcoholic and said so. I needed to get out of that relationship to continue my addictions. I used relationships the way I'd been used by my mother, to modulate my self-respect. I would gauge my self-worth by how someone else was interested in the woman that I would attach to my arm. That gave me a self that I could see, as opposed to my internal world, where there was nothing.

I moved to a little town in Florida and worked for a crazy cocaine addict in the parachuting business. The last time I used cocaine, I used a quarter ounce in eight hours. I came to lying on the ground next to my car, with policemen hanging on to my arm saying, "Son, you look like a pincushion. Where'd you get it?" They took me to an emergency room and let me go home. I never used cocaine after that.

I fled into the booze. I used that for another six months. My drinking got worse and began to interfere with the skydiving. I didn't want to jump; I wanted to drink. I wanted to get high and hole up. I finally went into treatment because I kept waking up alive. In treatment I realized that I had made up all the cardboard cutouts I could make up to get by. I soaked them all in alcohol, and they all caught on fire.

You can't work the Twelve Steps of AA and not start to become who you are. As you do, it starts to hurt. I see that everything I've done has made sense. The forty-two years of self-hatred is now turning into respect and admiration for how that little boy survived when his mother abused him and his father turned away in shock and horror. That little boy thought it was his fault, yet he survived. He survived by pulling the pieces he could from the two of them and putting them together to make it through. I am beginning to admire my own history and the grayness is starting to turn into rainbows.

Beth, a television producer, is the daughter of a father who was a workaholic and a mother who "suffered from low self-esteem." Because of that background, she says, "Most of the guys I've gone out with, and I've been engaged to two of them, were alcoholics." Beth also undervalued her talents and abilities and even reduced her self-worth by working jobs with long hours and low pay.

BETH ▸ In the last year or so, I've realized I didn't get enough attention or loving when I was an infant and that's made me seek physical affection from others in a way that's not proper for a young lady. My mom told me they used to put me in the farthest room because I cried all the time or cried so loudly.

By the time I was four, there were three children, and two more followed. We lived in a little house and were always doubling up or tripling up. We never had our own rooms, and a lot of fighting went on. I think it was fighting to be noticed.

At dinner Dad would be there for an hour, and then he'd go out to his civic and community meetings. We all fought for his attention. I guess we knew that we were supposed to have two parents, not just one. I remember very fond times at dinner, but inevitably somebody would leave the dinner table crying. Something was wrong when every single night somebody left in a tantrum.

The father-daughter relationship was very superficial, and the mother-daughter relationship was not good either. I think my mother suffered from low self-esteem and didn't seem to realize she was raising children and her children needed guidance. She never taught me how to put on makeup or do my nails. When I started my period, she gave me a book to read about it.

There was a lot of corporal punishment in our family. We were always getting hit with a belt or a hairbrush when we did things wrong. That was my mother's only way of controlling us. When there was a disaster in the family, they would take some action. When I was twelve, I was caught shoplifting. My girlfriend had stolen all kinds of things, and I had a few small items. They saw her and picked her up, and I was brought along with her down to security. My mom came to the store to get me and then locked herself in her room for two days and wouldn't come out to talk to me because she was so embarrassed. My parents sent me to a psychiatrist, and I was diagnosed depressive. They would buy two hours of time so that when I got to the office and when I left there would be no one in the waiting room. Although they were taking some action, they were embarrassed there was a problem. Last year my younger sister and I were talking, and she didn't even know that I had spent six or eight years going to a psychiatrist. It was hidden from the family.

My parents liked to keep up outward appearances. They were very civic-oriented, very "go to church on Sunday," and caring about the larger picture. I think they forgot that there was a smaller picture that needed attention. My parents didn't pay enough attention to our schoolwork and later on our staying out or drinking.

We had a very physical family in the violent sense rather than the affectionate sense. I remember going after my sister with a knife, quite frequently. We'd be in the kitchen and somebody would grab something. We'd throw heavy objects at each other, really having the potential to seriously damage someone. At an ice-skating rink I pushed my sister and she hit the rail and broke her tooth. It could have been a lot worse though: we could have poked each other's eyes out every week the way we fought.

In junior high I was accepted easily and became very good friends with the "popular crowd." They were the cheerleaders, wrestlers, and football players. I spent a lot of time after school either involved in the pep club or sports. In junior high school I had my first little boyfriend.

After junior high school, I went to a year of Catholic high school. It was a great education, but the social life was absolutely terrible. It was all cliques, and I just couldn't break in. It was a lonely year so I went back to public high school, and it seemed like things had changed a lot. People were getting into drugs really big-time. There was a lot of LSD, speed, and pot. Half of my friends got into drugs and half didn't. A lot of my friends took a sharp turn to the right or a sharp turn to the left. I kind of straddled the line.

During lunch we were allowed to go off campus. We'd go to the house of someone whose mom worked, smoke a couple of joints, and laugh a lot. I went to Latin class high every day in the fifth period. In high school I smoked a lot of pot, drank beer on the weekends, and did it all without my parents knowing.

I lost my virginity the summer between high school and college. I just wanted to know what it was like. College was when I started really going over the edge as far as the physical stuff was concerned. In college, I would tend to be a little on the easy side. It made me feel valuable for that night. It made me feel pretty that someone wanted me.

When I got out of college, I started dating a guy. That first big romance lasted three years. He had graduated from high school, was in the army for a couple of years, did all kinds of drugs in Germany, and got a discharge. It was probably all sex. He drank a lot and was probably an alcoholic. He had a photographic memory and knew history. I was impressed by that. He didn't have a job when I met him. He got a job finally and then got fired for stealing from the company. I was even engaged to him for a couple of weeks. He was sociable. He was fun. He had a good sense of humor, but basically he was just a bum.

After that first boyfriend, I went out with one guy who didn't seem to have any problems. After four or five months, I started putting too much pressure on him, wanting too much of a commitment, and I scared him off.

Then the next boyfriend was pretty much a loser. He had gotten two drunk-driving tickets and had been addicted to drugs. He got fired a month after we started going out. I kept dating him for a year and a half and ended up living with him. I left him because I fell head over heels in love with another guy who, between the time I started dating him and the time we broke up, went very far downhill. He was very deeply involved with alcohol. He severed every tie in his life, except one sister with whom he'd communicate on the phone long-distance. He lived in the woods and told me his dream was to live so far out that a helicopter would have to drop him supplies once a month. He didn't want any human contact at all. Breaking up with him was really difficult.

That's when I started finding out about alcoholism and dysfunctional families and realizing that by having a workaholic family I had had an upbringing similar to that of those raised with alcoholism.

I read *Women Who Love Too Much* and knew I should not be involved with all these people who were emotionally unavailable. Almost every guy I've ever dated was an alcoholic, and I never really dated anyone my own age. They've always been five years older, yet emotionally they were teenagers. I knew that there was something wrong with this pattern. So I got myself into therapy. I was also worried about developing alcoholism myself, because it runs in my family. I think it's something that I still have to be really careful with, although I don't drink very much anymore.

I see a therapist privately and also go to group. My therapist helped me see I was emotionally neglected as a child and had an emotionally unavailable father. Because my parents are so liberal and do so many good things, I didn't make the connection that mine was not a good, healthy childhood. Now my parents are wonderful. My father has learned how to relax and have fun and my mother and I are so close now. They've always been supportive since we became adults. I think relating to us as adults is much easier for them than it was relating to us as children.

I look back on my childhood, and I know it was a very dysfunctional home. My father was a workaholic, and my mom just didn't know how to deal with children. I don't think she was very comfortable with herself. I remember a lot of negativity and constant harassment on her part. This spring I had a nice talk with my dad, and I told him how much I loved him. It's something that never before had been said. He's a very, very good person, but back then he just didn't know how to relate to his daughters or his son. It would have been nice if my parents had been a little older. I think they were too young, and I guess coming from a dysfunctional home himself, my father didn't know what a father was supposed to do. Right now, they would make wonderful parents. They make wonderful grandparents.

I consider myself very, very lucky. I never wrecked a car, though there were probably lots of times when I was drunk enough to get into a very serious accident. I also could have been married and divorced, I'm sure, with five kids by now. I'm glad that at a young age I have been able to learn about the problems of the past and how they affect me today.

Brian's father was an abuse victim and his mother was the daughter of an alcoholic. Even though Brian was verbally, physically, and sexually abused as a child, he still fights his belief that he had a "wonderful childhood." He achieved the American Dream with his six-figure income as a publicist, yet found he was "miserable."

BRIAN ▸ I was the oldest of three boys. During my child-hood I always felt there was something wrong with me. I was very bright as a kid, and that was the best thing I had going for me. My ego was tied up in being that way, which made it very easy to piss off other kids, particularly kids that weren't as bright. In school I always got A's. I went through the second and third grade in one year, which was fairly common back then. It was my mother's idea; she also had done the same thing. So, not only was I bright, but I was also on display because I was a year younger than everyone in my class and still the brightest. My mother valued people for being intelligent, so she was al-ways encouraging precocious behavior, high grades, and not being a kid. I was constantly admonished to "Grow up," "Stop acting like a baby," "Don't play with the little kids," and "Act your age."

I used to run away to my grandma's because there was some kind of caring there. She used to feed me. She was a warm and loving person some of the time; the rest of the time she was telling me I was going to cause her to have a nervous break-down. My grandparents were sure I was going to end up in reform school. I remember one time they drove me right up to the gates of a local reform school and said, "Brian, see those kids over there behind those windows with bars on them? That's where you're going because you're such a bad boy."

Nobody knew there was alcoholism in the family. Relatives had drinking problems, and "Dad just can't hold his liquor very well." It wasn't alcoholism. Both my grandfathers, my father, and my brother were all alcoholics. None of this was known to me until my wife was in an alcoholic treatment center. I started to cry one night watching a film on alcoholism because all of a sudden I realized, "That's my family, all of these people are alcoholics, that's what the hell is wrong." That's when I also began to realize that all the bizarre things that had happened over the years that we accepted as normal weren't. A minor key that had been playing in the back of my head just screamed out, "Yes, there is something wrong, and it's alcoholism, and it's been going on in your family for generations." It was shatter-ing. It was devastating, but it was also an incredible relief to at last be able to realize what the hell was going on.

I began to put all the patterns of behavior together. I remember my dad being drunk almost every Christmas Eve. I can remember him coming home and passing out, his face going down into his dinner plate. We'd get him off to bed, and someone would say, "Well, Dad had too much to drink." I can remember when I was a kid, my father would drive with all of us in the car at a hundred miles an hour. I can still see the speedometer needle down past a hundred. At the time, it was exciting, but I realize now he was drunk. My mother ran the household. She was very controlling right up until she died. No feelings were ever expressed. She was very tough, very bright, very motivated.

I was in a bad car accident one time when I was in Boston, and it was my dad that came to visit, not my mother. My dad was visibly shaken and sad about it. My mother barely acknowledged the fact that I came home with my head in a huge bandage. My mother was hard and cold. A college friend of mine said one night, "I don't mean this disrespectfully at all because I really like your mother and she's a lot of fun, but she's the most unmotherly mother I've ever met."

My mother hated men. My dad traveled a lot because he was in sales. My mother was always telling me what a bad guy he was and how he was running around with other women just like my granddad had done. I constantly had this drummed into my head. She was sure he had a mistress, and I was always the focal point for all of this crap.

I always knew I was different, and I knew something was wrong deep down. When I was in high school, I was a loner. I hung around with the other kids who got straight A's. Good grades were the only way to get any love from my parents. I always basically hated my dad, and my mom wore the pants in the family.

I have a brother. The last time I saw him, I brought some of this up to see if I could pick his brain about it. He said, "You're a goddamn fool to go back to the past. The past is past. I only look toward the present and the future."

I had a second brother who, lately I've sensed, was a lot closer to reality than I was. He got into alcohol, had trouble getting through school, and spent some time in a mental hospital. He was judged insane at one point. He got into drugs, wrecked cars, knocked up a girl, and had a hell of a time. Every week it seemed like there was a new awful thing he'd done. The night before my brother's wedding everybody was drunk, and he yelled at my mother, "You're so fucking good you think you've got balls."

He committed suicide by overdosing on drugs and alcohol. In a horrible scene reminiscent of some awful movie, he knocked on my mother's bedroom door and said, "I've got to go to the hospital." She called the doctor, and the doctor said, "Let's let him sleep it off this time because this has happened four or five times before." She woke up an hour later and he was dead outside her bedroom door in the hall.

I guess the saddest thing about my life was the lack of love and acceptance I got while growing up. If you realize that there's dysfunctional crap from your past that's affecting your behavior today, you want to go back and change it.

I graduated first in my class in high school and went to college for four years and then to business school. I was the youngest in my class there with a scholarship. The whole preoccupation of my life has been intellectual achievements and "being successful." I never had any carefree times. I've done better at that lately than I did as a kid. I used to trust no one; now I find that I can be more trustful of men. Fear of women is still present, and low self-esteem still floats around a lot of the time. It's also still hard for me to have fun.

My wife's an alcoholic; her dad was an alcoholic. For a long time in our marriage we drank to preserve the relationship and we spent money to maintain the relationship. My daughter is very caring but almost too conscientious and has some anger in her. My son is the star student, star athlete, star pianist and is now compelled by all three of these things. I played piano as a kid, but gave it up because I didn't want to be a sissy.

In terms of sexuality, I used to shut myself down emotionally and perform. I can't do that anymore because of all the crap that's come out. I'm just fighting to be myself, fighting to be real. I've learned to love myself most of the time. I don't have a high sense of self-esteem yet, but I'm working on it.

Today I find myself in a life-and-death battle to be my real self, not this fake self that has been there for so many years. I can't be that way anymore. When I started therapy, I hated everybody. I've worked through most of my anger toward my dad. I've been able to pretty much forgive my dad and have some love for him. I'm left with this fear and anger toward my mother, though, which translates into fear and anger toward some women. It's not at an everyday level, but it's always there in the background, and I can see that sometimes in my behavior even today. I think back through all my relationships with women, and underneath them all has been a fear of a castrating mother.

On the other side of the coin, I do have a very powerful sense of being a survivor and a very powerful sense of being a good person whom I love some of the time. I'm not scared about the future, and I guess I'm much more accepting of myself. Before I was always beating myself over the head for what I imagined as lack of career progress or being a failure. I'm thankful I've done as well as I have and that I've gotten where I am almost in spite of myself.

Today I'm not so inclined to be down on myself for not being a vice-president of my company. I realize people who have six-figure incomes are generally viewed as being reasonably successful.

Manolito, a free-lance copywriter and television scriptwriter who grew up in Puerto Rico, describes his alcoholic mother as a "big, big screamer" and his father as "emotionally unavailable." His own low self-esteem, alcoholism, and workaholism are the answers to his own question "What could I expect in life if I was presented daily with the bleakest, loudest, most abusive and painful kind of drama at the age of two, three, or four?"

MANOLITO ▸ I can't help feeling very sad when I talk about the pain I've gone through since my earliest childhood. By forcing myself to deal with the pain, I have radically changed my life.

I compare the experience I went through as a child to living in the middle of a war. It's the same kind of intense terror a kid might feel when he hears bombs falling or machine guns being fired around his house. The stress is comparable. I had that type of feeling on a daily basis because my mother was a daily drinker. She was also grossly overweight—at least fifty pounds overweight. Her alcoholic behavior goes way back, as far as my earliest memories.

In my mother's family there have been alcoholics, drug addicts, and compulsive gamblers. My father had eating problems in his childhood. My grandmother was an overeater, I believe; so neither of my parents came from functional families.

When one of the parents is an alcoholic, the co-dependent partner in the relationship is there for the chemically dependent person, but is not there for the children. My father neglected his responsibilities to us because he was busy performing my mother's. He was filling her shoes and emptying his. He was unable to take care of his own needs either because he was taking care of the needs of my mother. In many respects my father assumed the role of a martyr, a victim, or a slave. A lot of my mother's rage and criticism was directed at him: "You are the cause of my unhappiness. You have created this terrible home. It's all your fault. I married beneath. You have no capacity to make money. You're a failure. You're nobody."

I'm the second of four children: three boys and one girl. My mother would complain about the hassle we were. She would damn the hour we were born. Every problem we brought to her was a crisis. She was violently unhappy. When she watched television, we couldn't study because she raised the volume so high. Then we would be spanked if we didn't get good grades.

The choking impact of seeing my mother act out her insanity, the hate she exhibited for my father, and her constant states of panic and depression were all quite damaging to me. You could hear her fighting as you drove away from the house, and you could hear her screaming as you drove toward the house. You could feel the screaming. It got worse as her disease progressed.

My mother would criticize my looks. If you get that from your mother, how do you feel when you go out into the world? You project the type of insecurity your mother projected on you. There was a lot of pain, and I had nobody to talk to. I was bullied from the first grade on, through high school. I had been subjected to such a great amount of punishment at home, that by second nature I attracted being beaten, punished, made fun of, and ridiculed by others.

With the shouting that was going on in my house, I went through high school with very little sleep. I developed a skin condition known as cystic acne and the doctor never made the connection to the lack of sleep. The acne was so bad that I was ostracized in school. My mother took me to the dermatologist, blamed me for the problem, and complained that she had to buy some medicines.

My mother would complain to us how she was a slave to her children. We'd asked her, "Why did you bring us into the world?" She replied we were God's punishment to her and that she was crazy to have done it.

I became very isolated, because I couldn't possibly have friends if I was the son of the crazy lady of the street. One of the things that I'm most aware of now was my fear of intimacy, my capacity to have relationships.

During my adolescence I was involved in one very sick friendship. He would put me down and I would put him down. We couldn't stop. It continued in college. He became an alcoholic and I became an alcoholic. It was a nine-year dysfunctional friendship that culminated in drinking and drugging together. Our capacity to isolate from the rest of the kids, not participate in their activities, and be enmeshed in our nucleus was how we lived. He was never emotionally available to me, yet he was the only measure of acceptance I had. Had I been more whole and self-loving, I wouldn't have put up with that sick kind of love-hate friendship. I didn't have the sense of self-worth to make choices and changes. I swallowed many things that I didn't like in my life without challenging or questioning. Life was meant to be hard, so I suffered and accepted the suffering.

In high school or college I was always alone. In Puerto Rico, it is not unusual for a young boy who is gay like I am to seek out gay relationships. I didn't, I couldn't. I was afraid.

When I came back to Puerto Rico after college, my drinking made me unemployable until a friend of mine got me into the AA program. I was able to stop drinking, and I began to get jobs in advertising and public relations. I didn't work the AA program well because I substituted marijuana for alcohol, so my growth was really limited and intermittent. However, it kept me afloat and allowed me to be very successful in advertising in Puerto Rico.

I became a workaholic. At one point, I had two jobs. Of course, there was no time for relationships. At the age of twenty-four, my translation of a play ran for three months off-Broadway. I worked in the largest Hispanic advertising firm in the United States. My campaigns were winning awards right and left, but not a day passed in the agency that I didn't think I was going to get fired for incompetence. I wasn't able to appreciate the scope of my success. I was never comfortable with my success, even though I was given a very big contract to come here to the mainland to work in advertising, which I did for over two years.

I didn't want achievement. I wanted struggle. I wanted tension. I wanted stress. I wanted to be running all the time. I needed that adrenaline fix. I became addicted to what I felt living in the house of a violent alcoholic, a rage-aholic, a sad-aholic person.

I chase people who are emotionally unavailable to me. I pursue relationships that lead to my being abandoned. I've never had a steady lover. Whatever relationships I've had have always cost me money. It's like I have to pay for their company by buying meals, movie tickets, and presents. They never loved me for me. I had to give to get.

I'm thirty now and I'm recovering. I'm not where I think I should be, but I am where I am. I have a lot of hope, and I have moments in which I feel very, very happy to finally understand what these thirty years are all about. That's a lot of relief.

It dawned on me when I began to attend ACOA meetings that the reason I was unable to control my chemical dependency was because I really didn't think I could be a success, that I was entitled to save my life. I finally saw I was good enough, and I was able to let go of the drugs and live happy, sober, and free. Then I took a second look at life. I've been able to rid myself of my lack of interest for life, and God rid me of my addictive job. Today I am happy to say I have a wonderful relationship with my father, and my mother, in the midst of her disease, is making an effort to change.

I see that the lack of love I had for myself was because I did not get unconditional love in my home. It was not a matter of not having parents or of being neglected; it was a matter of being abused.

It's very important for every adult child, be they chemically dependent or not, to deal with his or her childhood issues. If you're an addict or an alcoholic and you don't deal with your ACOA issues, you'll have a hundred times more difficulty getting your program because you'll substitute compulsive behaviors such as overeating, overworking, addictive love relationships, or addictive sexual behaviors for drinking or drugs. All of these are life-threatening, and I've had to deal with them all.

For Alice, a special-education teacher, " 'feelings' is the other f-word." She has used food since adolescence as a way of handling feelings that she finds extremely threatening. Alice is still influenced in her adult life by the neglect by her mother, who suffered from cluster headaches, and her alcoholic father's behavior, which caused her pain and humiliation.

A LICE ▸ I am the eldest of four children. My parents both came from farm families, and when I was very young, we were very poor. That was the least of our problems however.

My dad was the oldest of ten and was not allowed to finish school, because he had to work on the farm. His dad was quite brutal with him, so my dad was a very shut-down, nonentity of a person. My mother was raised by my grandma, whom I love dearly; but Grandma is seriously into controlling other people and very judgmental about how other people live their lives. I believe my mother married my father to get out of the house, and I don't say as I blame her.

My father was a quiet, passive man who didn't show emotion or affection very well. My mother was the strong, domineering one in our family. She had cluster headaches—like a knife wound to the eye—during all of her pregnancies, so she was extremely ill during my early childhood.

My mother was a slapper. Stories are told about my sister and I playing tea party with our dolls and telling them to "shut up" and slapping them. I'm a migraine patient myself and have a history of severe headaches. When I was pregnant with my daughter, I had headaches similar to my mother's, and I now know why she hit. Noise is excruciatingly painful. When my mother had a headache, she put me in my bedroom. She used lots of narcotic medications to control her headaches. I have real strong sensations of the smell of that room and the light coming in around the drawn window shade. I believe I spent a lot of time in that room. She knew she couldn't care for me, so she put me in a safe place. However, I also believe that food was not always forthcoming when it was needed. I now suffer from an eating disorder, and part of that may be because I wasn't always fed when I was hungry.

The rage I may have felt as a young child being placed in that situation has had a big impact on my life. I still have tremendous sadness when I think about it, even more since I've had my daughter. I've had fears I would repeat some of those patterns with my own daughter, and I love her so.

My early childhood was not one of the happy-go-lucky preschool toddler. I had a bit of a school phobia. I would get ill and the principal would take me home. I did not perform well academically throughout most of elementary school. I was very preoccupied. I didn't do much math, didn't spell, and didn't write very well. The one strength I had in elementary school was reading. I was placed with the smart kids in sixth grade and remember feeling angry about that. I was a fish out of water. The sixth grade was a very painful year. I had a teacher who used to throw wet paper towels at me because I could not do long division; however, the music program was made available to me and I had some successes in the band. I don't recall having close friends in elementary school. I recall seeing myself as the child apart from the circle of children playing. I was the little kid on the outside looking very painfully hurt but not able to communicate in any way that I wished to be included.

Even to this day I still carry around that image of myself as being just a little out of sync with the rest of what's going on. I'm always on the edge and in my own nonverbal, non-body-language way saying, "Please include me," and being mortified at the thought that they might.

As my early elementary years passed, my father was becoming more and more ill with his alcoholism. There were the frequent trips to see a man about a horse. "Where's Daddy going?" I'd ask. "He's going to see a man about a horse," would be the response. I always wondered where the horse was when he came home. In truth, he was going to the local farm-implement dealer and drinking. That kind of covering up took place in our family.

My dad's alcoholism really took hold in the family when I was an adolescent. What I remember most about those teenage years is the tremendous embarrassment that I experienced with his behavior. I recall being humiliated by my father's actions when he was drinking. He used to do something we called "The DJ Jig." It looked a little bit like a variation of a Mexican hat dance, but his eyes would be slits. It was very mortifying because people would not be laughing with him, but at him.

I was about thirteen when I realized that he wasn't reliable. A pajama party had been planned, and I was going to have my friends over. The night before, he brought home his friends. They all got drunk, fell off the porch, ripped the railing off the house, and trashed the place. It wasn't something that was ever talked about. I just endured the pain silently. I feared someone would find out and know. As I got older and dated, I would come home with my dates in the evening. My father might be sitting on the couch in his underdrawers with a beer.

He asked me intrusive questions about my sexual activities with boys. I was just at the kissing stage, but it was like he got some kind of pleasure asking those kinds of questions. As I got even older he would talk about fixing me up with his drinking buddies for dates. That made me horribly uncomfortable, and I never did that.

In high school I decided that I was not going to stay at home; I was going to go away to college. I fought the battle royal to get out of that house and not go to the local community college. My dad offered me cars and money if I would stay home.

I remember as an adolescent seeing some dumb movie where a woman became an alcoholic. At that point, I decided I was never going to drink and I've done very little drinking in my lifetime. Unfortunately, I didn't pick up on the "don't abuse food" message because that's what I have done. I use food as a drug, and I have abused food for much of my life from adolescence on. I overeat, I worry about my body, and I worry about fat. There's a part of me that would love to be anorexic, too, because I have gotten very thin on several occasions. I have a real control issue around food. There's a big body-image part of my problem that says, "If you get thin enough, life will be better."

I've spent most of my life shut down, not feeling emotion, just autopiloting. "Feelings" is the other *f*-word for me. I find feelings very painful. When the feelings start to perk up, I find myself eating. Broccoli will not do; carrots will not do, even in massive quantities—that's not the kind of food I'm looking for. I'm looking for the high-fat, high-carbohydrate kinds of foods. I'm very specific in what I want. The sweeter, the better. Dove Bars are a good anesthetic. At different stressful periods of my life, such as when starting a new job, immediately following my marriage, and at the birth of my daughter, I gain weight.

I also have tremendous problems with relationships, although I managed to get married. I married an alcoholic. He's now recovering. We have a marriage of emotional distance. It seems to have worked for us, although it's not always satisfying to either of us. Because of early experiences with sexual abuse by an uncle, I don't care for men especially. I like "grandpas," sort of nonsexual old guys that don't threaten me. I'm working on this in my therapy, and I hope I can be around men eventually and not be uncomfortable and feel threatened.

I went into therapy so I wouldn't gain weight. So it's been amazing how much weight I've gained. I think I've been taught, as many of my friends in the Overeaters Anonymous program have been taught, "Don't feel that way" or "You shouldn't feel that way." This message is something I heard in my childhood thousands of times.

I've been depressed a lot in my lifetime. As I look back I think it's a result of not expressing feelings in any kind of a straightforward way. When I get angry, it's very difficult for me to express it, so I turn it inward and I get depressed. I'm very limited in my range of emotions. I can feel some joy, more with my child than with anything else. With my work, I feel good when a kid I'm working with does well with something. I function real well on the surface. I look good, act good, take care of business, and raise a family. I'm very competent. But I'm told I have a Ph.D. in hiding how I feel.

At least now I know now that I have feelings. I know now

why I'm afraid and why I'm so afraid of being angry. I get little glimmers of joy, but I have a long way to go. I've been shut down for a lot of years. The conditioning was very, very strong.

The things that happened in my early childhood are finished. They're over, except they're not gone. My ability to live a freer kind of life and have relationships as an adult are limited because of my early experiences. I still experience a great deal of pain because I can't sustain a friendship. I'm looking at the kind of childhood that has made it impossible for me—without doing the things that I'm doing—to live life on an emotional level.

I've tried to "re-parent" myself through my daughter. I am extremely tolerant and affectionate toward her, which is the antithesis of what I received in my early childhood.

I think in the future I'll be able to have other relationships. I worry about being overly connected with my daughter. I don't want to put all my emotional eggs in her basket. I don't want to do that to her, and I don't want to do it to me. I hope that with ongoing recovery I can feel whole enough and healthy enough, so she can have her life and I can have mine.

Jan, a successful condominium saleswoman who grew up in a family with an alcoholic father, is a recovering alcoholic herself. Three of Jan's four children are chemically dependent; two of them are recovering. After a thirty-two-year marriage, Jan has moved out on her own after concluding that the glue that was holding her marriage together was her own "fear of abandonment."

JAN ▸ I was an only child until I was six years old. Up until that time, I don't really remember a lot of family problems. After my brother and sister were born, I became aware of my father drinking. When there were any family celebrations, it was very apparent that he drank too much. All four of my grandparents and my mother's two sisters were alcoholics. I can remember being excited about holidays and then having a fear and dread of what would happen. It depended on which relative had enough to drink first as to when the arguments would start. There were times when we didn't go near my mother's family because my father had had some drunken escapade and we were banned from the rest of the family. His binges and the family arguing were really bad. I remember going to both my grandmothers' funerals, and most of the aunts and uncles didn't speak to one another. They hadn't for years. I remember thinking, "When I grow up it's not going to be like this." I never understood why they didn't speak to each other. Now I know they couldn't have confrontations, work out their problems, and go on with their lives.

I remember my mother whispering to me when I was a teenager that maybe my father was an alcoholic; we never talked about it openly. I remember feeling very different because I didn't think there were any other kids I knew who had this going on in their homes. We always hid it.

I really felt a lot more anger toward my mother than my father. It was mostly for all the covering up that we were all expected to do. Being an alcoholic myself, I have a lot of empathy for what my father went through. I can look back and realize he was sick and did the best he could.

My mother was a music teacher, and we all had to take music lessons. We weren't allowed to be in sports because that would take away from our practice time or we might break a finger. There was always a tremendous fear of letting us do anything. We couldn't go to the circus because the tent might collapse. I was never able to stay overnight at anybody's house or go on scouting activities, because something might happen.

When I got into the adult children issues, the toughest thing for me to deal with was not my relationship with my father but with my mother. I had much more anger directed toward her. She died twenty years ago.

I think the biggest loss I felt in childhood was my mother. To be very frank, my father's a dear man. He happens to be an alcoholic and has a big heart. If I have anger directed toward him, it's really toward the alcoholism. A few years ago he was on a binge. He fell in his apartment and split his head open and almost bled to death. It took three or four days before anybody found him. If he hadn't been drinking, he could have picked up the phone and gotten help; but because he was drinking of course he couldn't tell anybody.

When I was in high school, I decided the one way I could

get out of the house was to go into a convent. It was a legitimate way of leaving, and I thought everybody would be happy. It is interesting that my brother went into the seminary and my sister went into the convent also. I was no sooner in the convent than I realized it was not the place I should be. Even there I felt different, but I could never put my finger on it.

I met my future husband two weeks after I came out of the convent. My parents decided they didn't want me to marry him, so of course, in my rebellious fashion, I ran away and got married. My reasons for wanting to go into the convent and for wanting to marry him were to get away from my family. I thought that marrying him against their wishes would finally do it. My mother wrote to me after I got married saying, "Of course, your father went on a tremendous binge; it was your fault he wanted to commit suicide."

When I was a teenager, I said to my mother, "If I ever get married, I'll marry somebody who doesn't drink." As it turned out, my husband didn't drink and that worked for me and against me. When I started to drink in my late twenties and when I subsequently got into a lot of trouble with alcohol, my husband had absolutely no understanding. The other side is that when I stopped drinking, at least I didn't have to come home to somebody who was drinking at night. So it did work both ways.

I really started to drink to escape. I found out when I drank that I didn't have to feel the way I was feeling. I knew I was pretty unhappy in my marriage, and drinking got me through a lot of it. I later took Dexedrine, which was given to me by a doctor. I ended up shopping doctors to get what I had to get.

I was in my early forties when I realized I was in a tremendous amount of trouble with alcohol. When Betty Ford went into treatment, I quit by going to AA. My own children got into a lot of trouble with drugs as well. It was difficult for me to accept, because it was another generation going the same way I had gone. I take no credit for their sobriety, but I was able to show them by my example and help them get into treatment that turned their lives around. My one son's been sober six years now, and my daughter, two and a half. I have another son who's still drinking, and my other daughter is okay. I have a lot of hope for my kids and my grandchildren that things will turn around and this family pattern won't keep repeating itself.

The most important thing is that we can talk about our feelings now; there's no covering up. As a child, I could never say out loud that I was unhappy. I couldn't talk when something was bothering me. I did the same thing with my own kids. I protected them from their father, who is not an alcoholic but is very rigid. I would say to my kids, "Don't tell your father." They grew up with the same kind of message I got, "No matter what's going on, don't tell." It's taken all of us a lot of work to get rid of that rule.

My thirty-year-old son tried to commit suicide a few months ago. He's really sick, but as a parent, I can only do so much. I have a really close relationship with my other two kids who are in AA. My fourth child is not chemically dependent but should be sitting in a group like this. I hope he will get around to that soon.

My relationship with my father is still pretty superficial. I went out to see him a few weeks ago to tell him that I'm going through a divorce. I got no reaction from him. I was so hurt and so disappointed. I had to say to myself, "This is a man who for eighty-six years was never able to say how he felt. Why do I expect it now?" I still have expectations that aren't real. I just have to accept that he is who he is. I'm sure my divorce hurts him and it certainly is going to change his life, but I can't make him talk about it.

What prompted me to seek a divorce was that I couldn't deal with my husband's anger anymore over the alcoholism in the family. I met my husband when I was eighteen and fresh out of a convent. He's eight years older than I am, and there was a tremendous control and manipulation of me by him. It was so bad he even bought all of my clothes. I used to say, "That's not so bad; he has wonderful taste and he'll spend a lot more money than I will." When I got sober I realized what was going on, and I knew it couldn't keep happening. We had separate bedrooms for seven years. I got up and looked in the mirror one day and thought, "I can't do this anymore."

I became involved with the adult children program after I had been in AA for a few years. I realized my childhood was one part of my life I hadn't dealt with at all. At AA meetings you say, "My father's an alcoholic," but you don't really deal with what it was like to grow up in an alcoholic household.

I've learned through the adult children therapy groups that I lived with the fear of abandonment. During the first twenty-odd years of my married life, I moved sixteen times all over the country with my husband on his corporate moves. I can often remember not wanting to move, but I packed up the kids and went anyway. The other part of some of those last moves was my thought that when I got to the next city and people didn't know I drank the way I drank, it might help. Of course, the geographical cures didn't work. My fear of abandonment played a role because I knew that if I didn't go, my husband would go anyway.

Now I'm going out on my own. To be very frank, I don't think it's very classy to be a fifty-two-year-old divorcée, but I couldn't continue to live like that, I really couldn't. I finally filed, and at least the process is started. I know I have more peace of mind being alone than living with all that anger. Today I know I can survive.

Jim, an auto line inspector, and his twin brother were born in 1930. He says, "I'm not sure whether we were the cause of the depression or made it that much worse." The son of an alcoholic, Jim became an alcoholic himself and got involved in two marriages and divorces from dysfunctional women. Repeating a predictable generational pattern, some of his own children have experienced dysfunctional problems.

J I M ▸ My father worked in the Kentucky steel mills; he was a machinist. My mother was a typical housewife. I have two brothers and a sister. Dad was an alcoholic and Mother was an enabler. I couldn't go to school when I was six because my twin brother, who had a motor control problem, was determined not to be capable. So they held my brother and me back a year. In my subconscious, I felt angry for not being able to go to school and having to watch after him.

We were brought up with a lot of double messages, such as "Don't do as I do; do as I say." My father would sit at the breakfast table saying we shouldn't drink or smoke, but he'd have a beer in one hand and a cigarette in the other. When there was drinking going on around the house, Dad gave us money to get us out of the picture.

We were isolated from anything that was important in the family; we were always shunted out of the picture. We weren't supposed to see things. We were also told not to play with certain neighbors. Mother didn't like me playing with blacks or Jews. I found the people she told me not to play with treated me better than my own family.

Both my father and my mother could get very angry. She would beat me with an extension cord. My father used a coat hanger. I reached a point in junior high where I had decided my parents were never going to beat me again; oddly enough, they never tried. I didn't have to let them know how I felt; they must have sensed it. I kind of took charge of me about that time.

I respect my parents in their efforts to keep me from becoming extreme on the bad side of life, yet I wasn't as good as they were hoping I would be. There was good and bad, and I was in the middle. I flirted with both sides. If I took the notion, I could work real hard and get the top grade in the class. On the other hand, if I wanted to be bad, I would go out and steal hubcaps.

Dad was into control. He wanted you to be quiet and "shut up." We were to be seen and not heard. "Don't make noise, don't interfere with me." His attitude was that "after all I've done, I should have all the space; you sit over there on the edge of it."

When my father was doing something around the house and we were helping him and it wasn't going well, he'd yell and scream at us.

My mother would make sure that his wishes were met. She would make sure that he didn't find out about anything unpleasant that happened during the day. If he was asleep when we came home from school, she would tell us to be quiet and go off and play. She would do everything in the world to make him happy, regardless of his behavior. My mother excused his drinking. She was very protective of him. She made sure that the boat wasn't rocked. Mother would routinely make meals with his favorite piece of chicken or steak or with his favorite pie. Her catering to him was her need for approval.

As a kid, I was very easily influenced by anyone, and I would do anything for attention. If I had a major defect of character, then that was it. Almost anything I did was wrong or shameful or guilty. I was told not to drink, not to smoke, sex was shameful, and if I played with myself, I was going to wind up being like the crazy man we had in town.

My father used to blame me because he didn't get promoted. He had to go to court one day because I broke some streetlights. He used to say he'd have been made foreman if it hadn't been for me. As I look back now, the fact that he had to go to court for his son didn't stop him from making supervisor. If he'd have been a good candidate for supervisor, if he'd have been the best person for the job, they would have made him supervisor regardless. I'm finding out this is true in my own life. Whatever happens to me is not anyone else's responsibility; it's only mine.

In the end all three of us boys wound up becoming alcoholics; all three of us are now in AA. My sister had some difficult times in her marriage, probably due to the way she was brought up by our father and mother as well.

I was definitely taught to suppress any feelings, and anything I saw or heard, I wasn't supposed to talk about. "You're not supposed to go there," "Don't play with them," "Don't do this," "you don't do that." I did what I wasn't supposed to do anyway, of course, and then felt guilty. I wound up finding out later in life that when I'd have a few drinks, I didn't feel the guilt or shame. I found out alcohol gave me a feeling of being myself. I know now it was a false sense of being.

I was once introduced to Morton Gould, the famous composer, as the only man in the service who was able to drink the sergeant under the table in twenty years. I thought that was great, but there was something in the back of my mind saying, "That's not very successful and that isn't what life is all about."

So I went on the wagon right before I got out of the service. I quit smoking, gained some weight, and went to work. That's when I got confident and decided to get married. I did and wound up having five daughters. I married a lady who was an adult child. Our relationship was doomed the day we got married unless we found some help, and neither one of us was ready to get help.

In my first marriage I was always hoping that my wife would change. If she changed and could be like me, I thought, she'd have a chance. Naturally I became an alcoholic just like her father, and she didn't deal with me any better than she did with her father. We got divorced after I was sober four years. She'd lost her identity, and my kids started going their own way. They were from our dysfunctional family. My children were brought up by me and my wife in the same mold that I was brought up by my mother and father. Naturally our children were going to be the same as us. It is amazing how much we are like our parents and how much our children's behavior is linked to ours.

My second wife didn't care as much about me as I would have hoped. I thought once we got married, she would change. That didn't work. She decided she didn't want to be married anymore and we parted. The day our divorce became final we went out for Chinese food. Chinese cures everything.

The last thing I was thinking about doing was getting married for the third time when I met my wife, Babs. The reason it's been so much better is that we decided there wouldn't be a problem we couldn't work out. She doesn't have to change and I don't have to change to work out a problem. We focus on the problem, rather than her having to change to suit my needs or me having to change to suit her needs. It's a wonderful way to operate because it works. There's trust now that's never been in any relationship in my life. I have a good feeling about it.

I'm me today, and I have a good feeling about me in all areas of my life: work, play, worship, and relationships. I have balance. I'm the same at church and the same at work. I'm the same at home and the same when I'm playing. When I was drinking, I wore a different hat everywhere I went. Any drug or alcohol we try to use to help us get through being all those different people eventually lets us down, and then we have to start being ourselves. I did.

When I was a child, my feelings and my behavior were motivated by what my parents said, did, and felt. As an adult child, I have an awareness today that when I react to something emotionally, it's not necessarily because of someone else. Someone or something outside of me may trigger an emotion. The old me would have blamed that someone for provoking that emotion and would have created a strained relationship between us. What I found in ACOA is that anyone can trigger my emotions, but it's really my problem.

When I get upset or angry today, I know it's something I have to look at inside. Knowing that stops me from trying to get someone else to change so they don't trigger my emotions. The old me would have tried to get the other person to change. I'd say, "If you wouldn't do that, I wouldn't feel this way." A wooden duck is not going to change because you love it; it's always going to be a decoy. Before I got to where I am today, I tried hard to get lots of wooden ducks to change. Today I don't create unrealistic expectations, and I don't try to get people to change.

I feel sincerely that any recovering alcoholic sooner or later has to get into adult children issues. I'm convinced it's only a "dry drunk" if an alcoholic stays sober for years and doesn't change. Change is important, but you have to recognize what to change.

Lynn, a social worker, is the adopted daughter of a "very cold and distant mother." The question "Who am I?" has colored her entire life. Because of a "longing and wanting" to get what she needed, Lynn stayed with her alcoholic husband for eleven years. Lynn has learned in recovery about the impact of her insecure childhood: "Someone who hadn't been adopted would have walked out on him earlier."

LYNN ▸ I was about four and a half years old when I found out I was adopted. My mother was pregnant with my brother at the time. He came along right after my parents told me. It was kind of a mindblower.

The adoption was an ongoing issue throughout my life. When I got to school, everyone knew I was adopted. I had a best friend who made it her business to go around telling everybody, and I think my parents had told their friends. In sixth grade, one of the boys in my class stood up and announced to the class that I was an orphan. After class I decked him in the hall.

I went to music camp because my parents were into music,

and I played piano and violin. Up there I dated a person, and he made the comment to me that my natural mother must have been one hell of a slut.

Adopted children are brought up with a "you're lucky" message. At Thanksgiving I'd be down on my knees saying, "Thank you, I'm not in the orphanage." The other side of my life was the sadness. I had lost my natural parents, and I had no blood ties to anybody. I was lucky in a lot of respects, but I also was unlucky too.

I managed to stumble through high school, ran for homecoming queen one year, and went to college. My therapist says it's because I happen to be fairly intelligent and could pull it off. Inside I was a mess.

My husband drank when I met him. It was the late sixties and early seventies, and I smoked a lot of marijuana. As the marriage progressed and we moved out to Colorado, I eventually stopped smoking, but he continued drinking. He beat me up one night. He'd been drinking a lot, got angry, and took my head and banged it against the wall about four or five times. I got in my car and went to my uncle's house; he lived in another town. I went back and told my husband that if it happened again I would leave him. This was about two years into the marriage.

He continued to get sicker. He was doing things like throwing up on the bathroom floor and falling down stairs. He picked me up at the airport one time and couldn't find the car. Watching this was a heartache to me because I loved him.

When he'd be drinking, he'd be really mean to me. He'd be critical. He was six foot two and about two hundred pounds at the time, so I was literally frightened of him.

The turning point was about nine or ten years down the road from the first episode. We had a ten-month-old baby at the time, and I couldn't leave her with him. I'd have to get a friend to baby-sit because he'd be drunk. I was lying in bed one Sunday morning and he was downstairs pouring a martini. I said to myself, "Normal people do not mix martinis at seven o'clock in the morning." Our whole life was being lived around his next drink. Later that day I wanted to put the baby to sleep. I went to turn the radio down and he slugged me in the face. I called the police. They wanted me to leave with the baby, and I told them, "Wrong—you get him out of here." So they threw my husband in jail. That weekend, I filed for divorce, and he ended up staying with a friend who was an alcoholic also.

After two or three weeks, he came back home with the stipulation that he could not drink. He didn't drink for nine months. It was wonderful. My daughter had a father and I had a husband again.

However, that summer his daughter from his first marriage was beaten up by her stepfather, so she came out to Colorado. A lot of stuff was going on with her, and this seemed to send my husband into a tailspin. He started drinking again, and it was terrible. He was so abusive to me verbally that I decided to leave. He got real angry, and I just went to the phone and made arrangements to get out of town. I went to the bank and divided up the accounts, packed my bags, took my daughter, and left.

As I look back there were turning points. When my husband went to jail, I met an old man there who was a recovering alcoholic. He said to me, "If your husband does not stop drinking, you need to leave." My friends and co-workers, who were professional people, advised me, "You've tried to save his life, but he started drinking again. It's all downhill from here. You're going to have to get out." My father, who's been my main support person for my entire life, told me, "He's not a smart man if he's still drinking and has a baby and a good marriage. He might be smart bookwise, but he's a fool." I put all this together.

My husband was killing himself, and I thought maybe my leaving would enable him to get some help. After I left, he entered a hospital, and he's sober now. Hopefully he can be a father for our daughter now; that's what I want for her. I want her to at least know him sober.

Because of his drinking he changed from one person to another. I hoped, I wished, and I hung in there. I did everything I could think of. I filed for divorce, threw him in jail, and called his family a couple times during the years. I said, "Hey, he is really drinking. You've got to help me." I asked his mother, father, and brother to come out and do an intervention. They would have no part of it. When I left, his mother said to me, "I don't know why you didn't leave him years ago."

It was tremendously hard for me to give him up. In a way, my husband was the mother I never had. He became almost the opposite of everything that I had looked up to him for. He disintegrated before my eyes. I was hooked in there, trying to get him better, trying to get him to give me what I needed, just as I spent my childhood trying to get my mother to give me what I needed. He and I would go days not speaking to each other because he would be drinking. We lived separate lives a lot of the time. That's how I felt growing up with my mother. She did her thing and I did my thing, and we never really connected emotionally.

Unconsciously I knew that he was an alcoholic when I met him. I knew he had a problem. Being adopted, the unpredictability of our lives was very familiar to me. I felt very insecure not knowing in my own head what was going to happen from day to day. It was similar to not having a mother I could really reach out to and with whom I could connect. It was very similar to my childhood. My husband would withdraw, and he was very critical. My mother's very critical of me, and she would withdraw. They're both real private people. I tried to get her to respond to me and be a warm, caring, maternal figure, which she was incapable of doing. I tried to get him to be a decent, caring husband, which he was incapable of being.

I hung in there with my husband eleven years, and about five years or six years were absolutely terrible. It was because of this longing and wanting to get what I needed that I just hung in there. I wouldn't give him up. I think someone who hadn't been adopted would have walked out on him earlier.

My entire life pretty much has been mourning. I've cried a lot and been fairly depressed, grieving the loss of what I thought was my natural mother. That's only part of it. The real loss was not ever having the mother I wanted. The mother I had did not make it. Giving my husband up was like repeating that loss again, and that's why it was so hard for me. I was so depressed when I left him, because it brought up all those other losses.

The question of who I am has been a real problem. I thought I was defective. I thought my natural mother actually saw me at birth and said, "Get her out of here. I don't want her." In those days, she probably never even saw me. I used to think that she turned me away personally. She never knew me; I was just a baby. I thought, "Something's wrong with me." Then when I couldn't get the mother whom I lived with to attend to me, I thought, "Boy, something really is wrong with me." I took everything on myself.

Even today I tend to see myself as the victim. I think I didn't get a fair start to begin with, and beyond that, I took an awful lot of abuse when I was married. I'm really making a conscious effort today to surround myself with people who give to me on different levels so I do get what I need. I'm trying to create a really positive life for myself, and anything that isn't positive, I make a conscious decision to get rid of or change. I'm not into suffering anymore and I'm not into being miserable. When I'm unhappy now, it's only for a little while; then I figure out what I need to do about it. It's not that feeling of hopelessness I lived with for a long time.

Dick is both a recovering alcoholic and compulsive gambler. He is the son and grandson of compulsive gamblers, and he describes his mother as "an emotional basket case." Dick began his own gambling at the age of seven and believes he was an alcoholic by the time he was a young teenager. Dick's shyness, inability to express feelings, and addictions were results, he says, of growing up in a home with "no love."

DICK ▸ My mother was a professional ballet dancer when she married my father. He was a good-looking man and a good conversationalist. He had chauffeur-driven cars and all the outer appearances of wealth. She married for money, however. He was a non-Catholic, and at that time it was unheard of for a Catholic woman to marry outside of the church.

My dad had been a stockbroker, and I came along two months after the market crash in October 1929. After my dad got out of the stock business, he became a tool salesman. Because of my mother's love for money, I knew then, and I know today, that I became a burden.

Anything that happened in the house was always blamed on my father, and it was always behind his back. My mother would talk about him to us when my father wasn't around. As soon as she would spot him coming into a room or coming in from outside, she'd say, "Be quiet, be quiet—here comes your father."

My mother's still living, and I still have difficulties with her today because of the lies that were told to me as a child. My father was a good man, even though he was a compulsive gambler. In her eyes, however, he was no good. I really believe the reason she married him was that his family had money. Money is god to her. She puts on an act with the rosary and other religious stuff, but I really believe she thought she would be set for life.

We lived in a nice home, and we were always well fed, but there was always tension in the house. I can remember as a child how good I felt when I went to neighbors' homes. At friends' homes there seemed to be love in those families.

During the war my dad made an awful lot of money in the tool business, but my mother would not go on vacations or enjoy herself. She never did socialize with anybody. My dad spent most of his time dealing with buyers in New York. We would see him only about every three months. He'd come home, stay for a few days or a week, and then go right back to New York. His father, my grandfather, who was also a compulsive gambler, was a horseplayer. My father was strictly a card-player, and he was good. He was a very talented bridge player and poker player, and I think a lot of the gambling he did was during the war.

We could not get involved in any type of game in the home that didn't involve a bet. Whether it was Ping-Pong, pitching money to the line, or playing croquet, any game we played always involved some sort of wager. I was the one my father usually chose to play these games with. We never knew what kind of gambling my father was doing outside of the house. For many years he did not work. He would get all dressed up and leave. I didn't find out until just recently that my father was a compulsive gambler. Everything was a secret in our family.

My father was an intelligent man, and he could talk with the best of them. Being a compulsive gambler, he could con anybody. People were impressed by his dress and his conversation. But deep down we were always afraid of him. My father had a terrific temper, and we never knew when he was going to get angry. We were all very nervous people. He could be sitting at the dining room table, and some remark that had been made many, many times before without a problem would be said by one of my brothers or me and all of a sudden his uncontrollable temper would come out. He'd get up, smash the table, and probably hit one of us. Afterward I think he always felt sorry. He couldn't say, "I'm sorry," but he would be extra kind to the one who he got angry toward.

We didn't take our problems outside of the house, and the problems that were in that home were unbelievable. Because there was no love between my mother and my dad, there was no love for the children either. I believe that because of the lack of any love in our family, I became a compulsive gambler and alcoholic.

During the war I was a young person, and we had a pretty good-sized home. I was afraid of the dark; and since there was no father in the house, I always felt insecure. At the age of fifteen I found out what alcohol could do for me. I couldn't depend upon my family, but alcohol was exactly what I needed. It removed all my feelings of fear and being unloved. I had a love affair with alcohol. It gave me security that I never had before. I was a shy person, and once I discovered alcohol, I could really express my true feelings. I really believe that at the age of fifteen or sixteen I was an alcoholic.

I can't ever remember carrying on a conversation with my mother and father about anything that meant anything, because he would disagree with her or she would disagree with him. I figured, what the hell, I'm not going to get any understanding. I have never been told, and my two brothers have never been told, "I love you," in our lifetime. Because my mother had told me so much bad stuff about my father, I never told my father I loved him. He died, and I never once told him I loved him.

My mother doesn't know anything about love. My brother had a problem with stuttering. It wasn't my mother who took him to a doctor; it was my aunt. They found out it was emotional. The atmosphere in the house caused him to be a stutterer. As a kid, my older brother had a temper that was unbelievable, and he was a fighter to boot. As a result of his anger, he was thrown out of high school in his sophomore year. He transferred schools and lived with my aunt and uncle. He became a different kid. It was like night and day. The temper left;

he got good grades and played sports. He had no problem whatsoever once he left the environment that we were brought up in.

I broke my wrist one time as a child, and the only thing my mother could say was, "Is your dad going to be upset when he gets home. It's going to cost money to get that wrist fixed." It wasn't "Too bad" or "Does it hurt?" or anything like that. I broke my wrist a second time playing football when I was in high school, and I carried it for two days for fear of saying something to them because of that first incident. I was afraid to go home and tell my parents about it because I knew there wouldn't be any understanding or sympathy. Finally it was so painful that I said, "I think I broke my wrist again." My mother was upset and said, "The doctor told you not to get involved in contact sports."

Even after I came into Alcoholics Anonymous, my mother wasn't happy. As a matter of fact, after I had been in AA many years, she once said, "Well, are you going to go see your neurotic friends again tonight?" This woman is one of the sickest women that I've ever met in my life. She's an emotional basket case.

My brother had an aneurysm, and at the time he had four young children. His wife had a heart condition, so my wife and I pitched in and took over the responsibility for my brother and helped raise those kids. A year or two later, my mother made the remark that we were "suckers" for helping my brother's family. I could not believe those words coming out of her mouth.

It's now been twenty-six years since I had a drink. I also had fifteen straight years without making any type of a bet. Right now, it's four and a half years since I've gambled. The last time out was a nightmare.

I have seen my father's temper and my mother's insecurity. I've seen it in other people, and I've seen it in myself. When you go through the stress, there's got to be an outlet for that stress. My outlet first of all was gambling, and then my drinking came along. After I came into Alcoholics Anonymous, I was addicted to food. I couldn't drink, I couldn't gamble, so I filled my face with sweet stuff. I'm still addicted to cigarettes.

These different addictions are all the same. They're all

emotional. We are all trying to figure out why we aren't comfortable. When we were kids, we didn't talk about anything, we weren't supposed to feel anything, and we had no trust in anybody. I used alcohol to overcome all the feelings I had bottled up inside. The feelings I had were not normal. All I wanted to do was be like my friends.

Audrey's childhood in the South was crucially influenced by her father's alcoholism, physical abandonment by both her father and mother, and sexual abuse by her father. A compulsive worrier, controller, and achiever, Audrey, a junior high school teacher, tried to live up to this advice: "Because you're black, you're going to have to be much, much better than the white person in order to compete."

AUDREY ▸ Early on, I didn't know about poverty or discrimination or alcoholism; these things just existed, and I just accepted them. We were very, very poor, and all of the people around us were poor also. It seemed as though most fathers drank heavily and beat up their wives and kids; it was just a fact of life. I didn't see too many normal situations.

I was the third child of four. I have two sisters and a brother. My parents were married when they were both tenth-graders. It was just something that they did one day because other kids had been doing it. They skipped school and got married. They had not dated. After getting married, my mother went to her home and my father went to his. The next day it came out in the paper where the marriage licenses were listed. My mother was living with her grandmother at the time. Her grandmother confronted her about it and told her that she would have to live with my father, which she did. After about two years my oldest sister was born.

When my father wasn't drinking, he was okay, although sometimes moody. He called himself a weekend drinker. After he got paid on a Friday, he would start and would drink and drink and drink. Then he became really mean and ugly, and would start arguments with my mother. It was so frightening. Once he went for two weeks without a drink. We were all aware he hadn't had a drink, but my mother told us not to say anything about it for fear he would start drinking again. He started anyway because he said no one appreciated he had gone two weeks without drinking. There you could get moonshine, and my father would drink anything. I have seen him strain shoe polish through a slice of bread and drink it. He would pass out from the drinking, and we were happy when that would happen because then he would be out for several hours and things would settle down in the family.

When my father first left home, I was five and things were very tough. My mother went to work as a maid, which was very typical for a black woman to do. Periodically he would send twenty dollars and she would buy four pairs of shoes. After a year or eighteen months my father appeared back at home with no warning. He went back to working in the coal mine, the fussing and the fighting resumed, and he left again. The second leaving was not as traumatic as the first. It was a blessing for him to be out of the house, so some of my anxiety could settle. I had internalized so much fear that I worried about practically everything. I don't remember a period in my life when I was not worried about something.

We moved to Mississippi after my grandmother died. My mother worked in a dress shop, but she was not earning enough to keep the family going. It was during that time in Mississippi that I came to really know starvation. My mother would come home at night and she would bring cinnamon rolls and a bottle of milk. We'd eat that and go to bed. There would not be more until the following night when she'd come home. Occasionally during that time a neighbor who became aware of our situation started bringing over a pot of beans and corn bread, but it wasn't continuous. I had to repeat the third grade because I absolutely could not recall any information that was being taught. I could not even remember the alphabet. When you're thinking about food and the essentials of life, other things are not relevant.

At one period my mother took us to Alabama to my father's oldest brother for the summer. They had no warning that we were all coming. He had eight children, and lived on a small farm. My mother left us there and did not return. My oldest sister contacted my father, who was in Chicago, and he came for us. He took us back to Kentucky, but not to the house where he had left me at age five. It was to a shack on the side of a mountain. It sat up on two stilts in front, this two-room shack with no electricity, no running water. We were so poor we didn't even own an outhouse. My mother did show up just before Christmas. There were no questions asked about where she had been. Not even to this day have we discussed it. You just don't talk about certain things. It's just something that happened.

The drinking and fighting were always very frightening. The arguing would scare me so much that even now I cannot bear to hear people argue. When my parents fought, I would go off someplace and shake and tremble. I never knew what my father was going to do next. My mother could say the least thing, and it would set him off.

My mother took all of this out on my oldest sister. When she punished and beat her, she would yell, "You're just like your old, damn dad—no good." My sister took to running away, and my mother would bring her back and beat her some more. Once when my sister was punished, my mother locked her in a closet. There were mice in there and my sister became hysterical.

During that time my father was there, he was working in the coal mines, providing as best he could for the family. He was showing me a lot of attention. In fact, I thought that I was his favorite. He was fondling me. I knew something wasn't quite right, but at least I was getting attention from him. We did things together. He loved reading, and we would read. He encouraged me to bring books home from the library. I would sit on his lap, and the fondling would be going on. He always insisted I take naps with him because he worked the midnight shift in the coal mine. It even continued when my mother was back home. She would give me a look to let me know that it wasn't okay, but she never intervened to stop it, so it went on.

The last time I saw him alive was a Tuesday night about 1950. I was about eleven or twelve. We were all living in the shack and I had been sleeping with him. I remembered feeling strange, experiencing strange stirrings from him. Every Tuesday night we went to the movies to see the serials; we never missed. This one particular night he just begged and begged me not to go, but he had scared me so in bed that I sensed that something was wrong. He told me he really needed me to wake him up to get to work on time, but my own fears and not wanting to miss the next episode compelled me to go with my sisters and brother. When we got back, he had torn that shack apart and was gone. There had been a fight between my mother and father. He went back to Chicago and continued his drinking.

In 1954 my mother received word that my father was very ill in Chicago and went to see him. When she came back, she told us he was dying of cancer brought on by alcoholism. When they notified her that he had died, she took the little bit of insurance he left as a result of his work in the coal mine, shipped his body back home from Chicago, and had the funeral. We didn't have many friends, so the church was just about empty. The funeral was on a Sunday. I was sixteen. I cried the hardest because I just felt someone needed to cry for this man. I felt embarrassed by the cheap casket, and no one sent flowers. My mother had bought one stand of plastic red flowers. I cried because that made me realize just how low we were.

I'm disappointed in my father's actions toward me. It's like I was tricked into trusting him. It was the one hope that I had of being loved by someone, and he let me down. I blame my mother for not intervening, but of course, she would have gotten it if she had criticized him in any way. He didn't allow it, and she never said a word, but I could just tell by her eyes that it wasn't right. She would often encourage me to go outside and I refused, and he refused to let me go outside. I remember my second sister once commenting that it seemed like I was getting sick, because I was getting petted and babied so much. It seemed to her as though I was getting younger. But I didn't try to change it, because I was getting attention from him. The fact that it was out in the open helped to make me feel that it was all right. Something abnormal looked normal.

My mother moved us from house to house until we finally had a white house with a picket fence. It had no running water, but it had electricity. It was the best we had ever known as children. We no longer lived on the side of the mountain; we lived at the foot of the mountain.

In my senior year of high school my mother took a job in Ohio and left us. I became head of the household and we made it. I had worked since I was fourteen as a maid.

I came to hate the woman I worked for. During the summer she would take me off to North Carolina, where she spent time with her daughter. It was awful how they made me work, but I survived. This lady hated blacks. She could be talking to her friends over the phone about "niggers" and I could be right there in the room dusting, but it made no difference to her. I remember once she said, "Well, you know niggers don't have morals anyway." At the end of the day, I thought, "I'm never coming back here again," but I discussed it with my teacher at school and she persuaded me that I should return. I can't remember her reasoning, but I went back and stayed there until I started college.

I married after my second year of college. I did not marry an alcoholic; in fact, my husband doesn't drink or smoke. We were very conscious of trying to bring our children up so that they could have many of the opportunities and advantages that we did not have. I spent a lot of time making sure my children were not faced with racial discrimination as I had been. If I saw where a situation could occur, I made sure that their lives were not touched by it, because I had known it.

I graduated from college with high honors. It was a black school, and in my head I feel that my education was mediocre. Black schools, even high schools, are not always up to par, but I can say those black teachers I had deserve a lot of credit for looking out for us, and especially me, in so many ways. Frequently I was given money, a coat, or whatever, without ever having to have asked for it. They saw a need and they took care of it. The special woman who watched over me just died this past May. She never ever allowed me to drop out of her life. Someone was watching over me.

Right now I'm going to therapy. I slowly have come to realize that if any change is going to occur, it has to occur with me. I learned that in Al-Anon and ACOA. It's such a slow, slow process, and I want it to change overnight. I have to remember that it took a long time to get this way and it's going to take a long time to recover.

It is such an eye-opener to know other people have experienced similar and sometimes even worse things than I have experienced. But my reactions have been all my own. They seem so unique, but I guess that's part of being me and how I am.

My oldest sister married a man, and she's now dealing with her alcoholism. She's trying to recover. My second sister has had two unsuccessful marriages; no alcoholism, but she's known ulcers and colitis. My brother is a recovering alcoholic. I am a compulsive worrier about my two children.

I also expect too much from other people. My daughter says I expected perfection at all times. I'm a master controller. Someone told me, "You control with a capital *K*." I suppose I do. I didn't want my kids to experience what I had experienced and I felt if they would do as I told them then they'd turn out all right. Well, they ended up rejecting everything I wanted for them. They were very obedient up to a point, and now they're both very rebellious and I'm powerless to change them.

I hope to find the miraculous change that I'm searching for. I'm working hard to stop trying to control other people. For so long I tried to control and change the kids and tried to control and change my husband. Sometimes I feel as though I've failed, but I'm coming to realize that I must change Audrey and not put out all of this energy trying to control someone else. Some days I feel hopeless, some days I feel unsuccessful. There's lots of frustrations and I'm in a turmoil, but I understand that this happens when you're getting ready to change. So, "Lord hurry up because this is very painful."

CHARLES L. WHITFIELD, M.D. ▸ The true self is who we really are. That's the child within. Most of the time we keep it private. Those who grew up in dysfunctional families learn to protect that true self from being injured, wounded, demolished, annihilated, destroyed, and pulverized. That true self goes into hiding. What emerges is a false self, because something's got to take care of business. That's what the Freudians call the ego. The term I have given it is the co-dependent self. "Co-dependent self" is a much richer, deeper, all-inclusive dynamic term than "false self" or "negative ego." Most of us walk around being a co-dependent self, being unreal. It's estimated that we are real only about fifteen minutes a day.

If I am real only fifteen minutes a day, who gets to see that realness? Me. I get to see myself being real and experience myself being real only for that short time. Therefore, I'm going to think I'm not real. I'm going to walk around not knowing who I really am, not knowing what I want, what I need, what I dream, what I want to create, or what I get excited about. I'm going to walk around most of the day dead, wounded, and numb—a robot.

The journey of recovery is to find out who I really am, to know that child within, that true self, to start to get my needs met, to support that true self and to make a safe and loving place for that child so that I can work through all of my past or current unfinished business.

Unhealthy independence is a trait of the person who says, "I don't need any help; I can do it on my own." That's needing to be in control. Rather than get to know oneself and rather than work on it, the unhealthy independent person says, "I can do it on my own; I don't need outside help. Thank you. Good-bye." That's the false self talking, trying to protect the true self against its pain. However, the only way out is to look outside of the false self.

It's very important to be able to reach outside of ourselves and ask for help because what we're really reaching outside of is not outside of our true self; we're reaching outside of our false self, our co-dependent self. We can reach out to any safe other. The problem is that we've grown up not being around safe others, including God. We believe God's not safe or he wouldn't have put us in a crazy family to begin with. It takes great faith to reach out and ask for help, but we must to know our true selves, to recover. Personal power in healing equals awareness plus responsibility.

The healing process starts out as pain, as a dreaded experience, as a fear. Then it gets progressively more exciting, interspersed with waves of pain. Increasingly, recovery moves upward toward freedom, creativity, possibility, choice, and love. Love is always there, but our ability to be open to it is more if we have worked through our unfinished stuff. The more we have worked through, the more open we are to love's presence.

Every issue we have with ourselves and others we also have with God. When we look back at the beginning of the journey, it doesn't at first look like a spiritual journey. It looks like drudgery, pain, abuse, or unfairness. But the farther along we get on the evolutionary journey of our life, we can see that the whole journey was, and is, spiritual. Every act we did or didn't do was part of a spiritual unfolding of our own life as a unique human being. We ultimately have to discover the divine within us. "The kingdom of Heaven is within."

To be happy, you go within, and God is within. So we are God in that sense. It's not our ego; it's not our false self; it's our true self. The true self is the higher self, which is God, in evolution.

We're discovering that the ego is nothing but an assistant, but we have given it all of our power. We gave away our power to the ego and to others' egos to run our lives. In the healing journey, we're taking back that responsibility.

THE

PROBLEM

4

SELF-WORTH

I have a photograph taken of me in the fifth grade. I was ten years old. I look at that picture now and try to remember myself back then. It's difficult because I have blocked out or forgotten many childhood memories. I see that youngster in the picture as a cute kid, but the eyes tell the real story. In those eyes I see pain, hurt, anger, fear, mistrust, and sadness. I see struggle and loneliness in that child's face.

For much of my adult life I have been trying to get rid of the pain, anger, fear, mistrust, and sadness. I have been trying to replace those negatives with love, acceptance, and security. We all want to be loved, respected, and valued. To love and be loved is part of what is wonderful about being a human being. I have experienced some of that along the way, but it hasn't been consistent. My striving for love and acceptance for much of my life has been excessive and obsessive. My judgment about myself has been so negative that I have looked to others to tell me I am good and worthy. In my personal relationships, I have often given away to others the power to make me feel good. In so doing, I have given them power over me. If they failed to deliver, I demanded it. My drug was a hit of their approval. I couldn't leave when others emotionally abused me, because of my need for their approval.

This struggle for self-esteem has been tiring. By constantly looking outside of myself, I have guaranteed my own depression. Only recently have I begun to understand that it is I who must change. I must change my attitude about myself, engage in behavior that makes me feel good, and surround myself with people who confirm my goodness. To expect others to create my happiness is a dependency and a fallacy; they couldn't do it —even if they wanted to.

I must admit to myself, I often form alliances with people who, I feel, will be good for me but who in reality aren't. In some cases, I must rid myself of those people in my life who cause me to feel less good about myself. My choices determine my level of self-esteem, and I know that the single most important key to my happiness is high self-worth.

Most adult children of alcoholic or dysfunctional homes have very low self-esteem.

Sharon Wegscheider-Cruse is the president of Onsite Training and Consulting, Inc., located in Rapid City, South Dakota. Onsite offers short-term residential programs on co-dependency treatment and family reconstruction. One of the most respected lecturers and leaders in the adult children movement, Sharon is the author of *The Family Trap, Another Chance: Hope and Health for the Alcoholic Family,* and *Choicemak-*

ing. Her newest books are *Understanding Me, Learning to Love Yourself,* and *Coupleship.* Sharon was also the founding board chairperson of the National Association for Children of Alcoholics.

S HARON   WEGSCHEIDER-CRUSE ▸ Self-worth is believing in the value of yourself. Self-worth is understanding, accepting, and loving yourself in order to have the courage to make choices and changes to protect the self. Self-worth is *the* basic personal need.

Self-worth entails how we feel about ourselves, how we teach others to treat us, and how we set boundaries and limits to ensure that we have nourishing lives emotionally, physically, or spiritually. Without a sense of self-worth, we need to get the approval of others, need to keep up an image for others, and respond to the demands of others. We live an other-directed life, which means we lose touch with who we are completely.

To have a good sense of self-worth means first of all that one has to know oneself. We've grown up in a culture in which many children, especially children who have come from any kind of a painful home, have learned at a very early age to discount the self. In those homes, we learn to monitor what's expected of us instead of what's really happening to us. We learn not to be angry, not to get too excited or silly, not to have trust or hope. We get serious and controlled about things. When we do that, we get further and further away from who we really are. With that value gone, we're dependent on others. If we have to depend on other people to tell us we're worthy, then we have to fit in to what those other people want, and we begin monitoring ourselves. Are we doing it right? Do we ever do it right enough? Are we doing enough of it? Do we look right? Do we talk right? Do we act right? Do we get good enough grades? Are we a good enough athlete? We become other-dependent. Then we become relationship-dependent, chemical-dependent, work-dependent, and success-dependent. We get caught up in all those self-destructive behaviors.

If people with low self-worth recover, they stop, look in the mirror, and say, "Hey, kid, you know you're doing all right. You've been doing all right for a long, long, long time." Some people never get to that point. Some people chase it to the grave. It's what I call a death-style, instead of a life-style. Energy that is wasted in being dependent on others is energy that can go into relationships with children, mates, a higher power, or a belief system—something that would give a sense of serenity or comfort. Energy could also go into play. There have been some marvelous studies done lately that say laughter, humor, play, and the ability to enjoy what you have accomplished are the best medicine for shame, hurt, and guilt. The energy that is needed for healing those kinds of feelings comes directly out of the ability to laugh.

For high self-worth one needs to go back and reclaim the part of oneself that was the natural perfect child before whatever happened that hurt that child. An adult child is a hurting person. It is someone who has grown up and developed mentally, intellectually, physically, and socially. Our society and our parents have rewarded that. The one area that people who have lived in painful families have not developed is the emotional. The adult child is a person walking around fully matured in every way except emotionally. Adult children are somewhat emotionally handicapped.

"Adult children" is a diagnosis of a wounded child, not a life-style. It doesn't work to blame, figure out, or just understand what happened. The challenge is using the adult self to go back and discover that wounded child which is the real self. That's where the worth is. The mission then is to give that child the tools, the affirmation, and the support to grow up and meet the adult who lives in the body.

The whole adult child movement is about reclaiming the lost child and nurturing it with self-worth and helping it grow up. What is healthy is to see that part of ourselves that was wounded as needing to be healed. We need to develop those qualities that a child would have that got thwarted in childhood —curiosity, joy, trust, spontaneous emotional discharge, being able to feel freedom, tenderness, confidence, and hope. The development of those qualities is what will bring us our self-worth. I see some misunderstanding that keeps the "child within" concept fairly superficial. Some people think they will recover from being an adult child if they carry teddy bears to board meetings. You can become a conference junkie or a book junkie too. I see some adult children who run to six or seven

ACA meetings a week but don't talk to their spouses at home. Some will play games with adults but ignore their own children. Finding out one is an adult child is a challenge to go back and develop new qualities that will give one self-worth. It's not a game.

Our cultural orientation drives us toward material success and performance. When we have parents who have low self-esteem and use work, money, prestige, and power to increase their own self-worth, those expectations are forced onto their children. Little children take on those expectations at a very early age and become other-directed themselves. A child who is driven around from preschool to dancing classes to the Y begins to believe that he's not okay just the way he is. Such children believe they have to do all these things and be something other than who they are to be worthy. The parents' intentions come from a good place in their heart, but they're misdirected because they themselves have been misdirected.

A dysfunctional family system is one in which the needs of the family members are not met. In a healthy family, there is open talk about sexuality, the body, and health. There are physical needs for affection resulting in a lot of physical touch. There are emotional needs that are met. In a dysfunctional family, emotional needs can't be met, because people don't feel safe enough to feel. In contrast, a healthy family is a place where you can go to cry or to share fears with the family members.

The message that is often given to the children in a dysfunctional home is that rather than feel, heal, and change their behavior, they should medicate for their own survival, with alcohol, food, or work. Parents teach children by doing. I wish I could stop the workaholic parents who are working their fannies off to make a better life for their families but, through work and frenetic activity, are medicating their own intimacy, sexual, emotional, and self-worth needs. They feel double-crossed when their kids, to whom they've given everything, become alcohol- or cocaine-dependent. What the parent painfully has to face is that "I taught my kid to medicate."

Symptoms of low self-worth are feeling overly responsible, busyness, and workaholism. Another sign of low self-worth is a tendency toward addictive relationships. Self-abusive habits such as alcoholism, drug dependency of any kind, food addictions, nicotine addiction, and relationship dependency are the kinds of things that keep us off balance and make survival difficult.

D ICK ► As a kid, I was never told by my parents I was good; as a matter of fact, I was always put down. I had a very low opinion of myself. What my parents did or didn't do stemmed really from their own inferiority complexes. They passed that along to me too. I was a very shy kid. I was the most lonely person you ever saw in your life, and the reason I was so alone was because I couldn't tell people how I felt inside.

J EFF ► When I came into AA, my self-esteem was so low I said, "My name's Jeff and I'm an asshole." I couldn't say I was an alcoholic, but I could admit to being an asshole. That's exactly how I felt about myself.

M ARY ► Growing up in my family, I was constantly told I wasn't good enough. My grades were never good enough. To this day, my father has not even seen my portfolio. I've had some of my photography work published in international magazines that he could pick up at a newsstand. He doesn't bother. My father is like a god to me, and sometimes I feel if he doesn't want to make the effort to look at my work, then no one else will. Therefore, what I'm doing is invalid.

When I was a child, my mother would say, "You're not pretty; you're ugly." I remember going through a very hard time thinking I was not physically attractive. For so many years I have believed what my parents were saying. I was nurtured by sick people. I was like a little piece of clay. Therefore, the end product was going to have a lot of cracks. With a lot of work, I can become healthy so the next set of dishes won't have as many cracks in it.

A LICE ► My mother was, and continues to be, very adept at pointing out my personal flaws, so I view my body and my personal self as not good enough. She was very explicit about what parts of me were not what they should have been. That lives with me still. Part of my overeating is a result of feelings I have about myself that are not positive. I have spent most of my life with no emotions and no feelings. I think this is a self-esteem issue. When I did have feelings, it was anger, but it slipped into depression because "good girls don't get angry."

I have taken care of my needs for self-esteem by taking care of others. What I'm working to do now is to turn some of those nurturing feelings and instincts and feelings I have onto myself. What I've done most of my life is nurture others at the expense of myself. I would find myself so depleted that there was literally nothing left to give to me. It's very hard for me to nurture myself. It's a foreign thought to me.

BETH ▸ All of the kids in my family developed very low self-esteem from our neglectful parents. It was emotional neglect, not physical neglect or physical abuse, although we did get beatings with a belt. We were called stupid by my mother and criticized constantly. A lot of time I felt like nobody in my family loved me. There must have been rage within me. I was always fighting with my brothers and sisters. A lot of time I felt like nobody in my family loved me. I developed a habit of biting my sisters and brother or torturing them by tickling. I guess those things fulfilled some kind of need for physical contact. Later I turned to men to provide physical validation or give me self-esteem.

I think that I finally discovered it comes within. I still don't treat myself the way I should, such as getting enough sleep or staying home at night to concentrate on myself. I'm always volunteering to do things like baby-sitting, helping people, or being with others to ease my own loneliness or the loneliness of my friends. I've been a very social person, but that's finally petering out. I'm finally giving myself two nights a week alone, which is something I really need. When I don't have time alone, that's when the big stresses build up and that's when things get out of hand. Having low self-esteem, I'm always trying to prove to myself I can do this or that. But looking outside doesn't work. I'm finally turning it around and looking inside to find my own love within myself.

LYNN ▸ The big message I got about self-worth while growing up was that it didn't really matter what was going on emotionally. Looking good, having nice clothes and jewelry, and real superficial things were valued; the soul of a person was never really appreciated. I can see that even more clearly now with how my mother relates to my daughter. My mother dresses her like a little doll. That's what she used to do to me. Outside I looked great, but inside I was a mess. I learned to use externals to get what I wanted. I could finagle and manipulate and get what I wanted by using how I looked. I also used the fact that I was female and I could act stupid. In college I found men to do things for me. Since leaving my husband, I discovered I can think for myself. I don't need someone else to think for me. There is something inside of me.

MICHAEL ▸ My self-worth was as strong as the mirror in which it was reflected, and the mirror for my self-worth was in your eyes and your acceptance of me. If you liked me, my self-image was strong. That is what I understood a self-image to be —what I saw reflected in your eyes. I got into people-pleasing to keep the mirror strong and positive. In the early stages of recovery the sense of "letting go" provoked a genuine fear in me. I thought I would disappear as an entity on earth and would atomize or evaporate. Gradually I began to realize there was somebody in there.

Now, for the first time in my life, I am seeing that I exist, regardless of the mirror. I am even coming to appreciate with a mixture of excitement, humor, and sadness how clever that person was to set up the gig he did to make the world like him. It was the real me who set up the mirror and pretended to be the image in the mirror that made you like and appreciate me. I'm beginning to realize that there was a little kid directing all that very cleverly back then, and that's the guy I'm accepting and hoping will put his energies to work in more-productive things than playing games.

MANOLITO ▸ I always had to prove myself to get any sort of self-esteem. But whether it was translating an off-Broadway show, being given a big international advertising assignment, or being named student commencement speaker at Boston University, the parental message was, "Don't count on us; we won't be there" or "You can do better." I went from wanting to prove myself, to being very uncomfortable with success, to sabotaging myself.

I have changed my value system completely to where I no longer seek my self-esteem in the exterior things. I cannot say I love myself unconditionally, but I can affirm I'm on the way. If I take an objective look at myself, in terms of my self-esteem, I know who I am today, what my potential is, and where I'm going. I like that; I really do.

B RIAN ▸ On a scale of one to ten, my sense of self-esteem as a kid must have been zero. One of the things I was always concerned about while growing up was being a man. After the early childhood sexual abuse by my mother, I had a hard time feeling like becoming a man, even though I could act, feel, and look like one. It's still there, but my self-esteem is better. As a kid, I got my self-esteem through grades. I was first in my high school class. When I first went off to college, I got horrible grades. That was very hard on my parents' self-esteem, because I was the perfect son who always got high grades. I was trying to please my dad by going to engineering school, which at the time I had no interest in doing.

Now I shore up my self-esteem with substitutes for grades: career progress, money, and trappings. The best indicator that my self-esteem is growing is that my interest in career progress, money, and trappings has dwindled. I don't care as much about them anymore. When I began to let go of those things, life got a lot simpler and a lot of things that would have been tough in the past suddenly become possible. I can see how wonderful things can be if I put energy into the right things rather than the wrong things. I sense that's what self-esteem may be all about.

A UDREY ▸ As a child I didn't get a lot of messages, positive or negative. I didn't get spankings, and at one time I wondered, Why not? I felt left out because the other kids were getting them and I wasn't. Being very timid and shy, I escaped all of that.

I started working at fourteen. I don't mean a little babysitting; I mean hard work. From a mail-order catalog I ordered a very inexpensive watch for myself. When the watch came, something very overwhelming came over me. I could not wear that watch to school. I would take it to school in my pocket and would peek at it. It had red stones in it. I was afraid my friends wouldn't like it, so they never saw it. I just carried it in my pocket. Recently I went shopping and saw a red suit. I said to myself, "Girl, you've never worn a red suit," but I'd always thought about having a red suit. I went in the fitting room, tried it on, and it was perfect. So I bought the red suit. Driving home, I said, "Well, you don't really have to wear it." Then I got up the courage to wear it to church because there it seems they don't judge as much. I wore it to church and it felt good. So something in my head said, "I bet you wouldn't have the courage to wear it to work," and I said, "You got that right." Because of my shaky self-esteem I only wore the jacket. I just couldn't wear the whole suit. The day I can go to school with the whole suit on, that's when I'll know that I have overcome a lot of this garbage.

K<u>AREN</u> ▸ I was raised by two parents who had very low self-esteem. I was surrounded by grandparents who had low self-esteem. I learned what they all taught me very well. There were lots of very negative, critical, and judgmental messages. We weren't wealthy, but I always got things rather than feelings. If I was feeling low, was sad, or cried, they'd always buy me something. Those material things became the gods I worshipped, but it was an insatiable drive because whatever I got was never enough. Later I came to find out that through sex or through being sexual or sexy I could get some of the attention that I had lacked growing up. So at a fairly young age I became sexually active. I was the performer, but never felt anything. I was not orgasmic. In fact, I couldn't figure out what the big deal was. I wanted the control, and if I were orgasmic, that meant I was vulnerable and no longer in control. I made sure the other person was pleased in order for my esteem to be higher. I chose to use sex, but the people that I chose to have sex with were usually similar to my father, in that they were emotionally unavailable or unavailable in some other way. Several were married men. That satisfied a need as well. That reinforced things I'd been told as a child and left me feeling I was really worthless and shameful.

The positive messages I got I didn't believe, because I saw

my mother using those to manipulate people. Whenever someone said something good to me, I immediately processed it back
to that and said, "Well, they want something from me." I became a chameleon. I had a desperate need for attention. It
wasn't until later in life that I found out that I was so numb that
the only way I could get the attention I needed was to do bizarre things.

To me, self-esteem is the cornerstone of my recovery; it's
the crux of everything in my life. If I don't have high self-
esteem, I have nothing. If I don't value myself, no one else will.
I wasn't taught that. I'm replacing all the negative programming
with positive programming.

J I M ► I had very little self-esteem when I was young because
of comments about my skinniness and awkwardness. My father
frequently called me a dummy or said, "You can't do anything
right." The harder I worked at trying to please him, the more I
got cussed at. For an engine to run, it has to be balanced.
There's a balance wheel in an engine, and if that wheel gets out
of balance, regardless of how fine-tuned the engine is, it's going
to run rough. There was a lack of balance in our family.

H A R R Y ► When my mother lost the daughter that was to
be herself and turned on me with an intense need to be taken
care of, things that happen in so many men's lives happened to
me: she explored my body through fondling and touching when
she could not explore her husband's. Our relationship got sexu-
alized, and my father found out and didn't do anything; my self-
esteem was the reflection of me in their eyes. My self-esteem
was my father's shock, horror, and flight back to medical school,
internship, residency, and career, and my mother's endless
neediness, complaints, and demands to be satisfied. My piece of
that was a sense of inadequacy and the belief that nothing I
could ever do would be enough. To merge with my mother, to
take on her depression, to become my mother's surrogate husband were the only ways I could give myself a father, and I did
it. Crazily enough, I survived.

It's not a matter of learning self-esteem; it's a matter of
uncovering. It's a matter of insight and then breaking free from
the chains. It was not a matter of learning something that would

give me self-esteem. I know five languages. I can quote you the *Iliad* in Greek, the *Aeneid* in Latin, and *Faust* in German. I can write poetry myself. None of those things worked. What did work was becoming alcoholic and falling out the bottom. Then I had no more choices but to face the truth. I came into a program where people cared about me; then I started to care about them. I looked across the table and cared about somebody and thought that's how I feel about me too. Then my self-worth started to come through.

J AN ▸ When I first started to turn my life around, my self-esteem was very low because I was still setting unreal expectations for myself. I tried to win the approval of others, beginning with my mother and then my husband. Today I can honestly say that there are things I do for my own approval. If I don't get approval from somebody else, it's okay. After a thirty-two-year marriage, it's taken me a long time to realize it's okay to admit I made a mistake.

I find today that I gravitate more toward the people who will give me positive messages. I used to be embarrassed if anybody told me I did something well. I know now if somebody says something good about me, they must have a reason. That's an indicator my self-esteem is getting better, because there are a lot of things I do well.

S HARON   WEGSCHEIDER-CRUSE ▸ There are three giant steps to self-worth. The first is to be detoxified of whatever is keeping all those feelings medicated. Those feelings are your clues to how to live life, how to recover, and where to get your self-worth. Get whatever treatment you need for alcoholism, eating disorders, nicotine, gambling, or addictive relationships. The second step is to get whatever professional care you need to go back, refeel, discharge, and resolve all the old conflict. We have to recognize that if we have gotten into medicating behavior, there's been something that's had to be medicated. Professional care is needed to bring one up to a starting point. Only after that are we ready to start another whole journey; that's step three, which is called recovery. Recovery has to do with exposing yourself to growth, self-worth, humor, laughter, playful experiences, healthy people, new choices, and new ways of being. Many people in recovery never get to this part. They detox and stop, detox and stop, and so on. They increase their number of meetings, but they're not taking the big step in recovery, which is re-creating a whole other life-style to replace the death-style they've been living in.

You never have a full recovery as long as you live carefully. When we're recovering from co-dependency and adult child problems, it's not a good idea to stick around people who have chosen to stay in their pain. I urge people to develop a family of choice. A person is responsible for finding at least five people who are recovering holistically and developing positive life-styles. So find at least five people who you make your family of choice and hang around them. Let them confront you until you get your own recovery program going stronger and stronger and stronger. Stick with those who are making those choices and be challenged into a riskier life-style.

You also need to make at least five life-style changes if you're going to recover. I don't know what they are. Each person has to find out for herself or himself. Maybe you won't be working at the same job. Maybe you'll be living in a new city. A woman I know closed down a fifteen-year effort to build a therapy practice and is on a two-year sabbatical. Some people have to learn how to make a commitment and get married. Some people have to realize their marriage was made in pathology and may have to end it. Some people may have to get a divorce from their family of origin or may have to go back to their family of origin and ask for forgiveness. Who knows what those changes are? If someone is in a place of stuck emotions, chances are that person has created a whole reality around those negative feelings. When those feelings are opened up, there are going to be changes that will have to be made.

You need to take responsibility for what you want to do in life. You can either wait for it to come to you or you can go get it. You need to learn how to respond and take charge of your own decisions. Doing that is your job. It's not your husband's or children's, and it wasn't your parents'. Responsibility means that you've got yourself a body and a head and a set of emotions and a chance—you're alive. Responsibility means waking up all those parts of yourself and walking through life the best way you can. There is a miracle of recovery, and it should be you.

If you're living, you survived and somebody was there for you. I call these people little angels. You have to go back in your mind and be thankful for them. I grew up in a family with two alcoholic parents and lost my father to an early suicide. That's a lot of loss, but I had a grandmother who loved me. I had a high school coach who was willing to work with me. I had a counselor who believed in me. People with high self-worth have the ability to reframe their experience, go through the necessary grief and anger about the loss, but also find the gratitude.

People with high self-worth are realists: they know that they didn't survive alone, that there's been somebody there somewhere. Another characteristic of those with high self-worth is that they can set limits and boundaries for themselves and don't respond to other people's demands. They also have a real healthy respect for the value of relationships. They may have an intimate relationship or they may have good friends. However, they do know they're going to need at least five or seven meaningful relationships to fulfill their needs, and they make sure they take the time and the energy to build those relationships. They invest in them and they don't take those relationships for granted.

High-self-worth people can make change. They're not married to any one particular way of life, one geographic part of the country, or one set of traditions. They can walk in and out of events and circumstances because they're not dependent on those for their worth. The worth comes from inside. Last and very important—rarely have I met a high-self-worth person who didn't have some sense of a bigger picture, a spirituality.

5

SURVIVAL

Adult children are survivors. We should give our-selves enormous credit for making it through those very difficult childhood years. We are alive, but not necessarily well.

Our survival was based on learning certain rules as children and playing by those rules in our dysfunctional families. We also adopted roles to survive. Those rules and roles protected us from even more-devastating consequences that could have occurred. However, the present-day life of an unrecovered adult child is testimony to the damage that did occur.

My first serious hobby was magic. The point of magic is to fool people, and I became the family magician. Misdirection is the essential element in magic, and I skillfully learned the principles of misdirection, both as a magician and as a person. As a child, my magic shows in the living room earned me praise and acceptance. Magic also gave me a sense of power and my own secrets. I was the class clown in school and used my humor at home to break the tension in the family. I'm sure my "success" as a showman back then caused me to pursue a career in broadcasting as an adult.

In my childhood I also learned lessons that haunt me to this day: don't trust anybody, do it yourself, sacrifice for others, be responsible, don't talk about sex, do better, life is serious, God is watching, be loyal, don't get angry, let it slide, people don't mean what they do, judge yourself, don't talk about anything but current events and what people are doing.

None of those rules or roles work today for me. They can't. They were tailor-made for my childhood. It's been a lot of work to get rid of some of those parts of who I am and I am still working on others.

The price adult children pay in their lives is enormous. We misinterpret our feelings (if we have any), fail to speak up for ourselves, disregard our own personal needs, involve ourselves in destructive relationships, and isolate ourselves in our depression.

When Claudia Black introduced her three classic rules of a dysfunctional home—"Don't talk," "Don't trust," and "Don't feel"—she opened the door to recovery for adult children. Operating by these rules in the past may have assured our safety: living by these rules today guarantees our pain.

Claudia Black, Ph.D., became the first well-known figure associated with the Adult Children of Alcoholics movement upon publication of her classic book *It Will Never Happen to Me*. Her other best-selling books are *My Dad Loves Me, My Dad Has a Disease*, and *Repeat After Me*. A past chairperson and current adviser to the National Association for Children of Alcholics,

her company, Claudja, Inc., based in Laguna Niguel,
California, presents workshops on children of dysfunctional families, produces materials to educate professionals, and trains personnel to implement family programs in existing therapeutic settings. An inter-
nationally acclaimed lecturer and trainer, Claudia is
featured on films and videos that focus on children of
alcoholics themes, including *The Sound of Silence,
Children of Denial,* and *A Child's View.*

CLAUDIA BLACK, PH.D. ▸ When I look at
adult children from dysfunctional family systems, the common
denominator I see is the issue of loss. I would probably be more
apt to use the phrase "children of trauma," as opposed to "children of dysfunctional families," because sometimes we can't
identify what the dysfunction is. It's more a dynamic than a
culmination of specific things. When we take a look at kids who
were raised in these families, we find that they are often kids
who experienced trauma. They experienced loss on a chronic
basis, and they experienced that loss at the time in their lives
when they were developing their worth and their identity. The
loss varies, but the loss is blatant. The loss is in embarrassing
incidents. The loss is in parents not showing up for events. The
loss is in parental anger that attacks being rather than behavior.
The loss could be childhood itself. The loss is often related to
normal childhood and adolescent development that the youngster didn't have. Therefore, the child couldn't grow spontaneously, couldn't grow up with flexibility, couldn't laugh, and
couldn't express his or her feelings with freedom.

A lot of children experience loss when they're raised in
homes with extreme punitiveness. In those homes kids aren't
rewarded for doing well or don't get strokes for being. They're
consistently reprimanded and punished for what they're not doing or not doing correctly. A lot of judgment, rules that are
inflexible, and a nonnurturing environment constitute the norm
for these homes. That is a very dysfunctional growing-up situation.

Kids from alcoholic homes and other dysfunctional family
systems end up with a defective sense of self. A child may end
up with a self, but the self becomes a co-dependency. Identity is

based in a reaction to a dysfunctional family system. Angry act-ing-out kids have an identity based in anger. For other kids, identity is based in performance. For some children, identity is based in humor and being cute, and others develop an identity based in nothingness. These identities are adopted to feel psy-chologically and often physically safe while growing up in these traumatic family systems.

Kids take on different roles to make the family system work and, even more important, to make it work for them. Roles bring about a sense of consistency and stability in their own lives. Whatever these kids do, they do to survive. It may not be physical survivorship, but it may be emotional survivorship. It is survivorship in the relationship to one's spirit, identity, and soul. Adult children behave in a manner that is psychologically safe.

Adult children say, "I became the other mother because my brothers and sisters needed me." While that's probably ac-curate, they really did it for their own survival. Taking charge and making some of the family decisions at seven years of age made the home a more stable environment. It also gave them a purpose, and children need a sense of purpose. It's a way of belonging. It also gives children a sense of power. It is also a much safer place for them, as opposed to expecting their parents to respond to them, because the experience is that they won't.

Responsible children are the nine-year-olds going on thirty-five. They are little adults within the home. Adjusters are the more nondescript children who don't want to draw positive or negative attention to themselves. They slide through, trying not to be noticed, and that's what makes it most safe for them. The placater is what I refer to as the household social worker. The placater is responsible for the emotional well-being of the family, while the responsible child takes responsibility for that which is tangible, such as food on the table and the car in the garage. The acting-out child is the one who walks through those early years with his or her arms raised, fists clenched, and fin-gers protruding. The acting-out child is probably the most hon-est kid in the home. All of these aren't just kids in alcoholic family systems; they are relevant to other dysfunctional families as well.

Children need love, hugs, and kisses, and in healthy families, parents are much more consistent and nurturing of children in terms of the child's whole being. In healthier families, kids get more quality time and focused time. Some literature today says that on average, children get fourteen and a half minutes a day from their parents. It's not a matter of sitting in front of a television set with them. Quality time means being active, taking walks, and playing with kids. In those ways kids learn they're special and they're loved. In alcoholic homes a child just prays that her dad's going to come home and not be drunk or that her mother won't pass out in the mashed potatoes.

It's important to look at the rules of dysfunctional families too: "Don't talk," "Don't feel," "Don't trust," "Be perfect," "Your needs aren't important," and "You're there to take care of others." Learning those rules is very much about survivorship as well. What adult children need to understand is that what once worked as a means of survival no longer works today. Adult children need to have a sense of appreciation that what they did was survivorship and took a lot of courage. It will take just as much courage to be willing to give some of that up now. Those old roles and rules no longer allow a person to function in a way that feels good and promotes happiness.

Look at the three classic rules: "Don't talk," "Don't trust," and "Don't feel." Kids learn not to trust because of broken promises, inconsistencies, unpredictability, and not feeling a sense of specialness. The result is that they always feel separate and removed from other people. If you don't know how to trust other people, you don't know how to be with other people on an equal basis. In personal or work relationships, you don't know how to act with your peers. That sets a person up for one-up, one-down relationships. So you either walk through life chronically in one-down relationships or you walk through life chronically having to be the one up, which means having to "sit" on somebody else so that person is in the one-down position. Not being able to trust means you can't utilize other people in healthy ways. You can't ask them for input. Without utilizing people in that way, you have fewer options. You also miss joy in life by not being able to have intimacy. You can't have intimacy if you cannot be vulnerable with others, and you're not going to have intimacy if you can't talk, trust, or feel. This lack of closeness results in incredible loneliness.

Feelings are cues. We walk through life not seeing the cues and signals when we don't know what our feelings are. For adult children it's not an issue of not knowing how to express feelings; they don't even know how to identify their feelings. It's a real numbness. For example, if you feel sad and know you're sad, that could be a cue that your feelings are hurt. Somebody said something to hurt your feelings, and you need to let that person know that. Otherwise, you're going to carry that hurt inside. If you find yourself getting angry, what that tells you is you're feeling abused by people, and that may be a signal you're not setting appropriate limits for yourself. If you're afraid, that may mean you're not asking enough questions. If you're afraid, that may also mean you need to say no.

Feelings can tell you something very important. When you don't see cues and signals, you often aren't going to see a problem until it's a crisis. Kids from dysfunctional families experience this all the time. They minimized their fear, sadness, anger, or embarrassment, and only at the final moment do they know that they should be angry. Often coupled with that is a high tolerance for inappropriate behavior.

Without knowing what your feelings are, you don't know what your needs are. Feelings are connected to being aware of what your needs are. The more aware you are of your feelings, the closer you are to being clear about your needs.

In childhood there is often very blatant negative behavior in reference to the expression of feelings. Some kids are told very angrily, "If you really want to cry, I'll give you something to cry about." Sometimes it is a lack of a response. When you cried, nobody gave you comfort. When you were afraid, nobody was there to help you solve problems. You had no way of making sense of feelings on your own, so as a survival tool, as a defense mechanism, you began to minimize and repress those feelings. If you do that chronically as a child, by the time you're in adulthood, you don't know what you feel.

The no-talk rule is absolutely fascinating. I've had people tell me that when their family home burned down, they were rushed out of the house in the middle of the night and stayed at a motel, the next day Mom and Dad got them into another house, and nobody ever brought up the incident again. The no-

talk rule isn't just about not talking about Mom or Dad's drinking or using drugs; it means not talking about anything.

If we don't talk about our feelings and we don't talk about
how we're seeing things, our perceptions aren't validated. We
learn not to offer our perceptions or feelings. We also learn not
to ask questions and not to tell people how we perceive things.
Then, as adults, we end up making lots of assumptions. By not
talking about things as we grow up, we don't get to see options
and choices as adults. That puts people into a greater state of
helplessness. They are not in the position to problem-solve if
they don't talk about what's going on. They minimize; they
discount. That puts them in terrible situations.

If somebody's done something hurtful to you and you dismiss it because "he's in a bad mood," that's going to cause
trouble down the road. Some people spend a lifetime of minimizing, rationalizing, and giving people the benefit of the
doubt. I have seen kids raised in battering homes who have
been so often pushed and shoved and slammed against walls
that when a boyfriend grabs them and pinches them so hard
they have a bruise, it doesn't even register that it was abusive
because "he didn't slap me; he didn't slam me up against a
wall." The whole adult child issue of "we don't know what
normal is" is tied into the "Don't talk" rule. For kids from
dysfunctional families, nothing's okay to talk about unless it's
truly significant.

B RIAN ► In terms of those models that you read about in
alcoholic families, my brother who committed suicide was the
scapegoat, my surviving brother's the lost child, and I am the
family hero.

A LICE ► I'm a good care-giver. I'm a good mother for the
world; I'd mother everybody if I got a chance. Doing for others
and seeing them do well gives me a feeling of self-worth.

M ARY ► I was most definitely the scapegoat of the family.
I put myself in that position to take on the problems of the
family. I would act any way I could in order to defocus from the
fights. If my parents were fighting, I would start crying or I
would hurt myself in order to make them stop. I did poorly in

school for a while, and when that didn't work, I did very well in school. I was always walking on eggshells. I was constantly trying to second-guess my parents and sacrificing myself to mend the family. My feelings didn't count. What counted was keeping the family whole.

MANOLITO ▸ I drank to disassociate from the core of my feeling, a single feeling always present. That feeling—which I tried to escape through drugs, alcohol, work, food, and the excitement of bad relationships—was the feeling of shame. The feeling of self-hate. It was the shame that I learned, the shame that was put in me. Instead of having love in my heart, I had shame about me because that's what I got.

I have no reason to be ashamed of myself, but I am ashamed of myself. As I come to understand what went on, as I liberate myself from old patterns, as I clarify where my shame came from, I will learn to love myself and this feeling of shame will disappear. The tape will be erased, and what will come out will not be a song of shame, but a song of love.

LYNN ▸ I didn't really express my feelings as a child. I always admired my brother, who's their own child. He would say to my mom, "Get off my back." I could never talk to her like that. I was very careful to toe the line. I really believed they could get rid of me. I express my feelings today, but I have trouble, particularly with men in intimate relationships. I almost tremble when I have to talk to them and say anything important; but I get it out.

DICK ▸ I was full of fears and anger. I had these feelings pent up inside of me, yet I couldn't express them. It was all right for my father to get angry, it was all right for my mother to get angry, but the kids were not supposed to express any emotions whatsoever. When alcohol came along when I was fifteen, it was amazing. It took the shyness and fear away from me. It took the anger away from me. Once I found what I call "the magic elixir," I was a sucker for booze. I had a tremendous fear of people, but with alcohol the fears all disappeared. I used alcohol for this purpose throughout my drinking, to the point where I could not drive an automobile, go on a job, eat, or sleep without alcohol. It was necessary for me to have alcohol in my system at all times in order to live. I came into AA only because alcohol would not do the trick anymore. After sixteen years it just didn't work.

In AA, I found a place where I could express my feelings and not be laughed at. Prior to alcohol, I thought that if people knew exactly how I felt, they would laugh at me.

I shouldn't have had the fear and anger I had. I shouldn't have had my inferiority complex. I had all these feelings, and I couldn't find any answer for them until I found people like myself who said they drank over the same feelings. When I came into the AA program, I felt a part of a group of people. I felt these people knew what I had suffered all my life.

If you get with a group of people like yourself, express your feelings, ask God for help, and try to help other people, I'll give you a written guarantee that all the negative feelings you have within you will disappear.

A UDREY ▸ The "Don't talk" rule in my household really applied to me. Being the third child, I followed the lead of my two older sisters. Very frequently I would hear the arguments and see the punishments that happened to my sisters as a result of them expressing their feelings or speaking out. I became the child who never wanted to rock the boat. I chose to say nothing and never would let anyone be aware of how I was feeling. All of the worries and all of the fear that was stirred up inside of me I kept to myself. I was too afraid of what would happen if I spoke up.

H ARRY ▸ Part of my not trusting my parents came from never quite knowing what kind of response I would get from them. If my parents were at odds about something, I knew I could get pulled into that and fail to please one or the other. To avoid getting involved with either one of them or to rely on them, I began to pride myself on getting by with very little. By not going to either one of them because of my lack of trust, I began to form a whole sense of self-worth as a reaction based on pride. By being so proud, I could get by on very little help, few pats on the back, or any interest in what I thought was important for me.

KAREN ▸ The message I got from my parents and my grandparents was that the best thing to do was not feel. My mother would pop pills when her feelings became too much. Now she takes them four times a day, just in case. She doesn't even wait for the feeling now. "Don't feel" was very much internalized, but of course, I did feel. "Don't feel" was really "Don't let me see you feel." If I felt, I was to keep it to myself. However, I handled it fine, so long as nobody knew about it. I was supposed to be a neutral being that didn't feel anything. As a result of that, I've had lots of physical problems, especially allergies. I go to chiropractors and massage therapists, and they say, "My God, your neck is so tense."

It's only been the last year that I started to really feel. Now feelings catch me by surprise. I will burst into tears, and it scares the hell out of me. It's frightening to me because I've never felt these feelings before. My immediate reaction is to suppress them.

As a kid, I would hear my parents fighting at night, and I'd ask, "What's the matter?" "Nothing's wrong," they'd say. "Go back to bed." I've come to realize through therapy and the program that, as a result, I've come to second-guess my feelings all the time. As a child, I knew there was something wrong, but these authority figures were telling me there was "nothing wrong." So I thought it must be me. Now it's hard for me to make decisions and follow through on them without checking with a lot of people.

Recently I called my mother to tell her I'd been to visit my grandparents in a nursing home. I hung up on her because she was screaming at me. I called her back later and said, "I'm sorry for the way the conversation ended. I was really angry with what you were saying." She then said to me, "Oh, honey, that's all right. We love each other; we don't get angry." And I said, "Mom, it's okay for people who love each other to be angry. That doesn't mean I don't love you; it means I was angry."

To her, if you have a feeling of anger, then you can't possibly also still feel love. If there's anger, that's it. That's shown itself in my family in extremes. My younger sister hasn't spoken to my mother in six years, I went four years without speaking to her, and my brother went a couple of years. Either everybody's acting like they're real happy or nobody's talking to each other. There's no middle ground.

B RIAN ▸ I've spent a lot of time in therapy being sad and feeling sorry for myself, sucking my thumb mentally. I wallow in self-pity and long for what might have been. One reason I do that is because I am terribly afraid of expressing anger. Anger is associated with loss of control. I have a lot of anger toward my mother. I remember it was so intense in a group therapy situation once, half of the people had to leave. They couldn't handle my anger.

I remember once playing a mind game and looking down my own throat. It was like opening a door down the basement stairs. All that was down there was a huge, black abyss filled with tears. When that happened, I could understand how people give up hope and commit suicide. I'm too much of a survivor to ever commit suicide, but I can see how my brother got to that place.

J IM ▸ I was the lost child, the loner, and sometimes the clown when I was insecure. I never took anything seriously, especially when family was around. It was to get attention mostly. I was always by myself or with just one other person. I was more prone to run away from the family than to run with the family.

B ETH ▸ Sometimes I was the responsible child, and other times, the angry child. I changed schools often as a child because I didn't feel at home, I knew I should be doing better, or I wasn't happy. I jumped around between Catholic and public schools a lot, and those were my decisions. I made the decision when I was nine years old that I wanted to go to public school. I was allowed to make that decision and I went. On the other hand, I acted out too. I was always a big screamer and physically violent. I attacked and bit people. I wet my bed until I was twelve or thirteen years old. As a young teenager, I smoked cigarettes, did drugs, and drank alcohol.

JEFF ▸ When my father came at me with his belt and beat me, his ultimate objective was to make me cry. I was angry and hurt that he would beat me, and I was upset with my behavior because I wanted to be perfect. I wouldn't give him the satisfaction of seeing me cry. I would take his beating until he was too tired to hit anymore. I would not cry under any circumstances. I face a lot of things that happen to me today that same way. I'll tough it out and go clear to numbness with it. I stop now, identify the feeling, and feel it. It's better to submit to a feeling at an earlier stage. It helps me get on with the business of living, and that's what all of this is about for me. I want to get out there, enjoy living, and have a better life as a result of time I've invested in recovery.

MICHAEL ▸ Nobody in our house talked about what was really going on between people. They only talked about safe subjects, such as world events or how good the coffee was. We didn't talk about our emotional lives. I got the distinct impression growing up that to talk about the emotional side of my self was rude, immature, and imposed on others. I understood that everybody handled emotions privately and quietly. I didn't know how to do that, and I felt sadly lacking. Everybody else in the house seemed to handle their feelings privately. They always said they were "fine." In our house you wouldn't talk about emotional things any more than you would urinate in the living room. It just wasn't done.

AUDREY ▸ I don't frequently feel for myself. I always feel the need to feel for someone else. At my father's funeral I found a need to feel for him because there wasn't enough sadness in that church to suit me. I outcried everyone in that church. I created quite a scene. I wasn't feeling a lot of sadness for me at age sixteen; I was feeling it for him because he was dead and people weren't that sad about it. No one's sad about a town drunk dying. I never saw my mother shed a tear during that time, at least not in front of me. So I did it for him, and that's the way I am.

A LICE ▸ In my therapy, I've had to work on having feelings, and it sucks. Feelings are not something I'm familiar with, except for fear, which has been my chief motivator throughout most of my life. When I look back at the life that I've had, there's a tremendous sense of sadness. It's part of my grieving. There's shame there too. It just is so painful. I can't even recognize positive feelings like happiness or joy. Feelings are hurtful, oppressive, and global. They're some horrible thing that's going to crush me into a nothing, a puddle. I've used food to control my feelings.

I learned very young to use food as an anesthetic. My goal is to not have those feelings be so oppressive that I have to hide. I was always deathly afraid of alcohol because my dad was alcoholic. I've lived my whole life fearing addiction. Nobody ever told me I could get addicted to food, but I do use food in an addictive way.

I feel so vulnerable sometimes, and one of the ways I can cope and get through my day is to numb some of my feelings. It doesn't have to be a lot of food. If it's a lot, I actually zone out. I get lolling, droopy, and very lethargic. If someone says hello to me, it may take thirty seconds for me to respond.

D ICK ▸ There was no communication between my brothers, mother, and father when I was a child. There was no talk about anything significant. We certainly did not talk about feelings. We never talked about problems because that would always start an argument. We never talked about wants or needs. We were always told we had everything we needed. If I felt uncomfortable about something in my own life, I couldn't talk about it with my parents.

M ANOLITO ▸ I was promised singing, dancing, and acting lessons. I was promised I'd be enrolled in a high school for the performing arts. And none of that ever happened. From the time I was five or six years old, I was told I was going to be trained for the stage. My mother talked about sending me to the Royal Academy of Dramatic Arts in London, but nothing was done in that respect. Instead, I was put in a school that emphasized mathematics and advanced sciences. My parents didn't even show up for the school performances I was in as my mother's disease progressed. I could barely practice the piano because it gave my mother headaches. It was all a big letdown.

JIM ▸ One of the resentments I nurtured for years was over a fight I had with a neighbor boy in school. We went at it for two days. I won the first round and he won the second round. His mother was very upset that I was picking on her son, so she went to the principal about it. The principal brought me in and gave me a paddling. I went home and told Mama about it. She didn't like that at all. She was very upset—not that I got a spanking, but that I got it in front of another parent. She was the kind to run down there, I thought to defend my honor. Well, I waited for years and years for her to run down to school and defend my honor, but she never did. That was the first really big disappointment in my parents I ever had. I never could depend on them after that. The disappointments were consistent from then on, with both my father and my mother promising to do things and at the last minute not being able to do them.

JAN ▸ Growing up in an alcoholic home, I had decided in my own mind I wouldn't be an alcoholic, and yet I ended up an alcoholic—and a woman alcoholic at that. I thought that was the worst. The first year and a half I was sober I literally spent in bed. I'd be up in the morning when the kids were around, but as soon as they left, I'd dive back into bed and sleep and sleep and sleep. In that way, I didn't have to deal with my feelings. I have a terrible fear of doing that again.

I'm dealing with loneliness now. After thirty-two years of living with someone, I'm living alone and I've never lived alone in my life. Rather than dealing with it, I'm getting around it by never being home. I work all day and I go out every night. I do not stay home, because I don't want to feel that loneliness and I know it's there. I think I'm afraid that if I stayed home one night, I'd go to bed at eight o'clock and I'd start that whole sleeping thing again.

MICHAEL ▸ There's a complete denial in my case of just about anything below my neck. I've come to understand in the last few years how I was basically a life-support system for a brain. That is how I lived my life. The only feeling that I would display was anger. I guess that's typical of men. I was generally baffled by people sitting around talking about feelings. One of the cardinal rules in the house I grew up in was "Don't upset Gram." I don't know that my grandmother ever demanded that, but not upsetting Gram was essential in that house. A lot of behavior was altered, and a lot of feelings got stuffed to avoid her getting upset.

I'm coming to an awareness that early on, I began to mistrust the whole idea of feeling, because feelings seemed to be used to control people. I had to walk on eggshells to avoid triggering emotions in other people and I resented walking on eggshells so much. That was a big reason why I turned off to the whole idea of feelings and climbed into my head. As I wake up, the numbness goes away, and I begin to come alive out of that emotional death. Another reason I avoided feelings so much was the sheer fear of their intensity.

At first, I feared that if I got in touch with my feelings, I would cry forever. It would never end, and I would be a total basket case. Indeed, I did experience an awful lot of hurt and crying. Sometimes for months at a time that seemed to be the only thing I could feel. There was a lot of feeling sorry for myself.

I'm beginning to see now why I chose to stay numb and stay in my head, where I could understand things and control myself and my environment. I think I was emotionally dulled as a child, and it turned into numbness as I moved into adulthood. It's a nice, comfortable, dead place to be. I was emotionally foggy for twenty or twenty-five years. I thought this was adulthood.

In the process of recovery, I have gone overboard in the direction of feelings, thinking that if I didn't feel every feeling that came along every minute, I wasn't emotionally healthy. That is beginning to come into balance. I appreciate that the emotional side of life is vital, but there are appropriate ways to handle it. To be aware of the feelings is most important, but I don't have to cry every time I'm upset. I also have come to realize that anger is the voice of my self-esteem responding to my hurt. Part of growing up for me is accepting feelings, learning how to respond to them appropriately, and communicate them.

BETH ▸ One of the major feelings I've always had has been longing. Longing equals love for me. I equate emotional distance with what a male-female relationship should be. I also think that I have a need for excitement. I've lived my life creating crises or working so hard and rejecting feelings so long that I get to a point where I crash. I take things to the maximum. If I'm going to have a feeling, I'll make it the most intense experience possible. If I'm sad, I'll just let that overwhelm me and burden other people with my sadness as well. I think I'm addicted to emotional highs and lows. I'll start getting angry with someone and feel a rush of adrenaline. That's important to me. For me, it's the opposite of numbness: "Let's have as many feelings as we can."

MARY ▸ I'm just an infant with feelings. Sometimes I have to go to my therapist and ask, "Am I feeling angry?" when I'm about to punch the fucking wall. And she says, "Yes, I think we could call that anger."

I'm twenty-four years old and I need to pay someone to tell me I'm fucking angry. I'm really angry at my parents for their lack of parenting and the pressure I got from them to be an all-perfect being. I go to a damn hard university, I've got three papers that are due, and I'm trying to figure out if I'm angry.

HARRY ▸ On the edge of my awareness was always a fear of liberating myself from the pain. If I broke free, I thought the needs that were never met would never ever be met. That's exactly how it felt when I was a kid. There was something wrong with me, and it was forever. No one would ever help me, and I was stuck with it. When the rock fell on top of me, I was going to be trapped eternally. That's what I spent my life trying to ward off. Feelings come and go. They're like weather.

CLAUDIA BLACK, PH.D. ▸ A lot of initial recovery is grief work. You need to go back and grieve the losses. It's important, though, to understand that this is only a part of recovery. You need to go beyond grieving. Recovery is not meant to be a blaming process. If you get stuck in the grief, it can turn into that. Recovery continues forward by asking yourself several questions: What does my past have to do with who I am today? How does the fact I didn't get to play affect who I am today? How does the experience of having lived with such fear affect who I am as a parent? How does my fantasy world as a child affect me today in my work? In recovery we learn the skills we didn't get to learn. We also learn how to negotiate, how to listen, how to ask for help, and how to identify feelings.

You've got to be willing to take some risks, in spite of the fears. You have to be willing to put yourself in front of other people. You do it in little bits and pieces. You don't do it in leaps and bounds. One of the first things to understand about the "Don't talk" rule is that you're going to have to talk. At the beginning, it's significant that you can say, "Hi, it's good to be here." The first time you sit down with somebody, you don't have to share the horror stories of your past. As you begin to open up, share the feelings that are most possible for you to share. Allow other people to facilitate greater exploration. You don't have to do it all yourself. That's why there are counselors and therapists. That's why there are special groups for people from dysfunctional family systems. That's trusting, and trusting evolves. Don't perceive it as black or white: "I don't trust anybody" or "How am I ever going to trust everybody?" You shouldn't trust everybody. Everybody's not trustworthy. Life isn't black or white. Appreciate on some level that you are trusting. You wouldn't be reading this book if you didn't trust, so identify with that. Adult children operate on a one-and-ten perspective; it's all or nothing. Recovery is learning the numbers two through nine.

When it comes to feelings, work toward a two or three. You don't have to get to nine yet. Make up a feeling list and carry it around with you. Three times a day pull it out and say, "Up to this point today, this is what I've felt," and check it off. A lot of people are really going to need a therapist to work with them on feelings. Taking care of your physical self is important, too, but your physical self is very much affected by your emotional self. A person can't be physically healthy and not be emotionally healthy. The payoff for really being in tune with your feelings is that your needs will be met; there's opportunity for

joy and intimacy in your life. Now, don't become so preoccupied with trying to find all your feelings that you have total
disregard for other people.

As devastating as some people's childhood and teenage
years were, they can live their life differently in adulthood.
Some people are going to have an easier path than others. For
some people the trauma was greater, but I see change all the
time in people who come from horrendous pasts. I don't think
people can make these changes by themselves, and they don't
have to. There's lots of help available today. Your past is your
past and you don't get rid of it; but the pain of the past leaves.
Recovery is not allowing the past to dominate how you live
your life today. It's being able to separate what happened then
from who you are now. Recovery is an ongoing process, and
adult children need to be patient.

6

CHARACTERISTICS

A couple of years ago a friend of mine who knew I had grown up in an alcoholic home sent me a list of characteristics of adult children of alcoholics. This list is often referred to as "the laundry list." I quickly identified with nine of the fourteen characteristics. The private therapy and the meetings of the recovering alcoholics support group I've attended never presented to me the essence of who I was as succinctly as that list did.

The laundry list of characteristics and my first reading of Janet Woititz' excellent book *Adult Children of Alcoholics* were the things that got me to investigate my own adult children issues.

The list came into being in the mid-1970s in New York City. It was authored by Tony A., a member of Alcoholics Anonymous. The list of characteristics resulted from his own written personal inventory. It was presented to a group he belonged to at the time, an offshoot of grown-up Ala-Teen members called Hope for Adult Children of Alcoholics. Here's the original list:

1. We became isolated and afraid of people and authority figures.
2. We became approval seekers and lost our identities in the process.
3. We are frightened by angry people and any personal criticism.
4. We either become alcoholics, marry them—or both—or find another compulsive personality, such as a workaholic, to fulfill our sick abandonment needs.
5. We live life from the viewpoint of victims and are attracted by that weakness in our love and friendship relationships.
6. We have an overdeveloped sense of responsibility; it is easier for us to be concerned with others rather than ourselves; this enables us not to look too closely at our faults.
7. We get guilt feelings when we stand up for ourselves instead of giving in to others.
8. We become addicted to excitement.
9. We confuse love and pity and tend to "love" people we can "pity" and "rescue."
10. We have "stuffed" our feelings from our traumatic childhoods and have lost the ability to feel or express our feelings, because it hurts so much.
11. We judge ourselves harshly and have a very low sense of self-esteem.

12. We are dependent personalities who are terrified of abandonment, and we will do anything to hold on to a relationship in order *not* to experience the painful abandonment feelings that we reveived from living with sick people who were never there emotionally for us.

13. Alcoholism is a family disease, and we became para-alcoholics who took on the characteristics of that disease, even though we did not pick up the drink.

14. Para-alcoholics are reactors rather than actors.

ACA literature states, "This is a description—not an indictment." Amazingly, the list seems to work not only for adult children of alcoholics but for adult children of many types of dysfunctional homes. If you can identify with some of the characteristics, ACA meetings can help you.

Timmen L. Cermak, M.D., is the past president, founding board member, and current Chairperson of the National Association for Children of Alcoholics. A practicing psychiatrist, he is the co-director of Genesis, a program located in San Francisco, California, specializing in treating spouses and children of chemical dependents and providing consultation and training on co-dependency and chemical dependence. Tim is Assistant Clinical Professor, Department of Psychiatry, at the University of California Medical Center at San Francisco and is the author of *A Primer on Adult Children of Alcoholics*. His new book is *A Time to Heal: The Road to Recovery for Adult Children of Alcoholics*.

TIMMEN L. CERMAK, M.D. ▸ There is no simple list of characteristics for children of alcoholics. Just as no alcoholic can have all the symptoms of alcoholism, no adult child can have all the characteristics of COAs. COA characteristics are a mixture of the following four categories: biology, stress, co-dependency, and underlearning.

Biology doesn't get passed on to all, but it gets passed on to a significant number of adult children and leads to an increased risk of chemical addictions. Some COAs were under incredibly severe stress as children; others were under less-severe stress. This leads to some COAs hearing about psychic numbing and being hit like a bolt of lightning, while others say, "Oh, yeah, I have a little of that." Co-dependency is a pervasive world view that suggests certain strategies for trying to solve problems which, if not unique to alcoholism and chemical dependence, are as intense there as anywhere else. Co-dependence relies heavily on denial and a uniquely distorted relationship to will-power.

Underlearning is a bit more of a general thing that can happen in other dysfunctional families. There are certain random gaps in the experience of adult children that surprise those who aren't.

One can assume that everyone who's an adult has been on a family vacation, but there are lots of children of alcoholics who've never been on one. They get to be adults, get married, and have a family. At thirty-two years old they get ready to go on their first family vacation and realize they've never done it before. They also may never have seen a fight between two adults lead to increased contact and intimacy. They may never have seen a fight that didn't lead to physical blows. A lawyer whom I had in therapy didn't know the usual way to tie his shoes. He had been taught to tie his shoes when his mother was drunk. She told him to figure it out himself, and he ended up never really learning the way most of us do it.

With all kinds of gaps in their experience adult children are left to reinvent the wheel as adults. We all can reinvent a couple of wheels, but if you've got a hundred to reinvent, that gets pretty hard. COAs often don't know what normal is. It's just simply a lack of information and experience. Some therapists who treat adult children believe that the person who says, "I don't know what normal is," is either resistant or neurotic. These therapists sometimes miss the fact that their clients really don't know what normal is. Their clients simply need to be told and then they're quite capable of doing what needs to be done.

The laundry list of COA characteristics performs a service. I don't know if there's scientific research on them, but they sure as hell work. COAs are bothered by the same problems we would expect people on the average to have, but to a much greater degree. Everyone can read the list of characteristics and have some reaction to it, but COAs have a profound reaction to it. They come to that list with a real setup. The setup is that they haven't talked to people about their problems and feelings. They've learned in a co-dependent way that you deal with problems by denying them, pretending they're not there, and keeping secrets about them. They come to the list often feeling they are the only people in the world who feel that way. Then, there it is in black and white right in front of them—a perfect outline of what they're feeling internally when they thought what they were feeling was idiosyncratic, unique, strange, and bizarre. Adult children say to themselves, "It can't be all that strange if it's here in black and white and someone else wrote it."

There are thousands of people reading the list and saying, "Yes, me too." The list is breaking the isolation for people. The average non-COA isn't walking around with the same intense sense of isolation. Even if they find things on the list they can relate to, it doesn't give them that tremendous relief of suddenly knowing for the first time they're not alone. The COA has the same relief the alcoholic has when he or she finally walks into a meeting and discovers that all the things they thought were special and unique about themselves really aren't. There are thousands of adult children who, in the same way and with the same sense of relief, are breaking their isolation, joining a group, and seeing themselves as one of many.

People from dysfunctional homes where there's no alcoholism read the list and see themselves as well. Sometimes they resent the fact there's not a place for them to go as there is for the COAs. Among COAs and adult children from other dysfunctional homes, there's more overlap than uniqueness. Some of it is simply from the stress-related characteristics, and some of it is from underlearning; then, too, co-dependence is not something that is unique to alcoholism. What's unique about COAs may only be 5 or 10 percent of what's going on, and what is in common with other adult children is the other 90 or 95 percent. Adult children from nonalcoholic families are more likely to relate to the characteristics if their dysfunction involved shame and secrets. Adult children from dysfunctional homes where there was sexual abuse, physical abuse, eating disorders, workaholism, compulsive gambling, compulsive sexuality, and schizophrenia all can identify. Chronic depression can fit in. Some families feel shame about that and keep it secret more than others. Physical ailments such as multiple sclerosis or chronic disabilities such as spinal cord injuries can fall in between. So much of it has to do with the shame-based aspect of it. Suicide is also interesting. Suicide happens for reasons. There's no such thing as suicide without something else going on around it in the family. And then there's the question of how family members treat the suicide. Is there tremendous shame, or do they talk about it? If you went poking around, you'd probably come up with some other family dysfunctionality. I've never seen anyone commit suicide as a random act.

Five major characteristics cut across all lines of dysfunctional homes. They are trouble with relationships; low self-esteem; the issue of trusting; issues of control (people from most dysfunctional families believe that unless they are controlling the world, what the world thinks of them, and what people are doing, then things are out of control and that's bad); and the inability to identify what is the authentic self, as opposed to the front put on for others.

Adult children from dysfunctional homes are often self-critical. That comes from having grown up in homes where all the blame was projected and kids were sponges for blame. Constant self-criticism is really a way of saying, "If I were doing this better, then the world would be different." It's really buying into the illusion of how much is really under a person's control. If you're a little kid in a terribly out-of-control world, you need as much of an illusion as possible in order to feel safe.

Adult children who were raised amid chaos may feel more substantial only when they are on a real adrenaline high. Without the continuation of chaos during their adult lives, their sense of aliveness and significance is lost.

Physical problems such as backaches, headaches, and allergies are also common in adult children from dysfunctional homes. The adult child has been under high stress. He or she has been taught, in the co-dependent style, to ignore that stress. The way adult children deal with stress is to deny it, but you can't fool Mother Nature. You can't fool your body. The body that is maintained in a highly stressful, highly tense tone for years starts breaking down.

Anyone who has difficulty with intimacy, closeness, and trust is going to have tremendous difficulties with sexuality. All the issues of low self-esteem are heightened by being in the concrete situations that sexuality pushes right in your face and right into your groin at the same time. Difficulties with intimacy are almost inevitably played out in the realm of sexuality.

Part of the healing process is understanding exactly what did happen in childhood—but not for the purpose of wallowing in misery. Little children are victims of their circumstances, but they can stop being victims in adulthood. There is a difference between "having an alcoholic parent" and "being the child of an alcoholic." Those are two very different perspectives. Having an alcoholic parent is a victim perspective. Being the child of an alcoholic recognizes that you have your own stuff to deal with. That's not being a victim anymore; that's being realistic.

1. **We became isolated and afraid of people and authority figures.**

D ICK ▸ Authority figures always bothered me. I balked at authority, but with alcohol I could talk up to anybody. I had a tremendous fear of people. I was very shy and introverted. I spent a lot of time alone if there wasn't any kind of sports being played in the neighborhood. In sports I could get out and do it, and I didn't have to socialize. I was afraid of people, including my immediate family. I felt uncomfortable at Christmas, Thanksgiving, and all the big family gatherings. When alcohol came along, it broke that barrier and I became a social butterfly.

2. **We became approval seekers and lost our identities in the process.**

M ANOLITO ▸ Advertising is a refuge for workaholics. I hated my job, but I stayed there because it was very prestigious and I couldn't disappoint anyone. My entire status, my entire world, and my entire sense of self-worth depended on where I worked and what I did. I was literally killing myself so that I could appear important to the world.

3. **We are frightened by angry people and any personal criticism.**

J E F F ► When confronted by an angry person, I often become flustered and upset, and find it difficult to focus on what the issue really is. More often than not, I back off and let someone else have their way, as opposed to standing up for what I might really believe. With the people-pleasing nature that I have, I want everyone to like me. I am affronted by personal criticism; I take it as character assassination and usually wind up rejecting the other person. I don't take criticism very well. I take it much too personally and not very often in the manner in which it was intended.

4. **We either become alcoholics, marry them—or both—or find another compulsive personality, such as a workaholic, to fulfill our sick abandonment needs.**

L Y N N ► When my husband and I left for Colorado, my therapist said to me, "You're really putting things on the line going out there, because he's got a drinking problem. By going out there and leaving everybody and everything that's familiar, you guys are either going to make it or break it." She told me I was smart to do that because I was forcing the issue. I was out there nine years. The last five or six years were horrible, but I wouldn't give him up.

5. **We live life from the viewpoint of victims and are attracted by that weakness in our love and friendship relationships.**

A L I C E ► When I dated in high school, I brought home the most mangy bunch of stray dogs for boyfriends. They were worse off than I was emotionally, but I was going to take care of them and make them feel better. I work with special-education students now. I've often needed to care for people who are handicapped. There's less of that now. I want to nurture everybody and care for people.

6.   We have an overdeveloped sense of responsibility; it is easier for us to be concerned with others rather than ourselves; this enables us not to look too closely at our faults.

H<u>ARRY</u> ▸ I was the oldest of eight kids, and by taking care of my brothers or sisters, I could get my own needs met in fantasy and never address the fact that nobody was taking care of me. I didn't even allow myself to acknowledge my core wish to be taken care of. I adapted to the abuse of nobody being there for me by constantly being there for other people.

7.   We get guilt feelings when we stand up for ourselves instead of giving in to others.

M<u>ICHAEL</u> ▸ If I stood up for myself in our house, I had the distinct impression I was hurting other people by so doing. They would get pained expressions on their faces, would turn away from me, or seemed awkward or uneasy. The impression I got was that I had done something to hurt them and that left me out in the cold. I loved them, and I was careful not to injure them by doing such a thing as standing up for myself.

8.   We become addicted to excitement.

B<u>ETH</u> ▸ The relationship was exciting. It was a lot of jet-setting and expensive dinners. Being apart and coming back together was routine. We hadn't been together for a month, met at National Airport, and flew to New York for an awards ceremony. He never stopped drinking, ever, but it was exciting. It was fun. It was romantic.

9.   We confuse love and pity, and tend to "love" people we can "pity" and "rescue."

A<u>UDREY</u> ▸ It's very possible for me to confuse love with pity. I tend to have such a sympathetic heart for so many wanting people. Being a schoolteacher, I very frequently see needy children. I reach out to them because it's so much a part of my nature to pity. I think it brings up a lot of feelings that I had as a child.

10. We have "stuffed" our feelings from our traumatic childhoods and have lost the ability to feel or express our feelings, because it hurts so much.

MARY ► When I was a little girl I went around the world with my father. I had jet lag. I was sick. I was running on an older man's schedule. We were staying with royalty. I was doing things that little kids have no business doing. My wardrobe was laid out for me every morning, and I was told how to behave. I remember I was throwing up in the restroom and we were landing in Bangkok. We were to meet the prince and princess. My father turned to me and said, "Turn it off. Turn it off now." Ever since then I've been a good little soldier. My feelings were no longer valid. That's where my spirit was really crushed— "Turn it off. Turn it off now."

11. We judge ourselves harshly and have a very low sense of self-esteem.

BRIAN ► I was convinced I was a bad kid and I was going to hell. I was convinced that God kept a big book of black marks against me for all the sins I committed. I knew that I was a bad boy.

12. We are dependent personalities who are terrified of abandonment, and we will do anything to hold on to a relationship in order *not* to experience the painful abandonment feelings that we received from living with sick people who were never there emotionally for us.

KAREN ► I bet I've been through thirty-five or forty relationships, and I did a lot to hang on to relationships, including getting pregnant in one relationship and then having an abortion. I followed one guy wherever he went and did anything for him. I look back at that and think, "Who was that person that valued herself so little that she would do those things?" He treated me like a dog. I thought he would now take care of me and that was the most I could hope for.

13. **Alcoholism is a family disease, and we became para-alcoholics who took on the characteristics of that disease, even though we did not pick up the drink.**

J AN ► I certainly had a lot of alcoholic behavior before I ever picked up a drink. I was rigid, and I didn't know how to have fun. The biggest thing was feeling guilty about doing something for myself. I also certainly felt a lot of guilt about the family in which I was raised.

14. **Para-alcoholics are reactors rather than actors.**

J IM ► I always followed somebody's lead. I never put myself in a position to initiate anything. That way I wouldn't be wrong. That way someone else was blamed if things didn't work out. I always had a buddy that was responsible in case I got in trouble. I reacted to life rather than leading.

T IMMEN L. CERMAK, M.D. ► We can have different relationships to willpower. Willpower is a tool that's appropriate for certain uses and inappropriate for others. You can, of course, abuse a tool. You can try to use it for things it wasn't built for, but you're usually not very effective when you do that. Willpower has absolutely no effect on laws of physics, such as those of gravity or the weather. A picnic is planned for Saturday and someone asks, "What if it rains?" So we say, "I just won't let it. I'll think positive thoughts." Most of us know that really isn't going to have any effect, but we pretend it does. That's an obvious example when our willpower isn't appropriate. It doesn't have any effect at all on the weather.

How about behavior? Can we simply by dint of willpower make a person wake up tomorrow in ecstasy? No, that's absolutely impossible. Willpower's totally inappropriate for that as well. Now take this a little bit further. Are we capable of using willpower to determine what feelings we're going to have ourselves? Willpower is totally inappropriate in that sense too. Willpower will not be able to determine how a person responds to something someone else does. You are either going to like it or not.

But willpower *can* be used on certain things. It's a tool useful to control physical behavior. An alcoholic cannot determine whether or not he is going to want to drink, but he can determine whether he walks into a bar or walks into an AA meeting. Willpower also has a lot of control over attention. We can use willpower to either pay attention to something or ignore it. We can decide to pay attention to pain or to brush it away. It doesn't get rid of the pain, but attention is no longer on it. Willpower has more effect in some areas than in others.

The prototypical example of co-dependence is really chemical dependence itself. Alcoholics get locked into a power struggle with the substance in a way that their self-esteem depends now on their ability to control what happens when they drink alcohol. Their assumption is that they will have no self-esteem if they can't control it. The alcoholic tries to control something that is uncontrollable.

Only when alcoholics acknowledge that they're powerless over the alcohol and that their willpower can't change how they react after they have something to drink can they begin to move forward.

People try to use willpower to make things happen that are out of the purview of willpower. It is no different in someone who's co-dependent than in someone who is chemically dependent. The prototypical co-dependent believes that whether he can get another person to stop drinking is an accurate measure of his own willpower and self-esteem. He believes, "If I can will it hard enough, I can get this person to stop drinking" or "If I can will myself to be good enough or rich enough, I will feel self-esteem about myself." The child of an alcoholic who's married to someone who's depressed believes if he can't get the person to stop being depressed, it's because he's not trying hard enough. If a relationship is not working, he whips himself harder to try to make it work.

The only people who really recover are people who have focused on willpower. People can stop drinking or stop some other compulsive behavior without understanding willpower and its limits, but their recovery remains partial.

7

COMPULSIONS
AND
ADDICTIONS

The profile of a practicing—or drinking—alcoholic includes anger, worry, depression, and self-pity. A drinking alcoholic is often called an egomaniac with an inferiority complex. From my conversations with others who have different compulsions and addictions, that profile and that definition fit as well for the compulsive gambler, overeater, the physical or sexual abuser, the workaholic, and the relationship addict.

Adult children of alcoholic or dysfunctional families are

addictive and compulsive. These addictions and compulsions are often passed on from generation to generation. While sometimes the substance or behaviors may change, the patterns remain similar. With alcohol, the addiction may skip a generation, but a close look will reveal alcoholism in the family history.

My father was an alcoholic. At sixteen, as I began using alcohol, I remember thinking I would never be like him. When I was a teenager, my father was in his forties. His behavior was very painful to my family and harmful to him. My drinking made me feel good and I had fun. My father was often angry and unpredictable when he was drinking. I was a kid having a good time on weekends. He was an alcoholic. Of course, I became an alcoholic, too.

While mood-altering substances or behaviors make us feel good in the early years of using, in the end our addictions turn on us, produce guilt feelings and shame, and may even destroy us. By the time we are addicted to our substance or behavior of choice, we have lost control and the substance or behavior controls us.

There is no way of honestly looking at adult child issues before dealing with a major addiction or compulsion. In addition, failure to examine adult child issues may cause relapse into addiction or compulsion.

Stephanie Brown, Ph.D., is one of the most respected figures in the Adult Children of Alcoholics movement. Author, lecturer, clinician, and consultant, Dr. Brown is the founder and former director of the Stanford Alcohol Clinic at Stanford University's Medical Center. A frequent keynote speaker at major health conventions throughout the country, she is the author of *Treating the Alcoholic: A Developmental Model of Recovery*. Her latest book is *Treating Adult Children of Alcoholics: A Developmental Perspective*.

S TEPHANIE BROWN, PH.D. ▸ The alcoholic family or family with problems is often quite functional. The family may stabilize in a very functional way around the pathology of one or more people in it. Pathology is a particular problem that causes severe consequences. In the alcoholic family, alcohol is the unacknowledged central organizing principle. It doesn't necessarily cause dysfunction. Often everybody functions very well. The word "dysfunction" as it's used today is an umbrella term. Now we hear people say, "I didn't have an alcoholic parent, but I come from a dysfunctional family." What they mean is that there were all kinds of problems in their family.

There are healthy or unhealthy families. Looking at it that way allows families to be functional or dysfunctional. Even a healthy family that has good communication and knows how to deal with crisis can become dysfunctional if something goes wrong. If a parent loses a job or there's illness, the family has to adapt itself to deal with the dysfunction. Healthy families have means to do that. They can solve problems that come their way so that they return to a new level of functioning, incorporating the problem or solving it. The unhealthy family often can't solve the problem and denies the problem exists. The family then quite functionally incorporates all its behavior, its interaction, and its view of itself around a myth or denial that someone is having a problem. The myth in the family could be that "there's no alcoholism in this family." The one who's got the problem is really the child who's acting out. The family then becomes very functional around believing the myth.

What happens in an alcoholic family is that the family has to actively construct explanations for what's happening to both explain the reality of the drinking and deny it at the same time. In one family, it's the child that becomes the problem. In another, it's a work situation: "Your mother wouldn't have to drink if she didn't have so much trouble at work." The problem becomes identified as something else, and the family then becomes functional around a problem that is misidentified.

When people use the term "dysfunctional family," it keeps them in the mode of asking, "What could we do to make it function better?" That's the heart of the problem, because it's functioning to maintain itself right now. To me, dysfunction doesn't label what's wrong. I call it unhealthy. Children who come from these unhealthy homes are set up themselves for compulsive behaviors and addictions. There are a number of reasons for that. First of all, there is a whole body of literature on the genetics of transmission. In other words, the predisposition to alcoholism or drug abuse is inherited, and that's a very important area. My area, however, is social learning and child-development theory. What I have done is try to understand why so many children become addicted themselves, and it can be explained by looking at modeling, imitation, and the process of identification. When you have the general theory, then you have to look at each individual separately because there's so much variance.

Children growing up with an alcoholic parent can't bypass dealing with the reality of alcoholism in terms of their own identity formation. What I have found working with people clinically is that regardless of their own drinking or chemical-use behavior, most children of alcoholics think they are alcoholic. That is important because it means they believe deeply that they are fundamentally out of control. They have grown up watching one or both parents chronically out of control. They've watched a variety of behaviors, emotions, and distortions in logic, and what they get from this is a norm: "I'm the kid in this family. These are my parents. I am like them." That's what development is all about. The kids of alcoholics are growing up watching both parents typically out of control, abusive, and perhaps violent. What they see as normal is what they learn. On another level, they are also missing key elements of attachment and emotional bonding necessary for their healthy development. Depending on the pattern of addiction, parents may be totally inaccessible emotionally or randomly so. The child may suffer tremendous deficits in emotional attachment. The consequences of that are severe problems, both in childhood and adulthood. The building blocks of an individual's development are missing. Often the child will develop a defensive core, a false self. The child manages to cope, but grows up without a healthy sense of self coming from within. These children have no sense of anything internal—of motive, wish, and feeling coming from within. As adults, they are very much other-directed, which brings about the need for approval—the co-dependent reactive stance, dominated by someone else.

Another consequence of the deficits in attachment and bonding is a tendency toward addiction. Early important dependency relationships have not been gratified, so the child never experiences having his or her needs met or understood correctly. The child then develops a sense of tremendously deep hunger and an inability to ever satisfy it. There is a strong link between who they are as adults and what they saw and experienced as children with their parents. They become like their parents, or they invest all of their energy to ward it off.

Depending upon environment, atmosphere, family, and the systems issues of role and function, the child can go in either direction as an adult. The daughter of a father who's an alcoholic may model herself after her mother, who was married to an alcoholic. The daughter may follow suit and marry someone who's out of control and needs to be taken care of. In this case, the gender roles are essentially replicated. She may also identify with her action patterns within the family, so that there's always a male out of control and always chaos. Her sense of self has developed as a caretaker. Here's somebody who thrives on stress or crisis. She may not marry an alcoholic, but finds herself in work situations that are similar. That is the kind of person who says, "I don't know why I'm always in crisis."

More and more people with different addictions are finding similarities among themselves. The common denominator is principally an internal experience of loss of control. There's also an area of great difference, and that has to do with the choice of substance or problem behavior. People will share the experience of compulsion, of being out of control, and the damage. They can readily identify with one another. Then they tend to form subgroups around whatever their respective substances or behaviors are. Picture a number of circles within a larger circle. There's the whole large circle of people with addictions and compulsions who identify with loss of control. Then there are smaller circles where there's more shared experience—alcoholics or overeaters or workaholics or sexaholics or abusers.

Most children from these unhealthy homes are in pain, but they do not know it. They have developed the defenses for, and the restrictions on, their own behaviors in the unsuccessful effort to quiet internal pain. It's not a conscious pain. People are not turning to drugs and alcohol by the millions to quiet pain that they are recognizing and labeling. In fact, that pain is there. What comes with abstinence is a tremendous amount of deep pain that was not known before. People choose to use because they believe it's positive. It's going to be enhancing. It's going to solve problems. It's going to be good. When it's said that people are coping with pain, that presumes much greater awareness than I ever find exists. If only people knew they were coping with pain, we'd be a lot further along.

My experience is that almost all adult children from unhealthy homes come out believing that they are out of control, that they are like one of the parents. It may be like the addicted parent or like the angry co-dependent parent who's out of control. There's a certain group that behaves like a parent. They imitate parental behavior, and they use and abuse. There's another core group, one of people who are not using substances. They may have another addiction, or they may be co-dependents. The core problem for both groups is arrested development. They're stuck. They're afraid to grow up because they will become out of control like the parent.

How can you grow up when you have unhealthy parents to emulate? Sometimes you find people who are not demonstrating any kind of serious problem. They're not coming to anybody's attention for addiction, but they are closed down emotionally due to intrapersonal problems. They're a huge percentage of the ACA population coming out of the woodwork. They're tremendously restricted. They have to keep a hold on themselves all the time, lest they be out of control.

D ICK ▸ By the time I was seven years old, I was involved in gambling outside of the house. At school the nuns would catch me matching coins, pitching to the wall, and shooting dice. At the age of eight I could play poker as well as an adult. I gambled heavily in the army, and when I got out, I gambled at the tracks. Apparently I inherited that from my grandfather. People that I hung around with were horseplayers. If I went out to the track with five hundred dollars I couldn't say, "I'm only going to lose fifty bucks." It was either win two or three thousand or lose every penny. When I won, I'd be the big shot in the bar, buying them all drinks. Sometimes I had to leave the track, go to the bar, and borrow money to drink. The last time it cost my wife and me thousands of dollars and my wife didn't know about it. My outlet was, first of all, gambling, and then my drinking came along.

COMPULSIONS AND ADDICTIONS

BETH ▸ I guess I picked up smoking at an early age, probably twelve or thirteen. My mom smoked. On the way to the pool in the summer, I would steal a pack out of her carton of cigarettes and smoke in the woods. I've been smoking now for seventeen years. It is an addiction.

MANOLITO ▸ I left San Juan to go to college in Boston. I began drinking and drugging from the beginning. By the third week, I was already in trouble with my roommate because of drinking. I had a blackout and I said all kinds of terrible things. My first drunk, my first blackout.

KAREN ▸ I was a compulsive shopper for many years. That behavior was modeled for me a lot by my mother. She shops all over the world, drags the stuff back, and gives it out. I did that for a long time too. I got a temporary high from it. It made me feel good, but deep down I felt terrible.

JAN ▸ The last two years that I drank, my husband traveled. He was only home on weekends, and I could hold it together pretty well for those couple of days. During the week, I used to drink so much at night that sometimes I would call him several times a night, all night long. I'd pick my husband up at the airport on Friday night, and he would never question me about my drinking and my phone calls. There were times when I'd ask myself, "Did I do it?" That's how strong my denial was.

AUDREY ▸ I used to observe my mother. She always looked worried, and I thought that was an adult thing. She had this worry mark on her face, so I developed it too. I am a compulsive worrier about my two children. In fact, I think it's my worrying that has driven them away from me. Right now, family is just everything. Whether that's healthy or not, I cling to it. I also cling to the material things I have acquired, because I still remember how it was when I grew up. It's like a sickness.

MICHAEL ▸ My habits were to drink about a fifth or a fifth and a half of vodka or whiskey a week. That would be in addition to any beer or wine I might have. I usually drank alone late at night "to relax" so I could go to sleep. It no longer worked to pace around and scratch my back. After all, I was an adult.

A LICE ▸ I can eat until I feel sick, but I don't throw up. I'm very into sizes and numbers when it comes to clothing and weight. I eat in spite of the fact that I know I'm eating many, many thousands more calories than would be necessary to maintain a clothing size. There are times that I feel as if I might literally die if I don't have something to eat. I feel afraid and that out of control. I just have to eat something. Anything will do, and I don't think; I just eat.

H ARRY ▸ I had been addicted to speed early on during my underground years. At the end of that time, cocaine appeared in very small quantities. Somebody offered it to me and I tried it. I remember snorting it and thinking this is what speed should have been. Then, I didn't do it for a few years, but later on, I would use cocaine and get paranoid. I would hole up and isolate from people and then come back beaten, whipped, and extremely depressed. During that time my drinking was constant.

B RIAN ▸ Using the alcohol progression of use, abuse, and addiction, I was in the abuse stage when I stopped. If I had kept up, I would have crossed the line to addiction. Once in a while I'd have so much to drink that I knew I shouldn't be driving. I could have been picked up for driving while impaired, I suspect. Right now, I have a compulsion to food. I used to be addicted to running, and I ran every day for seven years. I used to be forty or fifty pounds heavier but, because of the running, was able to lose. Work used to be an addiction, but it's less so now. I guess I have a money addiction too. Somehow there's never enough.

L YNN ▸ When we were in Colorado, I was probably stoned every day for two years. As soon as I'd come in from work, I'd smoke. If I had it in the house, I was stoned all the time. On weekends it was nonstop. I had to flush the marijuana down the toilet. I haven't had any in almost three years now. I can't smoke it like other people. I'm like an alcoholic with marijuana. I will not stop. I understand about alcoholism because I've been there with grass. I dealt with it in therapy, because it started to make me feel really terrible and paranoid. I decided I'm a parent now and I need to be respectable. I'm not twenty or twenty-five anymore. I just don't do it anymore.

J I M ▸ I had dropped my thermos bottle full of whiskey on the way to work, and I needed a drink. When I went to pour the drink, I found the glass inside the thermos bottle was broken. I got some toilet paper and made me a strainer and poured. It wasn't going fast enough so I punched a bigger hole in the paper, thinking, "A little bit of glass won't hurt me." I was sick, but that's the rationale of an alcoholic.

M A R Y ▸ I've always been involved in the arts, and I justi- fied my abusive behavior—snorting lines of coke, packing a bowl, and doing shots—by saying I was creative. That's really interesting because I've been more creative since I've been so- ber. I was a good addict, but I always knew within myself that something was wrong. I was hurting inside and I was miserable. I always thought I was such a good little actress, I was fooling so many people.

I was in New York working at Sotheby's, and I hit rock bottom. That's why I went to my first AA meeting. The night before, I went out with a bunch of brokers from Wall Street. My father was always trying to set me up with these noodle heads with no spines. We decided to go to the Limelight, and I got wasted. I remember coming home and binging. I wasn't even hungry, but it didn't matter. I was just trying to run away from everything. I opened up the phone book and looked up the number for AA. I went to my first meeting in the basement of a church. There was a bag lady to the left of me and there was an actress from one of the television soaps on my right. I was in so much pain.

J E F F ▸ Seven years ago I walked into a detox center in the ghetto. Out front, drugs and whores were sold wholesale. Ram- pant alcoholism was in my life. I don't remember signing in. I went through audio and visual hallucinations for three days. I shook for a month after I took my last drink. I'd been making stabs at quitting, but the last trip was the convincer for me. I was sicker and more afraid of losing my life than ever before. I didn't have as much fear about dying as I had about dying that way and under those circumstances. Dying in an alcoholic seizure wasn't the way that I wanted it. I didn't want that on my headstone.

STEPHANIE BROWN, PH.D. ► Research hasn't been done yet to understand choice of addiction or substance, or why particular children in a family adapt different coping mechanisms. We can see, however, that children from addictive-compulsive backgrounds, regardless of their choice of substance or behavior, tend toward becoming addicted and compulsive themselves. If they don't become addicted or compulsive, they are tremendously limited because of their excessive need for control to keep away from becoming addicted or compulsive. These people are rigid, frightened, and constantly warding off loss of control in themselves.

What's modeled in the family and what addictions and compulsions are popular in society at a particular period of time play significant roles in the addiction of choice. First of all, it's not uncommon to find multiple addictions within a family. There might be one person who is alcoholic, another person who is co-dependent to the alcoholic but also has an eating disorder, and someone else who may exhibit another kind of obsessive behavioral disorder, such as workaholism. Secondly, what's prevalent in the culture—what addictions and obsessions are currently the behaviors of choice—plays a role as well. Saying anorexia and bulimia were the rage is not incorrect. Young women were very attracted to being able to control their weight. Fashion dictated "Slenderella" themes and eating disorders. Workaholism is another good example of how the culture participates in building addictions. The culture dictates intense work load, drive for achievement, competitiveness, and the principle that you have to work constantly in order to keep up.

In working with adult children of alcoholics, one of the dominant issues all through long-term treatment is that adult children of alcoholics are terrified that they are out of control underneath all their defenses. It's the central theme. It has to do with processes of identification with the parent and the belief

"If I let myself go, if I let go of the control, if I relinquish my defenses—I will become like my parent." And that means being out of control, violent, hostile, vicious, or angry. That was the behavior in the home that was related to the substance.

The parent may be drinking alcoholically, and the child may react in a way that imitates parental behavior in terms of being out of control behaviorally, but with an entirely different substance or even entirely different behaviors.

Frequently adolescents, as they begin to experiment with drugs and alcohol, say, "I am in control and I am not addicted to alcohol." Let's say the parent drinks and the adolescent chooses a substance, such as marijuana, that represents the peer culture, as opposed to the adult culture of alcohol. The adolescent says, "I'm different, I'm not going to be like you." That is often looked at as rebellion. It's not. It's rebellion on the surface; it's identification underneath.

We don't know yet how to predict a particular response in children. We do know there's an enormous range of response. One thing the responses have in common is that all such behavior disorders are based on something being out of control and an attempt at self-control. Children see parents who are out of control and therefore experience a lack of modeling of behavior, control, self-control, and acceptance of limits and boundaries. That whole range of disturbance in the parent creates the same problem in the children.

Growing up in an alcoholic or severely dysfunctional home does not necessarily mean that you're going to become alcoholic or compulsive; but it does mean you're going to have to struggle with the lack of healthy models, and that could result in an excessive need to control.

8

CO-DEPENDENCY, ADDICTIVE RELATIONSHIPS, AND INTIMACY

Children who have been raised in alcoholic or similarly troubled homes usually have as role models one dependent parent (who may be chemically dependent) and another parent who tries to change the dependent partner's behavior. That caretaking, controlling, other-directed parent is the co-dependent.

However well intentioned, co-dependents, by focusing on

other people, are never free to improve themselves. They can blame others for their unhappy lives. Co-dependency allows the co-dependent to live as a hero, martyr, or victim. The co-dependent believes that if the compulsive behavior—such as the drinking, gambling, unfaithfulness, or overeating—stopped, life would be wonderful. It wouldn't. The co-dependent has an illness or condition that needs to be identified and treated.

Just as the alcoholic is dependent on, and compulsively attached to, his or her drug, so do many of us use people as our drug. Adult children often look for "self-love" in others, and we respond to them co-dependently. Frequently our adult relationships re-create the parental relationships of our families, and we therefore choose our mates poorly. We choose excitement, chaos, and pain because that is what we know. That is what we learned. We do it over and over and over again.

A co-dependent person myself, I have frequently found myself attracted to people and situations where I perceived myself as the rescuer of someone I saw needing help. Past relationships were often predicated on getting self-worth, sex, and security. However, by focusing on others I was able to rationalize my self-centered search.

Most experts agree that all children of alcoholics and most from other dysfunctional homes suffer from co-dependency.

Robert Subby, M.A., has worked in the field of addictions for the past fifteen years and is a pioneer in the development of family-centered chemical dependency and co-dependency treatment. He is a founding board member of the National Association for Children of Alcoholics and is the executive director of the Family Systems Center located in Minneapolis, Minnesota. A frequent lecturer on co-dependency, Bob is the author of *Lost in the Shuffle: The Co-dependent Reality*.

ROBERT SUBBY, M.A. ▸ When defining "co-dependency," the prefix "co-" means "with" and "dependency" means "reliance on something for support." From my perspective, "co-dependency" means dependency on outside things, such as work, spouse, position, title, neighborhood, and social contacts as a way to define oneself as a person. With those things in place, the obvious conflict people live with all the time is, "If I lose these things, who in the hell am I?" As people get older they invest themselves in the maintenance of those outside things to the exclusion of investigating, questioning, and looking at their own relationship to themselves.

Different studies look at what happens to mothers when their children leave home or what happens to men who lose their jobs or retire. These people fall into an identity crisis of sorts. If you look back at their lives, you see how much of their self-worth was placed within the context of those external things. Outside of work and family, these people are often very lost and confused about who they are. Whatever emotional investigation or resolution hasn't taken place usually catches up with them, and they get overwhelmed with free-floating anxiety. We look at such people and say they have been suffering from a delayed identity development that was brought about by the mistaken belief that if they did all the things the social script told them to do, they were going to be happy, feel secure, and feel good about themselves. As long as they're living within that external context, they can be quite unconscious of the fact that they haven't investigated very much of life and really don't know who they are. Much of the adult world depends on people's ability to be comfortable with themselves, where they came from, the experiences they've had, and a recognition of what their strengths and weaknesses are.

Co-dependency is an emotional, psychological, and behavioral pattern of coping that has been brought about by the practice of, or prolonged exposure to, dysfunctional rules: Don't talk about your feelings. Don't talk about your problems. Don't let people in. Don't ask for help. Try to avoid conflict and maintain the status quo. Try to build acceptance based on not being who you are versus being yourself.

The co-dependent is an individual who believes that doing the right thing will bring love, acceptance, salvation, and happiness. The pursuit of the right thing in the co-dependent realm is manipulation. The reverse of that logic would be a healthier, clearer, identity-based logic: "I do the right thing because love is already in me, and with that love in place I can intuitively sense, know, and understand what I have to do to be content with myself, and that doesn't mean always pleasing everybody."

That's different. That's an identity built from the inside out instead of from the outside in. Co-dependency is the evolution of identity from the outside in.

I don't think happiness is—though our culture has sold it this way—the arrival at some place measured by how much money you make or whether you had a marriage that lasted thirty years. Happiness is being able to look in the mirror on a day-to-day basis and say, "I'm still as confused as I was yesterday and I don't understand all the things I think. I don't understand all the things I feel. I certainly don't understand what a lot of people around me are doing. But given all of that reality, I can still be okay with myself, even if the best thing I can say at times is I'm lost and I know that."

In our culture we mimic the adult model, follow the adult script, and eventually abandon our natural need to investigate who we are. Many of us wake up in really successful situations at thirty, forty, or fifty years of age and, when we look in the mirror, say, "I don't know who in the hell you are." We end up at odds within ourselves and go about in the crisis of co-dependency projecting this intrapersonal conflict onto our outside activities. We pick wives, bosses, or friends that we couldn't possibly get close to. And we live by a covert set of rules that doesn't challenge us to change and doesn't challenge us to take risks that scare us. The rules include, "I don't know if this is normal or not. I don't know if I'm an okay human being or not. I think I'm a bad person. I don't want you to know that, because if you knew that, you wouldn't want to be with me."

The co-dependent is an individual who is basically manipulating the outside world to find validation and okayness. All co-dependents are playing a game of manipulation in order to acquire some sense of security that they don't know how to create on the inside themselves. Their goal is to feel good about themselves; it's a fairly self-centered exercise.

If you identify an adult child, you know that he or she comes from a definable, recognizable, exaggerated category of dysfunctional family. Adult children are always struggling with co-dependency in adulthood. Yet, co-dependents are not always adult children. Some co-dependents come out of a decent, consistent, nurturing, loving, and accepting family background. They get involved with a co-dependent and get distracted, tangled up, and then seduced into playing unwittingly a game of co-dependency. It's a different reality to treat these people, because once you sit them down and get them into a sane environment, they very quickly fire up the old memory and can go back and start building again. When you deal with adult children, they have no memory of ever having had it sane, so it's much more a total reconstruction process.

Co-dependency is an addiction to outside issues in whatever way we orchestrate them to make us feel comfortable within ourselves. If somebody is used to failing and was reinforced in this pattern by his family, he will often create scenarios in which he will fail. This keeps him in a comfortable or familiar struggle. Manipulation of the outside helps a person maintain control of what is familiar, rather than take the risk of stepping outside.

The false sense of security in the co-dependent's life comes from sincerely believing that by manipulating the way he is, he can control what will happen to him in his life and that if he stops manipulating, he would stop being okay. It's as though the person in an adult body is, like a kid, looking to his or her parents for something that the parents didn't give the child in the first place: unconditional love, positive regard, and a sense of self-worth. Parents are responsible for giving those things to their children through the model of their own behavior and through their attention and care during the children's developmental years. A lot of the time they don't do that.

Adult children are not raised to expect the best, because they don't see themselves as people who deserve that. For someone who unconsciously doesn't feel worthy, to get anything is better than to have nothing. Abuse victims often stay in physically violent relationships because they get almost addicted to the routine. It's a terrible consequence. It's extremely mood-altering to be constantly worried about the next time you're going to get physically abused, but as with alcohol, being abused keeps people effectively out of touch with feelings that would overwhelm them if they didn't have this kind of behavior to distract them. What would sink them would be all that bad family history and all those feelings of "I'm no good. I'm not worth anything. I don't have anyplace I belong." This is a very immature but powerful way of thinking that says, "If I lose what

I have, then I will have nothing. I will be nothing and I will be all alone." Then, with childlike logic, the person thinks, "If I'm left alone, I'll die. That will be the end of my life."

These are the classic rules of co-dependency: Don't talk about your feelings. Don't burden anybody with your feelings. Feelings are weakness. Negative feelings, such as anger, rage, hostility, pessimism, and self-pity, are unacceptable. Don't talk about problems.

"Don't rock the boat" is the rule that governs all the other rules. As children, we believed, "Mommy will drink more. Daddy and Mommy will fight. Mommy and Daddy will get a divorce. I will be left alone and I will have nothing. It will be my fault. I'm a bad person. I don't deserve anything and I'll die."

Adult children in recovery figure out that that fear isn't real and come to trust in themselves. Co-dependency is not a lifetime sentence. Emotionally you can grow up and say, "I'm a recovered co-dependent." The truth is that co-dependents haven't even been parents to themselves. They haven't even been real adult guides in their own lives. They don't know how to look at the child part of themselves and love and care about that child. As parents, they have a responsibility not to abuse themselves and put themselves down. They should be accepting of themselves and recognize themselves as human beings who are vulnerable like children. Once individuals recognize and make peace with their own rejection, denial, and abandonment of themselves, and begin to enlist in equal measure participation from all those untapped good parts of themselves, they don't worry so much.

If you are going to recover, ultimately you have to recognize your own culpability. Even though you were unconscious and blind, the potential for choice was always there for you. Ignorance of the choice is no excuse. In the long run, you have to own up to that so that you can begin today to make those choices. Co-dependency is a denial that you have a need to learn, that you're lost, that you don't know that you are a victim. You're really not anymore. Recovery is change, getting back to yourself, getting rid of the hype and building from the inside out.

In co-dependent relationships it's not only that we are taking care of people; we use them as an alcoholic uses alcohol. People become a medication, a drug of choice as a way of staying out of touch with ourselves. We don't like how we think, so we stay busy and we don't have to think. We don't like how we feel, so we work on our husbands or wives in order not to deal with our own feelings. We don't like the way we look, so we stay at the office sixteen hours a day so that we don't have to do anything about it. All of these things are really drugs in lots of different forms.

You think you have power, but the truth is, you're powerless. You think you have to win when the truth is, what you have to do is surrender to win.

Co-dependency is not a guarantee that you're going to feel bad about yourself, but is a guarantee that you're never going to know who the hell you are. All co-dependents are clinically definable as depressed. The cumulative effect of not talking about what you feel or not expressing the things you think is that you have to repress who you really are. Another word for repression is "depression." The opposite of "depression" is "spontaneity." If you've got something you'd like to do for fun, but you think you can't because you're an adult and it would look childish, that might be true. On the other hand, it might be that you're afraid of being yourself, and maybe everyone else would love to do exactly the same thing you're thinking about doing. We have a largely depressed society because so many of us follow co-dependent rules.

What do you understand about co-dependency?

M A N O L I T O ▶ I've become convinced that I am addicted to humiliation, failure, attention, excitement, and self-pitiful depression. When I'm feeling comfortable or good or I'm on the verge of achieving something, I tend to sabotage it. This is perhaps the most amazing pattern that I have been able to recognize and act upon. My goal has not been to succeed but to struggle and suffer and keep on going. There's a Greek myth about Sisyphus, who was always pushing a stone up the hill. There is a lot of Sisyphus in me and, I suppose, in most of us. I believe this is the disease of co-dependency.

Were your good feelings about yourself linked to being liked by other people?

J I M ▸ Before I got to the age of forty, all my feelings hinged on someone else. I was dependent on other people. They were responsible for the way I felt. I was insecure about everything when I was little; and even as an adult, so I tried hard in all the wrong ways for a response to make me feel good. Then I got into alcohol. In that sick behavior, I would shortchange the people who really could make me feel good. The old me would have felt responsible if I made them feel good and I didn't want to be responsible. Some time ago I learned I wanted to be able to think whatever I wanted to, so I had to allow others to feel and think whatever they wanted to. Recently my daughter, who lives in New Jersey, was home for a visit. I felt real good with her because we have a detached relationship now. There was no responsibility on either of our parts for each other's feelings. It was a beautiful experience.

In your relationships, have you placed others' needs ahead of your own?

D I C K ▸ My father was not a giving man and my mother was not a giving woman. It disgusted me to see that they never would help anybody. If it didn't involve making money, they were not interested. I was brought up in a home like that. My mother still feels to this day that receiving is a lot better than giving.

I always felt sorry for my mother. Everything that ever happened in the house was my dad's fault, according to her. I more or less grew up with the idea that he was no good and she was good and I had to help her out. Guilt feelings were instilled in me—so I felt more or less responsible for her. I was driving her to the church at six o'clock in the morning.

When I was drinking, I would help people who couldn't drink like I drank. They would get into trouble and I would help them. They'd be someplace and need a ride and I was the one that took them home. I was the one that was always taking care of their problems for them.

Have you neglected yourself in favor of other people?

A UDREY ► There were times when I was so consumed with worry and fear that I developed stomach disorders. I've experienced high blood pressure and spastic backaches too. When I entered college, I worried so much that my hair started falling out. I was always worrying about how things were going to be for others. When I had children of my own, I always worried about what could happen. In worrying, I tended not to look at my own health, and when I did look at myself, I found myself deteriorating. Then I was forced to look at myself, and it made me go to the doctor. I've experienced lots of physical problems because I failed to focus on myself. One of the things I do best is to notice what's wrong with other people and try to get them well.

In past relationships, did you focus on others?

H ARRY ► My sense of selfhood was greatly derived from the image I saw in a woman's eyes and also the image that I saw in the eyes of rivals for her. If I had a pretty girl on my arm and you admired her, my worth went up in my own eyes. I used women as used cars and traded up the ladder. I was involved in a mad scramble to enter into a relationship that would allow me to meet that other person's needs in a way that would restore some sense of self to me. The payoff was that I was never allowed to look at the one thing that I got as a kid for keeping a depressed woman alive: If my mother died, I was going to be motherless, and you can't live without a mother. So I had to keep her alive. In adulthood I was constantly re-creating the same relationship.

When my mother turned on me emotionally and sexually, I learned there's a hell of a payoff for taking a woman from depressed to orgasmic and that encoded itself in my life. I would seek out relationships where I could have an external sense of health and vibrancy and an internal depression. When I filled that void, that was the payoff. That payoff was better than I ever got filling my own needs. I learned early on to say, "Fuck your needs. Not only do your needs not exist, you don't exist."

In your relationships, have you focused on people you could help or rescue?

A LICE ▸ I gravitated to people that I could help. The other type of person I sought out was someone I thought could help me. I always looked for surrogate mothers. Typically I would find a female supervisor or someone in that kind of role. Against both of our "better judgments," we would develop a personal relationship that got very close and very entwined. I was involved in her life in ways I was not comfortable, knowing about marital problems or sexual issues. We would go so far as to discuss being parents to one another and taking care of each other. I was always listening and providing consolation.

When I had needs, they wouldn't be acknowledged. I would feel like a depleted prune because as the relationship wore on, the lifeblood would disappear and I would feel like I was being sucked dry. I had a number of those relationships. They've been real painful experiences for me because I was always frustrated and disappointed. They reinforce my whole distrust of people.

In your personal relationships did you try to solve others' problems?

B ETH ▸ Four out of the five long-term relationships I've had were with guys who had drinking problems. I was very co-dependent with them, often ignoring that there was a problem. Some of them lost their jobs, and I'd help them start a new career. I tried to improve their lives. I would ignore my own family to concentrate on one needy person. I would let them lie to me about what was going on. I've always tried to help solve other people's problems, not realizing it was creating new problems for me.

In past relationships, have you tried to please others?

K AREN ▸ I always tended to gravitate toward relationships with people who would not validate my feelings. There's one relationship that I was in for five years off and on. It was with a person whom I perceived as being very powerful. He had lots of money, and we were always focused on him and what he was doing. Whenever I would bring up something that I wanted to do or something I felt, he would ridicule it, ignore it, or tell me I shouldn't feel that way. I gave up "me" a lot to please him. It's not just been in relationships with men either. I can think back on my relationship with my mother. I was afraid to say what I had to say, because of her anger. In many relationships I went along with things so that people would not attack me emotionally or physically in any way.

In past relationships, have you lost yourself in another person?

M<u>ICHAEL</u> ▸ When I married the second time, I watched myself create the disappearance of me as a separate entity. I became essentially an appendage of my wife's personality. I did not like it and she did not like it. Yet, I did not know how else to act in a relationship. It was one of the most maddeningly frustrating things I've ever experienced, because there was a lot of good in that relationship and I kept it going down this other track. I was very angry about that, and it came out in negative, snide, biting little ways.

Were your dreams linked to someone else's life?

M<u>ARY</u> ▸ My dreams have always gone on the back burner whenever I've been in a relationship. To this day, when I'm around my father, my dreams are irrelevant and what I do is irrelevant. So I don't talk about it. It's not important. I was recently in a relationship that ended, and I had to make an incredible conscious effort to keep my dreams alive. A lot of my addictions were a result of shoving myself off in a corner and asking others, "What is your dream?" I became a chameleon in regard to what that other person was about. I always thought of myself as a piece of dreck. I never got any recognition from my parents for anything I did. I just assumed that anything that I did was irrelevant.

Do you confuse love and pity?

A UDREY ▸ It's very possible for me to confuse love with pity. I tend to have such a sympathetic heart for so many wanting people. One particular child that I have right now comes to mind. She's so pitiful, docile, and unresponsive. I catch myself being angry with her. So often I would like to tell her to speak up and to be strong and assertive: "The way you are now is going to follow you." I project that she's not going to be happy as an adult. I see that right now in that child. I want to respond a whole lot to her because it stirs up so much emotionally in me.

Sometimes I let her be by ignoring her, and I feel that that's wrong. Other days I'll be very responsive. I have come to realize it's what's inside of me that I see so much in her. Yes, pity replaces the love.

Was your self-worth raised by solving others' problems?

J EFF ▸ I was the cheerleader: "Well, your problems are here and let's work through them together. I'll help you out." I was so preoccupied with trying to find a way for others that I really wasn't looking at the ways for myself. My relationships with my brothers and sisters worked much the same way. I was trying to fix their problems before I even took a look at my own. With my dad, his business was more important than my own time and energy. I wanted to be accepted by people and the way I did that was by doing for them. If there was no payoff, then I was hurt. All the way along, I can see that pattern. It's good for me to cheer other people on, but not at my own expense.

Did you find yourself preoccupied with how others responded in your relationships?

B RIAN ▸ In a relationship, how the other person was responding was 98 percent of the pie. How I responded was really not important at all. Three years ago that was the game: "What do you want?" "How do you feel?" "How are you going to respond?" "What do you feel toward me?" Whoever it was, was the reality. How I felt was not important. What you wanted was important. There are very few areas where I did what I wanted. It's really incredible. It makes me so furious, I could fly into an enormous rage. That was then, and now I don't do that anymore. It's what I want that's important.

Has fear of someone's anger determined what you said or did?

M ANOLITO ► When I was a very little kid, I was subjected to life-threatening explosions of anger from my mother. If the abuse had gotten out of hand, I could have been injured very seriously. I've developed a defense against anger. I consciously and subconsciously do anything in my power to avoid any sort of anger in any situation. The same goes for abandonment in personal relationships. I fear abandonment in every situation, and that's why I suffer from acute people-pleasing.

In your relationships, was there a sense of trying to control someone else's feelings or behavior?

J EFF ► My boy fell off his bike. I picked him up, and he was crying. I said, "Now, stop crying. You'll be all right," rather than allowing him to cry because he was hurt. I do try to control relationships a lot. After my wife had gone to her first AA meeting, I wanted to work her program for her and tell her what she should do.

In past relationships, would you characterize yourself as a dependent person?

M ICHAEL ► I acted very independent, but I was in fact very dependent. In both my marriages, my view of myself hinged upon how my wife viewed me. If she went on about her work the way anybody should, I felt ignored. The mirror that I needed to define myself was gone. I was very dependent on my wife's continued attention and admiration. I suppose it was a vestige of the experience with my mom, who was always fawning over me. It was a two-edged sword. It was a real love-hate thing. I desperately needed their attention, and a part of me was very angry about desperately needing their attention. It was a hell of a battle. It's where all my energy went.

Were you ever in a co-dependent relationship?

J I M ▸ Unhealthy dependency is the co-dependency. After I got the alcohol out of my system, I went into several unhealthy dependencies. There was something there for me. I felt needed. In almost every relationship, there was the question of who was getting what. This kind of relationship feeds on itself, and it can get so bizarre that no one believes you would stay in a relationship of that nature. Often it blows up or falls apart of its own accord because it's unhealthy. There's no substance to hold it together. Once each person has taken everything he or she can take out of it, it disintegrates. Then you step back and say, "Next time I'm going to do it differently." The next relationship starts feeding on itself too. You're getting what you need, and your partner's getting what he or she needs, and, boom, you're right back in a co-dependent relationship. Until you start finding out what you need and what's healthy for you, the pattern continues. What's healthy for you is that you don't need that kind of unhealthy relationship. In a healthy relationship, you share; you don't need. If you can't be friends, you'll never work as lovers.

Have you had difficulty in your personal relationships expressing your feelings?

J A N ▸ I never talked about how I felt, because my husband could never hear me. That was how I grew up too. I think my husband had a very distorted view of who I really was, because it was so difficult for me to say how I felt. When I did say how I felt, he'd say, "You shouldn't feel that way." After I had been sober a couple of years, I was having a hard time. I can remember telling him, "This isn't easy; it's difficult." His response was, "Oh, you're strong, you'll be fine."

Looking back through my whole life, I realize that I tend to gravitate toward "broken-wing" people. I was attracted to people who were very similar to the people with whom I had grown up. I tend to worry more how the other person feels and how my behavior will affect them.

Have you denied the reality of your relationships?

MARY ▸ I didn't see any of the warning signs that my relationship was unraveling. I just denied there was any sort of problem. I saw what I wanted to see. That goes back to my early childhood, when I denied any sort of problem existed. I call it "shutting that elevator door." I don't want to look at it, I don't want to see it. In this relationship that just ended, there probably was a problem. I put myself in a situation where I was very vulnerable. This person was living under my roof, and he left with no warning. Why was I unwilling to see the signs? For years and years people would say, "I think your mother has a drinking problem" or "Your father has a drinking problem." To this day, when my therapist says, "You know your father's an alcoholic," I have a blank look on my face. It's seeing what I want to see. I'm very good at that. That's been what's protected me.

Did you try to control the relationship with your husband to make it better?

LYNN ▸ Up to a year before I decided to leave, I actually thought that I could get my husband to stop drinking. I didn't realize his alcoholism was a disease; I didn't realize there was nothing I could do. I drank with him for a while; that didn't work, obviously. I went along with whatever he wanted. I covered for him with friends and relatives. Looking back on it, I find it hard to believe it was actually me there, but it was. I wanted that marriage so bad and I wanted him so bad, a part of me believed it was my duty to get him better because I was married to him and marriage was supposed to be forever. I was real angry that I couldn't get him well. I had no life. I went to work and I came home. I quit being a social worker, because I couldn't stand treating people when I was having so many problems myself. I had hardly any friends. My whole goal was keeping a lid on what my husband was up to. I tried all different methods to get him to shape up. It was one of the most frustrating experiences I've ever had. I finally realized I couldn't get this man together.

Have others been more important than you in your relationships?

B ETH ▸ One guy I was involved with would be physically violent toward me and give me black eyes. I would ignore it. I wouldn't see anything terribly wrong. It wouldn't be the cause for me to break up with him. I've often gone out with guys who might have a high school education, denying there would be anything different with our aspirations. There were always enormous differences. I tried to make myself believe these guys were the greatest. In reality they were no-good bums. I denied the reality that they had drinking problems. There was one guy that I really wanted to marry. The first time we had a date, we closed the restaurant; we sat there after everyone else had gone. We were there until two o'clock in the morning on a Sunday night because he wanted to keep drinking.

Have you found yourself attracted to people who were compulsive?

K AREN ▸ Many of the men I've been involved with were compulsive. One person in particular comes to mind. It was nothing for him to call fifteen or twenty times a day. I didn't understand this was a compulsion on his part. I was flattered by the attention. I would say to him, "You know, you really shouldn't call me so often," but I would pick up the phone and still talk with him. My words and music didn't jibe. I can recall times when he would not call and do what I said I wanted. Then I became really upset because he was not calling me, so I would start calling him. We would trade compulsions. As long as he was calling me, I could sit back and act a little bit superior and say, "I see what you're doing and you need to change." That was okay; but the minute he took that control back from me I was real uncomfortable. Other people I dated were compulsive and addictive in terms of alcoholism, drug abuse, or workaholism. I was very much attracted to those with that type personality, because they were so busy in their compulsions that it fed my need for abandonment. They were so busy being compulsive, they were leaving me behind.

Can you identify with the idea that we re-create our childhood in adulthood relationships?

A LICE ▸ I always looked for people—and even to a certain extent still look for people—who can take care of me and protect me, because what I needed in my childhood was someone to care for me and protect me from things that were happening. Although that's what I desire the most, the people that I choose are not able to provide those things for me, so I have effectively re-created my early childhood experiences.

How did your relationships keep you from looking at yourself?

K AREN ▸ One extremely compulsive relationship that comes to mind was with a man who was married. I had an authority figure whom I feared, yet I was drawn to him. I viewed him as powerful and me as powerless, and I needed to get my power through him. The fact that he was married made him totally unavailable to me emotionally and physically. That brought out a lot of my compulsive behaviors. I tried to control something over which I had no control. I can remember waiting for him to acknowledge me or to want to see me. I totally denied my own needs. I would do insane things. Somebody would call me and I'd tell them I couldn't talk because he might call while I was on the phone. I would run home just in case he might call. I would stay at the office late in case he might want to come by. I would do absolutely everything and anything he wanted. He would drop me little notes, and I would go downstairs in the middle of the afternoon and have sex with him. It was horrible.

I get so sad and so emotional when I think of how little I valued myself. I sold out. It was attention to me. I'd never had any attention good or bad. At the same time, to my grave I will be grateful to that man for what he did to me, because it brought me to my senses. It brought me into this program, it made me change, it made me look at my life because it was totally unmanageable. It's absolutely the power of the human mind to deny the reality of a situation. I continue to be amazed by that, and I also continue to be so grateful for having gone through that, because now I know and it will never happen to me again. That victim is gone. I'm still very tempted to fall into the victim role. It's a very seductive thing for me to fall back and play victim and give control to someone else, because then I can blame and resent the person, and not me.

How did your childhood influence your relationships?

M ICHAEL ▸ I've had a continual need to make sense out of the world by proving myself correct about my beliefs of the world. The basic psychological beliefs I formed were that I'm not entitled to love and acceptance from another person just as I am, women need to be pleased, and it's in relationship with a single woman that I have any chance of getting love. That's not the way the world is, but those are the beliefs. As I look back on my relationships I always chose women who appeared to be "strong." In all cases there was a need on my part to be emotionally dominated to a degree and to have to please someone. In so doing, I kept proving to myself, this is how the world is and that is how women are. It helped me to make sense out of the world. I've had a constant need to prove my beliefs correct. They were wrong to begin with, because they were formed in an incomplete and inaccurate environment.

Can co-dependency be viewed in a positive way?

H ARRY ▸ I was born dependent on my parents to put things inside of me so that I could use them to relate to people as I grew up. However, by the time I was three, I was co-dependent. My cocaine addiction, my history of wreckage in relationships, and my alcoholism were the evil that I internalized.

I'm proud of a lot of the relationships that have graced my life. I used the behaviors that I used to survive. The neat thing about my co-dependence is that it is making me healthy now by making me aware of what it was I was repeating. That's what I always wanted to do: separate from the pain, the hatred, the abuse, the loneliness, and the engulfment, and be free.

Therapist, lecturer, and consultant Terence T. Gorski, M.A., is the president of the CENAPS Corporation in Hazel Crest, Illinois. The Center for Applied Sciences works in the area of addiction and co-dependency and serves as a bridge between the professional and the layperson in research and education. Terry is an acknowledged leader in relapse prevention for alcoholics and has coauthored, with Merlene Miller, *Counseling for Relapse Prevention* and *Staying Sober: A Guide to Relapse Prevention,* among other books. His excellent audiotapes *Intimacy and Recovery* are distributed nationally.

TERENCE T. GORSKI, M.A. ► In a healthy family a child learns that relationships are basically a source of joy, comfort, and cooperation. A relationship is a place to which you go to find satisfaction, to get bolstered up, supported, and nourished. The family is the refuge you go to when you are burned out from the world, when you have a problem, and when you need love, caring, and kindness. When you are chewed up out there in the world, you can come back to the family. You have a place where you can truly be yourself. The healthy family affirms the unique individual and says it's okay to be you here: "I am interested in your pain. I'm interested in what you think. I'll tell you whether I think you're right or wrong, but I'm going to love you whether you're right or wrong. I'm not going to abandon you. I'm not going to kick you out." It's an unconditional relationship. "I love you. You're my child. I love you for who you are. You don't have to be what I expect; I love you anyway and I am interested in you. I am concerned about you. If you have problems, I want to understand them. I'm going to help and support you in doing what you need to do." That's a healthy family.

In a healthy family parents treat each other with dignity and respect. The parents find a legitimate sense of joy and satisfaction in being with each other. Periodically they experience problems or struggles. They view those things as temporary setbacks to the norm, which is a pleasant, satisfying, comfortable, and rewarding experience. They model that to children. In a functional family the norm is peace, calm, comfort, and joy periodically disrupted by problems that are temporary. Then it returns to the norm of being happy.

In a dysfunctional family it's just the opposite. The norm is struggle, chaos, confusion, and pain. Relationships chew you up. Sometimes a relationship gets really good for a short period of time, but doesn't last. It returns to the norm of being a painful, horrible place to live.

In a dysfunctional home the child learns that relationships entail a difficult, painful struggle; they temporarily feel good, but will rapidly decay back into a difficult, struggling, and painful situation. The child learns that at five or seven or ten or fifteen years of age.

Children from dysfunctional environments often end up in bad relationships because they believe on a fundamental level, "I'm not worthy of being loved and the only way I can get somebody else to love me is to trick them into believing I'm someone that I'm not."

Four general relationship stances come out of families of origin, depending a lot on how the adult child internalizes the parental role-modeling. The first is a person who comes out ruggedly independent. He or she denies totally all of their soft, caring, and vulnerable sides. Second is the dependent, a person who will overemphasize all of their vulnerabilities and disown all of their strengths. The third is the ambivalent; ambivalent people see themselves vacillating between the best thing in the world and the worst thing in the world. They don't believe they're lovable; neither do they believe other people are lovable. Fourth is the detached person who's given up totally on other people; this person just slips off into the woodwork and doesn't seek relationships.

The classic concept of the co-dependent is that he or she is a dependent personality. Such people lose themselves in another. But not everyone who comes from a dysfunctional family is dependent; many of them are viciously independent. They still have problems with intimacy, but the way they manifest it is different. There's a neurotic link.

An addictive relationship has an extremely independent

partner who is grandiose to the hilt and believes, "I'm entitled to the world," and an extremely dependent partner who feels, "I'm really not worth anything and I need the sanction of another human being to survive." That combination creates the addictive relationship. The self-centered partner says, "So here I am. The world ends at the tip of my nose. The only people who are worthwhile are people who reflect what I think I am." The other-centered person comes along and is able to mirror back the image the self-centered person wants to see. The self-centered person is saying, "As long as you're mirroring to me in the correct way, I'm going to reinforce you like crazy and it's going to be bliss." It works until the other-centered person runs out of steam one night and doesn't have enough energy to mirror back what is needed. The relationship is going to blow up. Addictive relationships do not necessarily have to have self-centered and other-centered partners, but it helps.

People who come out of a dysfunctional home unconsciously either re-create their family of origin or the polar opposite. A person either blindly conforms with, or blindly rebels against, what he or she was unconsciously taught as a child. In both cases there is no free individual choice. The female child of a male alcoholic may marry an alcoholic; that's conformity. The daughter of a fundamentalist minister may get involved with totally irresponsible men; that's rebellion. A man who was a superachiever all through school can conform by joining a company and marrying the president's daughter; or he can rebel by dropping out of mainstream society and living in a commune with a "free spirit."

In making the decision to conform, the child decides that the family of origin is good and he or she therefore is bad. To be good, the child must make the family right. In making the decision to rebel, the child believes that the family is bad and he or she is too good to live like that. To be good, the child must do the opposite, whether or not it is in his or her best interest.

Every family of origin instills in the children a profile of strengths and weaknesses. A family of origin is not all good or all bad. A person needs freedom to choose.

An addictive relationship is marked by a swing between intense pleasure and intense pain, swings between feeling extremely good and feeling extremely bad. The glue that holds the addictive relationship together is the desire to feel good. Personhood is secondary.

There are seven major characteristics of an addictive or dysfunctional relationship. The first characteristic is magical, unrealistic expectations: "If I get into a relationship with the right person, that person will fix me, and my whole life will be okay." In a healthy relationship the person has rational, realistic expectations: "I want to have a good relationship because I would like to have good sex, a companion in life, someone with whom to share recreation, and someone to mother or father my children. I have a partner to do things with, but it's not going to make me someone different from who I am."

The second characteristic of addictive relationships is the desire for instant gratification: "The most important thing in my relationship with you is your ability to blow my mind on demand. I am using you like a drug. Your job is to change my mood and make me feel good. If you do it now, I'm happy; if you are not able to do it now, I'm not." In a healthy relationship short-term pleasure is nice but the person has a long-term orientation: "If the sex tonight isn't mind-blowing, that's okay; it will be again in the future. If you're tired tonight and if you need space, that's okay. Your job is not to be my drug; your job is to be a human being with whom I interact."

Third, dysfunctional relationships are dishonest: "I lie about who I am; you lie about who you are. There are certain things about me I can't tell you." There are no-talk rules. Healthy relationships are rigorously honest. There's a commitment to being fully conscious. In a healthy relationship, "I know who my partner is from A to Z. I know my partner thoroughly and intimately, and I accept my partner fully."

The fourth characteristic of a dysfunctional or addictive relationship is compulsive overcontrol: "I only am interested in the portion of you that can produce a good feeling in me. I'm not going to let you shift; I'm not going to let you move. You have to act in a certain way, damn it, or you're no good." This is why addictive relationships are so often marked by love-hate, love-hate, love-hate. In a healthy relationship there is voluntary and free-flowing cooperation: "I'm with you because I want to be; you're with me because you want to be. I don't *need* you." The addictive relationship stance is: "I need you; if you walk out on me, I can't make it." There's psychological coercion, and both people feel pressure. In a healthy relationship, "If you decide to leave it will hurt, yes; but I'll survive."

The fifth characteristic is lack of trust: "I don't really believe you love me; I don't really believe you care about me. I don't really trust you're going to be what I need when I need you to be it." In a healthy relationship there's rational trust: "I trust you to be who you are. I like who you are. I trust you're going to be who you are. I don't distrust you."

The sixth characteristic is social isolation. In an addictive relationship the couple becomes the whole world and nobody else fits. In a healthy relationship there's social integration. The male partner has friends and the female partner has friends: "There's my friends, there's your friends, and there's our friends we have together." People are welcome into the relationship.

The final characteristic of an addictive relationship is a recurring cycle of pain. The cycle goes from intense pleasure to intense pain, into disillusionment, blaming, and then desperate attempts to make up. Intense pleasure: "Boy, you blew my mind." Intense pain: "I'm really mad because you can't do it again." Disillusionment: "I guess you're not the person I thought you were" or "I'm not the person I thought I was." Blaming: "It's all your fault, goddamn it," and then, "No, maybe it's my fault; I've been a fool." Then there is desperate action to go to the other person and fix the relationship. The partners make up and the intense pleasure comes back, and they start the cycle all over again.

In a healthy relationship there's a repeating cycle of pain-free pleasure. Episodes of pain are tolerated because they're bridges to more pleasure and greater intimacy: "We'll solve this crisis together; we will bond closer and be better partners because of it."

There are also cases of passive dysfunction, where partners quietly vegetate together. They're miserable together and do not meet each other's needs. Typically the partners are two detached people who get together. That's a passive relationship. You can't call it addictive, because there's no drive to it.

People who come from a background of addiction or compulsion disorders very often are sensation seekers and very active individuals in their pursuit of life. The climate in the family will shape the personality. There are active and passive family environments. As we develop as children the range of our usual experience becomes our psychological norm. If a child gets emotionally beat up every day by his or her parents, that becomes a norm. When that child becomes an adult and gets in a relationship and psychologically gets beaten up every day, that is normal: "I'm within my comfort zone. I know how to survive this." If there's no psychological abuse, such people don't know what to do. They feel uncomfortable and unconsciously they set their partners up to reabuse, to redo what brings them back into their comfort zone.

To recover from an addictive relationship, you must recognize it's not healthy and understand you can change and have something different. You must admit that your life is all screwed up because of how you learned to relate to others as a child. You must also believe there's hope. There is some power greater than you, some source of help that can show you a way out. Search for that person until you find someone who you believe can help you and then follow directions. What they're going to tell you to do is going to make you feel uncomfortable, because that person is going to pull you out of your comfort zone very quickly.

Intimacy is a close, personal relationship between two people that reflects affection, love, and a depth of knowledge about each other. These two people share common individual characteristics and distinctive relationship characteristics, which causes an intermixing or interweaving of interests and activities. This results in the relationship assuming a high level of importance, value, and priority in each partner's life.

First of all, there's a close, personal association. If intimacy's going to have a chance, two people have to spend time together. (One of the biggest problems with people who come in for marriage counseling is that they're never together.) Second, it's between two persons. Third, it reflects affection and love. Affection means, "I like you." Love means, "I care about you and I'm concerned about your well-being on a very deep level." Love is the genuine and sincere concern about the other person's well-being. Fourth, they share things in common. There's a commonality of experience. They have similar interests in significant ways. There's a natural common foundation, which allows each person to feel, "I know you and I'm interested in you, and you know me and you're interested in me." The frames of references are close enough so that they don't have to get out of their own comfort zone in order to relate to each other. Fifth, there are also distinctive relationship characteristics. When they get together, there are enough things that happen that are new, novel, exciting, interesting, or intriguing. There are enough complementary relationship characteristics to make it work, and they cause an intermixing or an interweaving of interests and activities. So it's not just two individuals; there becomes a we: "This is our thing; this activity exists because of us." If either disappears, it won't be the same thing anymore. There's a sense of we-ness. Sixth, this interweaving of activities results in the relationship assuming a very high level of importance, value, or priority. What they do together is important and valued. "I choose to be with you over anybody else."

You can't create intimacy. When people say they can create intimacy, they're making an error. What they are saying is that they can engage in behaviors that increase the likelihood of affecting another person in a certain way. However, if two people are emotionally mismatched, you can do all the right things and intimacy won't happen. The societal standard right now is to confuse the concept of infatuation with the concept of love.

Infatuation is the intense feeling of physical and sensual attraction that leads to, and culminates in, sexual gratification. It is intense passion, plus intense sensuality, plus intense sexuality. You can have a long-term relationship based on just infatuation, but it will be addictive. People get into infatuation thinking that they're getting into love, and they're not satisfied. Something doesn't happen; there's something empty; something is missing; they don't get along. There are problems, and the couple doesn't understand why.

Passion is an intense desire, and sensuality is the ability to take pleasure in a partner. It's very primal. Does her body odor turn you on? Do you like the way your partner tastes when you kiss? Do you like the sound of his voice? The more the person matches your natural sensual preferences, the greater the potential for dynamite sex. You get close to each other, and you like the way the person smells. Then your partner starts talking, you kiss, and—zammo! That makes the potential for good sex. When you get into bed, if you are able to abandon each other to the sensual enjoyments, if there're no sexual hang-ups, if the sexual rhythms and routines and intensity are right—then BOOM! it's the Fourth of July. Bodies dissolve into atoms and reassemble. This is infatuation. It's more powerful than most drugs. This is the nature of the addictive relationship, because when all you have is infatuation, the partners don't love each other; rather, they love how they make each other feel. People get married for the wrong reason. People are taught to over-identify with the sexual.

A number of years ago researchers interviewed long-term married couples. The feeling of infatuation, passion, or intense love was found not to be a predictor of long-term success in marriage. As a matter of fact, marriages almost seemed more likely to survive in the long run if the initial passion was not too intense. The predictors of success were shared levels of self-esteem, mutual expectation of autonomy and freedom, common interests, common values, common life-style preferences, complementary differences (Does the person have enough intriguing differences to keep the interest and sparks alive?), and a common sense of spirituality, an active identification with some vision bigger than a person that gives life meaning and purpose.

Infatuation is a state of temporary insanity that is marked by a sense of euphoria and the inability to see another person realistically. When you get infatuated, say to yourself, "I am temporarily insane."

The basic mistake people make is to say to themselves, "I've got to find someone to love." What they mean is, "I've got to find a victim for my love."

People coming out of a dysfunctional home always feel unlovable. They feel they have been loved for the role they play, not for who they are. You are only capable of re-creating with another human being the nature of the relationship you have with yourself. If you punish yourself, you will punish your love partner. If you hate yourself, you will end up hating your love partner. If you are afraid of yourself, you will be afraid of your love partner. A person is incapable of establishing a level of intimacy with another human being that is greater than the level of intimacy he or she has with himself or herself. You can't go out and find intimacy. What you can do is adopt a policy of attraction, and who you are limits who's going to be attracted to you. A woman who needs to be victimized will attract a brutalizing man. Healthy people attract healthy partners.

A relationship addict is a person who compulsively needs excitement in a relationship. The relationship addict needs the intense emotionality of an intimate, mind-blowing, passionate relationship. Some 20–30 percent of the adult population is hooked into chronically addictive relationships, and the figure is higher for younger people than it is for older people. However, my impression is that 40–60 percent of adults periodically go out and opt into short-term intense affairs.

If you are involved in an addictive relationship, you can change. You need to declare abstinence from high-risk addictive partners. Ninety percent of people in addictive relationships will misread that statement. It is typically misunderstood by most people that they should declare sexual and relationship abstinence. What I'm suggesting is that you identify the type of person you get involved with addictively and avoid that type like the plague. High-risk partners can be difficult to spot. Sometimes there's no common denominator in physical appearance or physical behaviors; it is totally in the kind of person they are. Often it's totally in the life-style the person lives. What the relationship addict is really addicted to is the feeling the person creates inside. However, to know that doesn't help. You have to know what *type* of person creates that feeling. When an alcoholic takes the first drink, he loses control. Certain personality styles are like booze for a relationship addict. Certain types of people create the rush they desire. Abstinence means living without the rush.

Begin getting involved in casual, superficial dating relationships with the type of partner whom you would find dull and boring. Make a decision to date without making any significant commitments. Always date at least two people at a time and abstain from sex for the first three dates. There should be no exchange of money, and you should not live together for at least three months. Build the relationship slowly. Keep it superficial.

Before you spend significant time alone, observe the person and see how he or she interacts with other people in your presence. Go to parties and see what they do. Slowly reveal a little bit more about yourself, sit back, and see how the other person handles it. Go to the next step and share more and more intensive, exclusive activities. Then begin spending time where you're alone without the protection of other people or structures. Then move to the final step, where you share progressive intimacy. Do it responsibly with no dishonesty. Make sure you have the capacity to get out, because if you do not have the capacity to walk out of a relationship, you can never be free. You have to know that at any time you choose, you have the capacity to leave and survive on your terms. If two partners are involved in an addictive relationship and they're married, they have to abstain from the behaviors that create the superhighs and the superlows. That may mean a break from sex or certain sexual practices. It may mean taking a vacation from each other. The decisions get more difficult.

For anyone who is in an addictive relationship, the chances of working it out without professional help are slim to none. It's not a bad idea for one partner to have his own therapist and the other partner to have her own therapist. They can go together to a marriage counselor.

The goal is moving from a style of ready, fire, aim, which is the addictive style, to ready, aim, fire, which is healthy. A healthy person prepares before he executes, and evaluates when he's done. A sick person overreacts, has a disaster, and blames somebody else.

PART
III

THE
SOLUTION

9

ASKING
FOR
HELP

Back in college a priest took an interest in me. He observed that I lived life either on top of the world or horribly depressed, so he suggested I go to a couple of psychiatric sessions for consultation and testing. The doctor's recommendation was that I should begin therapy immediately or I might end up committing suicide. From the time I was eighteen I have seen psychiatrists, psychologists, and therapists regularly.

I am still at a loss to explain why none of the therapists addressed my obvious alcoholism—except to see it as a symptom of deeper problems. Those therapists did provide some outlet for my depressed feelings, monitored my manic-depressive behavior, and may have kept me alive. However, I now know that none of those therapists understood the adult-child syndrome as we know it today.

I left my PBS position as host of "LateNight America" to write *Are You Happy?*, to see how it would feel to be out of the limelight for a while and to learn about being raised in a home with alcoholism. While on the air, I never seemed to have enough time to investigate it.

As a recovering alcoholic, I knew I had made great strides in my growth; and while I certainly was happier than I had ever been, I still had the feeling that something was very wrong. After three meetings with other adult children of alcoholics, I knew I wanted more. I read a couple of books but still had a thousand questions. I wanted to understand how growing up in an alcoholic home had affected me. I decided on private therapy. Joan Pheney was one of the experts on alcoholism I had interviewed for *The Courage to Change.*

In a telephone call, I asked Joan, "Who is the best COA therapist in southeastern Michigan?"

She never missed a beat. "I am."

"I'd like to come to see you and spend a couple of hours," I said.

There is an old saying, "When the student is ready, the teacher appears." I was ready.

For the past year and a half I have seen Joan on a regular basis, digging into my past and looking at the adult problems that came out of my unhappy childhood. It's been difficult but I am making progress.

Adult children get to the help—therapists, counselors, and support-group meetings—for different reasons. The important thing is to get there, and excellent help is available today. Since we learned as children not to ask for help, frequently we don't when we should. Maturity is knowing when to ask for help.

Joan Pheney, M.S.W., is in private practice in Ann Arbor, Michigan, specializing in the treatment of eating disorders and adult children of alcoholics. She is a consultant on eating disorders with Glenbeigh of Tampa, and the Naples Counseling and Research Center in Florida and the Ardmore Health Care Group in Birmingham, Michigan. Joan is the former director of outpatient services at Brighton Hospital, an excellent alcohol rehabilitation center in Michigan, and the former executive director of the National Council on Alcoholism in Flint, Michigan.

JOAN PHENEY, M.S.W. ▸ The adult child movement is giving a lot of people nowadays the green light to go into therapy. People ask me, "God, how can you be a therapist? How can you listen to all those people who've been physically addicted, sexually abused, or stay in a bad relationship?" What I see is the recovery process. I see people who are beginning an exciting journey toward getting to know themselves, and I'm in on it. I can't imagine being anything else but a therapist. I love it because I see them leave that adult child past behind. I get to see people grow and become what they can become. It is like a jigsaw puzzle. A client comes in and gives me three little green pieces over in a corner. We start there. We start where the client is and fill in other pieces over time. It's exciting to see that jigsaw puzzle come together. In the end you get a whole picture instead of three little green pieces.

Pain is bringing adult children to ACA; pain is bringing them to therapy. Until recently therapists did not see people come into treatment as "adult children." We saw people come in with anxiety, depression, substance-abuse problems, headaches, and personality disorders. Nowadays, adult children might see a television show and watch a very good expert on adult children issues speaking about the list of COA characteristics. They may read an article in their local newspaper about issues of adult children of dysfunctional homes and say, "Oh my God, that's me." The article or the expert might say, "There are adult children meetings you can go to and talk about your own experience." They may be motivated to go. Some may already be attending AA, Narcotics Anonymous (NA), or Overeaters Anonymous (OA) meetings, hear about COA meetings, and try them.

People from dysfunctional homes often get addicted to some substance or get involved in some kind of compulsive behavior. If they come from an alcoholic home, they're genetically stacked for alcoholism. If you had one alcoholic parent, you have a 50 percent greater chance of becoming an alcoholic than someone who did not. If both parents were alcoholic, the figure rises to 80 percent. Kids identify with their parents; that's part of the developmental process. If you happen to be a young girl and your mother was obese, you have a good chance of being obese too.

Addictions cause an enormous amount of pain. The substance works for a person at first, but then the addict becomes consumed by the addiction; it causes more and more problems and starts to work less and less well. The consequences of addictions and compulsive behaviors often bring people to support-group meetings, which in turn may bring them into therapy. If you're an adult child seeking therapy, you may want to go to someone who understands adult child issues.

AA, NA, and OA all are Twelve Step programs. The original Twelve Step program was Alcoholics Anonymous. According to one expert, alcoholics got tired of dying, so they banded together and started talking about their experience. AA is a spiritual program. The only requirement for membership is a desire to stop drinking. AA, OA, and the rest get a bad rap for being labeled religious programs. They are not. They actually ask you to leave your religion at the door. You are never encouraged to join any kind of religious organization. You are simply asked to look inside yourself, share your experience, and believe in a power greater than yourself. You define what that power is. If you choose to believe in God, that's fine; if you choose not to, that's fine too. By and large, therapies do not work very well for addictions, and we do know AA is the single most effective self-help program in the world. ACA, COA, and ACOA are all Twelve Step programs.

Recovery from alcoholism, drug addiction, eating disorders, and workaholism is more involved than putting the cork in the bottle, staying clean, coming up with an abstinence program, or changing your work habits. Obviously, those things need to be done. That's the first step, and maybe that's 10 percent of the work. It's a very difficult 10 percent. I don't want to minimize that. A therapist can't even touch an alcoholic unless the person is sober. People with eating disorders, however, do tend to get back into food. They need to work with that, along with the therapy.

Therapy is a process of working with clients to help them understand who they are, how their past relates to what they're doing now, why they do the things they do, and what is working for them or not today. People often enter therapy repeating a very destructive behavior but not understanding why. If simply *telling* them to stop worked, the therapist could do that, but it doesn't. It's not as simple as that.

The therapist's role is to provide a reparative relationship, interpret the unconscious, look for patterns, and help with feelings. In therapy clients are free to say anything. The therapist's job is to help them understand why they're doing what they're doing.

In a dysfunctional home, children don't get what they need emotionally or physically in order to grow up to be healthy adults. If you grow up in a family where you had a cold, rejecting mother, that's going to have a tremendous impact on your ability to choose a mate or friends. Most kids don't say, "Maybe there's something wrong with my mother." They ask, "What's wrong with me?" An alcoholic father may promise to see his child's basketball game on Wednesday but then comes home drunk on Thursday unable to even remember his promise to go to the game that night. You can imagine the child's disappointment. The child looks up to his father and learns his father is untrustworthy. How children interpret things makes a big difference. At eight years old the child doesn't know the broken promise is because of alcoholism. He thinks, "What did I do wrong?" So in both cases the child asks, "How can I fix this? What did I do wrong? How should I act differently? Why aren't I lovable?"

In a home where a parent is alcoholic, workaholic, a physical or sexual abuser, or eating-disordered, you'll see a lot of dysfunction. All kinds of erratic behavior will occur. A parent could be preoccupied with food—getting food, eating food, hiding food, and denying there's a problem. In eating-disordered homes there's no mention of the fact that Mom or Dad weighs three hundred pounds. Attention that should be paid to the children is being paid to a substance or behavior. Children who are emotionally neglected pay a tremendous price as adults and all kinds of problems may arise.

Adult patterns of behavior that might be looked at in therapy are relationship problems, isolation, the inability to be assertive, inability to identify and express feelings, and addictions and compulsions. In therapy clients may ask, "Why do I allow people to speak to me in a rude manner?" "Why don't I ever buy myself anything?" "Why am I always tired?" "Why don't I ever do anything that's fun?" "Why is this relationship not working?" "Why do I choose this kind of man or woman?" "Why am I so uncomfortable around my parents?" "When I go home why do I want a drink?" "Why do I want to eat and throw up?" Therapy is an exciting process of discovery, learning, and change.

JEFF ▸ A fear of the way I was disciplining my children after I was sober a couple of years scared me one night to such depth and with such fervor that I called a telephone number on TV for child abuse. My daughter had wandered off from home, and it scared the hell out of us. When I found her, I yelled at her all the way home. She was scared in the first place because she had been lost. Without taking any of that into account, I put her down on the floor, put my knee in the middle of her back, pulled off my belt, and spanked her. She was screaming and afraid. My wife was screaming at me and trying to pull the belt away from me. I just could not stop myself because I wanted to do it so much. Not only was I spanking her but I was spanking myself and feeling the fear that I felt when my dad was beating me with the buckle end of his belt while I was lying down on the floor writhing in pain. The same goddamn thing was happening. I was dealing with my kids the same way my dad had dealt with me. I hate like hell to admit that I ever did such a thing, but I did it and it scares me today. The abused child becomes the child abuser.

Somebody suggested that I get counseling, and I started going. It was never suggested that COA might be a place where I could find help for this kind of issue. This year my AA sponsor suggested I try it. Going to those meetings and finding other people who feel the same things and are going through similar things, I find has been most helpful. The more I'm with these people, the more I feel like I'm dealing with these issues, working through them, closing them out, and moving on. All I ever wanted was to have happy, healthy kids. In the past, when they got energetic and full of life, I told them, "Shut up, sit down, act right." I wanted them to act like adults; but they're not adults—they're children.

As a child, I was told, "Sit down, shut up, act right." I was not allowed to be a kid. If my kids can be kids, the cycle can stop now. One of the most important things in my life is to be able to stop it so my kids won't have the same issues to have to deal with that I have.

It's an exciting revelation to find out that there's a broader picture and that I haven't looked at all the aspects of it. I'm capable of growing and changing and becoming better. I'm not doomed to remain the same. I can change and people around me can change. I am capable of becoming something other than what I've been. I stepped outside of my boundaries and found out that I was capable of bigger and better things. It feels good.

J A N ▸ I had been in AA about six or seven years, and I was getting a pretty good handle on why my behavior was the way it was while I was drinking. But I could never explain to myself, and it was never explained to me, why my behavior was the way it was while I was growing up and again that same way while I was sober. I could explain the drinking behavior, but I couldn't explain the before and after. When I heard about the adult children movement, I realized that I hadn't dealt with my childhood and what happened then. When I did become involved in pretty heavy-duty ACOA therapy, it caused me to understand a lot of things. The secrets were out. I had never been able to talk about my feelings, and I learned how to do that. The other thing I learned was how my fear of abandonment had controlled my whole life, not only when I was drinking but long before and again in my sobriety. I don't think I would have gotten anywhere unless I understood that.

The biggest thing that's happened to me is getting out of my long-term marriage, which was constant abandonment. I couldn't have done that if I hadn't understood how I kept set-

ting myself up to be hurt. I had lived with abandonment all my
life. My comfort level was abandonment.

MICHAEL ▸ At a talk I attended, the speaker asked the
question "Are you tiptoeing through life trying to make it safely
to death?" That hit me like a ton of bricks. I had done everything right in my life, as I understood it: I got the college degrees, married the pretty girl, did my bit in the service, had
been a school board president, and nothing was working. I was
miserable. That question—"Are you tiptoeing through life trying to make it safely to death?"—forced me to break through
my denial and realize I was dragging a huge boulder with me. I
didn't know why. I didn't know how. I just could not stop. I
couldn't get going with my life. That simple question is what
had driven me through a number of major events, another relationship, then therapy, and finally ACA meetings.

I have the clear-cut awareness and understanding now that
I have lived the story of Oedipus, which Sophocles wrote about
twenty-five hundred years ago. As a little child, I blamed myself
for my father leaving—that is, I'd killed him. I was all my
mother had and felt responsible for her well-being. I have never
made that break, though I have postured as if I were independent. I'm sure everybody in my life could come up with my
problem in ten seconds, given the family structure within which
I was raised. I've emotionally realized recently at a very infantile level that that is what happened. This overwhelming insight
is opening up the doors to looking at women as people instead
of goddesses.

BETH ▸ Another relationship had ended. I was devastated
by it. I saw a perfectly talented, wonderful human being destroyed by alcohol. I started reading everything I could about
co-dependency and addictions. I became aware that childhood
has a lot to do with what's going on with you today. I started
understanding why I kept repeating my behavior, and I began
going to private therapy.

The most amazing discovery I've made is that if I value
myself, others will value me. I've always been the perfect em-
ployee because I'll work for practically nothing. I'll work fifteen
hours a day, Saturdays and Sundays. I did whatever needed to

be done at work, and I got used and abused. It's been the same thing in relationships. I'd always be there. If I got stood up, I'd say, "That's okay. I'll forgive you." Forgiveness is my middle name. I forgive everything. Not having the validation of being a real human being from my father and sometimes having criticism and little support from my mother, my self-esteem wasn't very high. As soon as I realized why I acted as I did, I could start seeing what life would be like if I didn't act like a push-over. In both personal and work relationships I shouldn't be such an easy mark. Just realizing where the behavior came from has helped me to start combating the syndrome.

The thing that seems nice about COA is that it's probably easier to find a group than it is to find a good private therapist. I haven't been to COA, but I'd like to start looking for that in my area.

A UDREY ▸ In my son's second year of college, I became very, very aware of his drug use. My husband and I had to intervene, and my son was admitted into a treatment center. Little did I know that if he had a problem, so did we. As part of that program, I was introduced to Al-Anon. As a result of the things I said at those meetings, someone told me I could possibly benefit from ACOA. I began immediately attending ACOA meetings. Even though my father had been dead for over thirty years, I had never dealt with those feelings. I could not believe I had not addressed the situations that occurred when I was growing up.

For practically all of my years I've been living only a partial life and not feeling certain things. I felt a lot of fear, guilt, hurt, and shame. I didn't know that there were other wonderful feelings such as joy, peace, and excitement about simple things that could come from inside. I've just been overwhelmed by that. I did not know that all of this wonderful stuff was already inside, needing to come out. I have asked myself the question "How did you cope for so long?" I didn't feel. I didn't want to feel that pain I felt at age five when I was abandoned, and so I set out to make sure that it never happened again. To the outside world, things were great, and yet I continued to feel miserable inside. Through therapy, Al-Anon, and COA meetings I feel an emerging now that is so great.

BRIAN ▸ The process started when my wife went into treatment. Both of us were heavy drinkers. She became an alcoholic. I stopped drinking once she was in treatment, because they suspect that spouses may have alcohol problems. After stopping, I found out one of the reasons I drank was to feel good about myself. So I started therapy for the second time. I had gone once before when we were on the verge of divorce. The therapist this time was in the program herself. I got in touch with some incredible anger, and the therapist recommended I try primal therapy. That's where I really got in touch with the fact that I'd not had a happy or normal childhood, that I'd had a disaster. It was shortly after I started the primal therapy that I first went to COA meetings. My reaction was "Thank God, there're other people besides me that are in so much pain and are trying to work their way through it."

I've started to discover myself, who I really am, and how suppressed and covered up I have been all these years. I've become far more aware that events unfold and things change. The most important thing I've learned is that I can love myself and I can be loved by other people. I always felt that I was unlovable, and I hated myself. I don't feel that way at all anymore. I've gotten in touch with how much power and strength I have, and I can pat myself on the back for going through all this pain and turmoil to become better, to recover and become healthy. I'm willing to let go of all the negative baggage that I've carried around all these years.

ALICE ▸ Six or seven years ago I decided I wanted to have a child, and the question that popped into my mind was "Do you want your child to be raised the way that you were raised?" The answer was an emphatic no. Initially I thought that the change that needed to be made was for my husband to stop drinking. As I worked in therapy and the program I found out what I had experienced as a child was much more devastating than I was aware of. I've gone to Al-Anon and OA, but I've done all of my COA work in individual therapy and I've learned a lot.

The number of limitations I've placed on living my life is amazing. Prior to my recovery program, I thought I was living a full life, but actually my life was very empty. Having gone back digging and finding out why it is I behave the way I do, I realize the tremendous impact those early experiences have had on my life thirty-five years later. It's painful but relieving at the same time. The truth about what happened gives me some freedom. I had all these fears, and I didn't know why I had them. I just knew I was afraid. Without the program, I never would have had a child. I've been afraid my daughter would be sexually abused since she was born. It's only in the last several months, when I realized that I was sexually abused, that I understand that fear. I could have spent my life doing all kinds of strange things to protect her.

D ICK ► I hated myself as a child. I was very angry. I was very fearful. With alcohol, I could express feelings. What brought me into Alcoholics Anonymous was the fact that my love affair with alcohol ended. I could not get any more security out of the bottle. I was forced to go to an AA meeting, and there I found people exactly like myself who had stuffed negative feelings all their lives and had found good feelings with alcohol. I found a group of people who had suffered the same way I had suffered and found a program in which people understood how I felt inside. I was able to identify with them. They were able to identify with me and give me the help that I needed to overcome the feelings I had all my life.

H ARRY ► I have created crises all my life in order to try to get well. One of the crises I engineered was alcohol and cocaine. What they did for me was to help assist in the destruction of my own experience to the point where I would feel good. It became the problem. I had no choice but to either die or deal with it. I decided to die. That didn't work, so I ended up having to deal with it. Because of my recovery in AA, I had to do a fourth step: I had to make "a searching and fearless moral inventory." "I'm never fucking doing that" was exactly the way I felt at the time. I always thought if somebody found out what I was really like, I would have to kill that person. In my inventory and fifth step in AA—to admit "to God and to ourselves and to another human being, the exact nature of our wrongs"—I found out somebody had always known. Things started to knit themselves together, and for the first time my life became like a motion picture instead of a bunch of snapshots with holes in them where Harry was.

When I was teaching and counseling I was showing Sharon Wegscheider-Cruse's movie *Family Trap* to a group of people. I found myself one night watching the film thinking, "How much longer do these people have to suffer before they understand that some of them are becoming alcoholics?" They were there to learn why they got arrested for drunk driving, and my job at the time was to show the film. The group was sitting on one side of the screen and I was sitting with my head in my hands on the other side. I heard Sharon say, "You have to separate the personal part from the professional part of your life." I got up off my butt that night and the next day started to seek information on COA meetings. A little door opened and some caring force said, "Come on."

The single most important thing for me has been uncovering the truth about my mother's behavior of using me to meet her needs, my response to it, and my excitement and participation in that incestuousness. I have boundaries now for the first time in my life. I can allow myself to think, "That's what you say (or feel or want or need), but that's not necessarily what I say (or feel or want or need)." I have begun to have my own thoughts, feelings, wants, and needs that are personal, shareable, and don't need to be kept hidden. My innermost self is free, not secret and false. It's authentic.

KAREN ▸ I always knew there was something wrong. I read a lot of self-help books and a lot of books by very angry women who were very angry at men. Those books made me be able to blame men for all my problems. I hit bottom and got into the program when the relationship with the man I've talked about ended. I was suicidal. I was plotting my death at home. I kept getting involved in relationships with people that were not very healthy. I started to notice a pattern and saw I was getting involved with the same type of people over and over again. I was the hero in my family, and it was even harder for me to admit I needed help because I'd always helped everybody else all my life.

I've had three pregnancies. Each one of them I've aborted because I was so terrified that I would do to that child what had been done to me. I couldn't face it. I wasn't married any of those times, but I easily could have been. It was an option that was available to me, but I ran from it. After the last abortion I had, I got very, very ill. I never read the newspaper from cover to cover; I just read different things. Because I was home and had nothing better to do, I found an article on adult children and read it. Talk about God working in my life—He threw me flat on my back and said, "You're going to read this, lady." I went to my first meeting that night and have never stopped going since then.

The most amazing discovery I've made is that I'm not in control of my life. There is a higher power. As much as I thought I had things under control, I didn't have them under control at all, nor could I ever. I needed to recognize that there was a plan and a will and a force that was much greater than I that was in control. I had to get comfortable with that and build that relationship. That higher power had always been there waiting for me to get my act together. It wasn't until I did that that things began to change for me. It's a matter of recognizing the powerlessness. It really is.

LYNN ▸ I got back into therapy after I left my husband because of his alcoholism. In therapy I learned my adoption was directly related to why I had picked him. I also discovered unconsciously that at some level I knew that he had a problem when I met him and that I didn't pick up the cues. For some reason, I didn't really want a whole relationship with somebody; in a lot of ways, he fit the bill. I also learned a lot in therapy about my role in his alcoholism, my co-dependency, and how I enabled him to continue drinking all those years. A real benefit was discovering that even minus his alcoholism, we were not very compatible. The marriage probably would not have lasted.

Being adopted, I had a fantasy in my head that my natural mother had looked at me at birth and said, "Get her out of here." All through my childhood, I felt I was bad and defective, that something was wrong with me. I was always looking for evidence so I could validate those negative feelings. I came to learn in therapy that since I was just a baby, my mother probably never even saw me and what she did had nothing to do with me personally. Finally, having put myself together as a whole person, I don't believe there's anything wrong with me.

M ANOLITO ▸ I went to an AA roundup in Boston in 1985. A woman there mentioned how important ACOA meetings were for her. I went to my first ACOA meeting out of curiosity and I exploded. In that meeting I felt something I have never felt anywhere else in my life. What I felt was very powerful. Those people touched something that was very sore and painful in my life. The room was full of people who understood what I had gone through, and suddenly I could simply let go. A huge door opened. It's something I can't describe.

I wasn't enjoying the fun, love, and joy that God wants me to have in life. Now I'm learning why and I'm learning how. As a child, I was cast in a very bad, grade-B war film. My responsibility as an adult is to produce and cast myself as the star of my own big, multimillion-dollar musical comedy. If I skip ACOA meetings, I go back to suffering, humiliation, and stagnation. I really have to learn to love myself. If I hadn't found ACOA, which helped me to get rid of the pain, I would probably be dead. I've had suicidal tendencies throughout my entire life because of living the life I had. I would not be sober today if I didn't deal with my ACOA issues.

M ARY ▸ I have an incredible love for animals, and they're big teachers for me. When a dog is biting people, it's probably because the owner keeps hitting the dog for no apparent reason. I had gone to AA and OA, but it was the culmination of working in therapy and working on Mary that brought about the realization that the cause of my symptoms of bulimia and alcoholism was my family. My problems were a reaction to my dysfunctional family. I, too, want to have children someday. I know I have the capabilities to be a really cool mom, but I won't be a good mother if I don't do the footwork and clean out my closet now.

Up until a couple years ago my whole life was a total reaction to my father. Discovering who I am, letting myself be who I am, and respecting and nurturing the individuality in me is such a revelation. I did everything to be what I thought my father wanted me to be. I acted the way he wanted me to act. I dressed the way he wanted me to dress. I even tried to convince myself I wanted to be a business major. I don't have to repeat old patterns. If I just remain consciously aware of my life, I'll learn. That has been my big birthday present to myself.

JIM ▸ I went to Toronto and heard a speaker give a dynamic talk. He started out by saying he'd been drinking and drugging from the time he was fourteen. I thought something really had to change in his life between then and now because you could see the evidence of his serenity, humility, and honesty. He said he'd been dry for seventeen years, achieved a lot, and was very miserable. That's common in AA. He decided to do something about it. He went to a counselor and the counselor said, "Tell me about yourself." He said, "Well, I started drinking and drugging when I was fourteen." She said, "You weren't born fourteen. Let's go back and take a look at the three-year-old." It registered with me, but I put it on the back burner.

My daughter in New Jersey got acquainted with ACOA. She'd been going to Al-Anon but couldn't relate there because she'd never been married to an alcoholic. She also couldn't relate to a father who drank because I'd been sober almost all of her life. She was unhappy, depressed, and suicidal. She told me about her going to ACOA and how it changed her whole life. I found out there was a meeting in my area here, and I started going. I jumped at the chance for ACOA. I knew that I had to take a look at "the exact nature of my wrongs."

I read in "Twelve Steps and Twelve Traditions," which is AA literature, that the problem with keeping long-term sobriety was a lack of taking a thorough fifth step: to admit "to God and to ourselves and to another human being the exact nature of our wrongs." I also read that we've got to go to any length to stay sober.

Once I digest and deal with the past, then I start looking at the now. I'm still just as capable of doing all those things I did in the past over again unless I change. The ACOA program has brought me back to the reality of the things I really need to change. I was brought up to feel inadequate and unimportant as a child. Today I can make all those same mistakes I made in the past and forgive myself real quick. If I make a mistake, I can promptly admit to it and let it go. The old me hung on to something forever. I kept wanting to go back and make it right, which is impossible. What is, is, and you can't change that. We have to learn what is.

JOAN PHENEY, M.S.W. ▸ It's important for people to know the truth about their families. Therapy is not about "Oh, weren't Mom and Dad horrible." There can be some of that for a limited period of time. In a successful therapy, people will move from that into self-forgiveness. A lot of people want to begin with self-forgiveness, but most adult children need to identify what happened to them and understand how that affects their thinking, their relationships, their work, and their view of the world. People make progress as they understand the consequences of their past and begin to have some empathy for that child who grew up in that situation.

Often adult children of alcoholics think they caused the alcoholism. Most adult children think they had some control over the dysfunctionality of their families, so it's very important to go back to that little person inside and let that child know there was nothing he could have done to cause the alcoholism, to cure the alcoholism, or to influence the co-dependency. Adult children have to appreciate that they were smart at that time for going to their rooms and reading books. That can look like isolation now if the person is having trouble with relationships. Back then, it made sense. Now the person doesn't know why she's isolating. As the client and therapist work together and put more pieces of the jigsaw puzzle together, they can see that child went into her room so she could have some peace.

All people who come out of dysfunctional homes have problems with relationships. Look at the role models they had. You can't have an alcoholic system and not have chaos. I have never seen a recovering alcoholic who didn't have co-dependency issues. Your family was your first classroom. You watched everything that went on and made decisions about yourself and other people. Kids don't sit down in a little chair and say, "Gee, I'm going to do this." It's an internal process. Part of therapy is talking about the things you didn't talk about in your dysfunctional family. Recovery is not as simple as unlearning; it's understanding what happened to you and how that's affecting you now, and then making changes.

I strongly encourage my clients to involve themselves in a Twelve Step program. I can help with the inner journey, but people are multidimensional. I believe people are happier if they come to terms with their own spirituality. Twelve Step meetings provide people with a social outlet too. If I see clients once a week, I can be supportive for one hour. But going to meetings opens up for them a network of support and friendship. They can tackle some of the really tough, in-depth issues in therapy. My clients who go to Twelve Step programs get better faster. I think it has to do with the support.

People who are successful in recovery have the ability to look inward honestly. They're willing to take that risk. I think I should have a brass plaque over my door that says, "None but the brave." The recovery process is a very brave, unusual journey. Our society doesn't encourage painful inner honesty. I think it takes a very brave, motivated person to come into therapy.

10

RECOVERY
ISSUES

I t is much easier to define the problems of growing up as adult children than to grasp the solution. Recovery is much more individualized, and each person gets better at his or her own pace. Recovery requires work and patience. If your body is out of shape or you want to run a marathon, you have to go into training. To achieve the desired results of change will take time. Recovery is a process, not an event.

To look at the pain of the past and stay there is not recovery. However, if your goals are discovering who you are, making changes, and enjoying happiness, get ready for a slow, uneven, but richly rewarding journey. Adult children want everything yesterday. Realizing that the journey of recovery takes time comes as both a shock ("I want it now") and a relief ("If it's going to take time, then I don't have to have it all finished by next Tuesday or next fall").

Central to recovery are grieving the losses of childhood, achieving self-esteem, and dealing with co-dependency. Specific issues for each person may be control, dependency, expressing feelings, honesty, personal needs, relationships, powerlessness, fears, trust, and love. Recovering adult children may relate to some issues and not others. It also seems that each person identifies some major piece of emotional baggage from the past that becomes a significant key to recovery.

Members of our group responding to questions about recovery issues are at various stages of growth. Their responses tell us where they are right now. Any of the topics suggested by these specific questions can take weeks or months to work through in therapy or support-group meetings. The bottom line of recovery is change.

Earnie Larsen is a nationally known author and lecturer. In the past twenty years he has written more than three dozen books on topics ranging from interpersonal relationships to spirituality. His latest books are *Stage II Recovery: Life Beyond Addiction* and *Stage II Relationships: Love Beyond Addiction.* His own company, E. Larsen Enterprises of Brooklyn Park, Minnesota, conducts seminars throughout the country on such topics as healthy adult relationships, recovery, and building self-esteem. Earnie's fifteen audiotape programs include *For Adult Children of Alcoholics and Those Who Love Them.*

EARNIE LARSEN ▸ Recovery is primarily an intimacy issue. The only place intimacy exists is in relationships. Dysfunctionality relates to learning negative traits that impede healthy relationships. Every family is dysfunctional to some degree. There are no perfect people; there are no perfect family systems. As children, we should learn traits, habits, and patterns that promote our ability to function in healthy, loving relationships; but sometimes we don't.

Co-dependency is not primarily an alcoholic issue any more than the term "adult children" means solely adult children of alcoholic family systems. Co-dependency means those self-defeating learned behaviors and rules that result in a diminished capacity to initiate or participate in healthy relationships. These behaviors are learned because they were modeled for us. What you live with you learn, what you learn you practice, what you practice you become, and what you become has consequences.

Some of the symptoms that suggest people come from a severely dysfunctional home are depression, low self-esteem, and relationship problems. The greater the dysfunction in the family, the more damage is done to the children growing up in that system. Some families are much more dysfunctional than others. There are a lot of adult children who do not come from alcoholic families but are horribly abused.

The real key to the whole family of origin experience is not what happened back then but what you took away from what happened. It's not what your parents mean; it's what you heard. The two deepest needs all of us are born with are the need to love and be loved and the need to be accepted by significant people. The greater the dysfunction of the family of origin, the more a person is willing to sacrifice or prostitute self-esteem, dignity, and even sexuality to buy acceptance and love as an adult. Of course, that doesn't work.

We've all been affected by the past, but none of us has to be a victim of it. Recovery is not an endless process of rummaging through the past. Adult children need to get to the point where they can say, "Here's what I need to do to change."

Everybody has a family of origin. It's where our very best traits and our virtues come from. But our best stuff is not what gets us in trouble. The traits and habits that get us off base and cause us and everybody around us a lot of pain are the dysfunctional parts. Remember, it's not what happened; it's what you took away from what happened and the lessons you learned. If adult children say, "I have difficulty sharing my feelings" or "I have a terrible time asking for what I need in my personal life" or "I can't stop working," it's important to start with that specific issue and focus family of origin work around it. That begins with looking for a pattern: What happened? Who was there? What was said? What were the consequences? How did you feel about what was happening? Habits also are feelings, and you started to learn back then what felt normal. Normal means you've done it enough so that it has become the norm. What were the lessons? What was the rule? How are you still acting out that rule today? In recovery you begin to tie up past learned patterns with today's activities and results. The crucial question is what are you going to do to change?

Typical adult children characteristics are a general sense of alienation ("I never feel that I belong; somehow I'm always on the outside looking in") and not knowing what is appropriate ("I'll wait to see who's laughing at what and then I'll laugh" or "I'll wait to see who's ordering what and then I'll order"). Another characteristic is shame. Shame is the basic assumption that a person is inadequate and flawed, and therefore does not deserve happiness or success beyond that which the person already has. No one can outperform his own self-image; it can't be done. If your self-image is that you're going to strike out, you will strike out. If your self-image is that you cannot get a particular job, you won't get it. If you do get the job, you will find a way to lose it to bring you back to normalcy in terms of your self-image.

Another characteristic is fear of abandonment, which is almost universally present in adult children. They go into relationships with enormous fears. If you do not believe you deserve happiness, chances are the only people you are going to choose to be in a relationship with are people whom you can't be successful with in the first place. Shame-based people sabotage their success. They fall in love with people that they cannot have because they're already committed to someone else or they're so broken that they are emotionally unavailable.

Another adult child characteristic is violence, either as the perpetrator or as the victim. Both of those are violence issues. In healthy homes people learn healthy ways to deal with conflict. In a dysfunctional home people learn that the way to deal with conflict is either to become violent and abusive or to assume the role of victim and tolerate abuse.

The last characteristic of adult children is defiance or hypersensitivity. What adult children with this characteristic learned is that they are going to be overcontrolled or abandoned. Many adult children get to the point where they're so hurt that they adopt a defiant attitude or they take everything personally. These characteristics of adult children of dysfunctional homes are all going to have a severe impact on a person's self-image and his capacity to function in healthy relationships.

Another way of getting a handle on the effects of coming from a dysfunctional home is to look at the roles we play in our adult lives. The caretaker learned that self-esteem is based on taking responsibility for others. The people-pleaser learned that "my rights, my thoughts, my needs are not as important as yours." The martyr learned that "if it doesn't hurt, there's something wrong." The workaholic learned that worthiness is based on production or being busy. The perfectionist learned that either "finally I'm going to get it right" or "there's no such thing as right enough." The procrastinator learned that "no matter what I do I fail, so don't try." Lone rangers learned to "do good things but never let them know who you are."

The last one in this little lineup is the tap dancer. The tap dancer learned that "commitment is an invitation to devastation." These are the people who early on desperately wanted to be accepted and wanted a commitment from their parents, but it wasn't there. Rather than make a real commitment as an adult, a nonrecovering tap dancer ends a relationship. The closer it gets to exclusivity or marriage, the more a tap dancer must run away. Tap dancers never tell the total truth; they're shifty. They'll tell you a truth, but you never get the whole truth.

Recovery is primarily learning to love. The quality of our personal relationships dictates the quality of our life. Begin by looking at yourself and determining your capacity to function in a healthy relationship. The central, primary issue in recovery is the willingness to deal with co-dependency, which is always a self-image question. Co-dependency involves the ways we have learned to define ourselves. Adult children must break those old negative habits and learn to function in different ways.

Have you changed your belief that your self-esteem is based on other people?

JAN ▸ For so long I couldn't really let people see who I was. It's been amazing to me that the more I become myself, the more accepting people are of me. I didn't think people would like the real me. I spent my whole lifetime not being real. It wasn't okay to be real in the family in which I grew up. It wasn't okay to be real in my marriage. It wasn't okay to be real in my relationships with my kids. Getting real is very painful. I worked for so many years to be this other person whom I thought people would like and approve of. I didn't have nearly as many friends as I have now. I am feeling better about myself because I've become honest with who I am. It's how I see me that's important today. That was never important before; it was always how other people saw me.

Are you beginning to let go of trying to control?

AUDREY ▸ I'm letting go of situations in my household that I have come to realize were holding me back from growing. I'm not as involved in the lives of my family. I'm concentrating more on myself and letting other people be responsible for themselves. For so long I thought it was up to me. I felt if things changed within the household it would be due to my efforts. How wrong I was. I am saving energy by not concentrating on my son, his whereabouts, or his doings or where my daughter is and how things are going for her. I'm getting a little bit beyond that. It's more relaxing.

Are you learning how to say "no"?

KAREN ▸ In many ways more than just saying no, I'm learning how to say what I want. I'm not accepting what other people are trying to deal me. I'm leaving my job after eleven years in the spring. That was a big way of saying "no" for me because it was something I could easily have stayed with for the next twenty years until retirement. It wasn't working, I wasn't happy, I didn't like it. My self-esteem has improved because of the decision. I thought that if I don't stay, people won't like me.

I found it's just the opposite. The outpouring of support I'm getting from the people I work with is amazing. A luncheon was arranged for me with a woman who's an outside consultant with the company to talk with me about consulting. It's incredible. When I say I'm going to do something, it's because it's what I want to do. When I say, "No thank you" or "I don't want to do that," people are okay with it.

Are you learning how to trust?

M ICHAEL ► I always considered myself a deeply trusting person. That was a real, genuine, honest, strong belief on my part. Because of the total trust and faith in the relationship I had with my mother, I transferred that trust to my first wife. When the marriage fell apart, my sense of devastation was incredible. In the last couple of months I have finally touched the deep level of anger, mistrust, and betrayal that I've had. As a baby, I had to make an adjustment because the man in my life was gone. I began controlling to survive. It makes me realize how I really haven't trusted much at all ever. I feel like I'm just starting to crawl in regard to trust. Through the program and the unconditional acceptance of men and women at meetings, I'm taking little steps. The biggest thing for me has been uncovering how little I ever did trust and how cleverly I posed looking like I did.

Do you think it's okay to be selfish?

A LICE ► I think it's necessary. It's hard to do but it's necessary. Meeting some of my needs that haven't been met in the past is crucial to my ability to live in the future. To meet my own needs is often viewed by others as selfish. If the word "selfish" has a negative connotation, then so be it.

How do you take care of yourself today?

J IM ► I practice being selfish. I decided my sobriety was so dear to me that I wasn't going to let anybody interfere with it. Today I get out of the mainstream when I get tired. I work and I give that a good effort. That makes me feel good. Comparing my old behavior with my new behavior gives me a boost too. When I get a feeling there's a knot in my stomach, I do something to alleviate that, such as taking an evening off, going to a meeting or movie, or going to bed early. If I really need a lift, I go to my favorite restaurant for dinner. Today it's not as necessary to go by myself as much as I used to. It's not nearly as important for me to be that selfish. Today I can take my wife, or my wife and a friend, or my wife's children with me while doing something good for me. I can share that now.

Do you think it's okay to get angry?

M<u>ANOLITO</u> ▸ In my house you couldn't express anger, and when I came into the AA program, they told me never be hungry, tired, lonely, or angry. So I haven't dealt with anger very much. I think it is all right to be angry at somebody you love if it's a natural thing that pops up. The important thing for me is to keep the anger in perspective and speak up for myself. I'm capable of holding my anger forever and nurturing resentments. If I do that, I'm only hurting myself.

Can you make mistakes today and feel comfortable about them?

L<u>YNN</u> ▸ Yes, I can, and I make a lot of mistakes. I make mistakes with my daughter, but I apologize. I tell her I don't know what I'm doing some of the time and I don't have all the answers. I make mistakes at work; but that's okay too. I don't take things personally anymore. If something happens at work and I could take it personally, I try to distance myself from it and look at things professionally. I used to think, "They're abusing me." That's not true; it's not a personal issue. My mother was always critical of me as a child. So when I made a mistake I heard about it. I was very tense as a kid. I'm not that tense anymore.

What are you learning about your feelings?

B<u>ETH</u> ▸ Trusting my feelings is getting easier. I've always been an intuitive person. Trusting my intellect is harder. My feelings often will override what I know in my mind is right.

Intellectually I'll say, "This person is a no-good bum," but the feelings will overwhelm the thought. I'm working on trusting my intellect. Feelings are easy for me. Someone recently complimented me on how I'm so open and free with my feelings, and I said, "Thank you very much, that's just my problem." I don't have enough boundaries on my feelings.

How are you handling fear today?

JEFF ▸ I'm a lot more careful about getting myself into situations where there will be fear. I've made some pretty good choices lately about who I spend time with and the places I go. I'm still not free from fears, but they're not crippling fears like they were once. They're fears I can work through. For a long time I was afraid to ask for help for fear I'd be rejected. It's taken a lot of practice. Getting help was always there if I took the risk to ask. The fear of failure or the fear of success are not as present in my life today. I'm beginning to learn to enjoy my success. I was always afraid that once I did accomplish something, it would be yanked away from me. I have some insecurity from time to time, but I'm making progress.

In what new ways are you learning to accept yourself?

BRIAN ▸ I view self-acceptance as a process. I'm learning to accept that I don't have to do everything perfectly and that I don't have to always be right. I used to be an "I'd rather be right than president" person. I've learned I don't have to be president to feel successful or to love myself. I've learned to accept that it's okay to relax and goof off. I accept myself as is and love myself for who I am and what I'm becoming.

What's changing in your relationships with people?

MARY ▸ I'm working on not trying to control and I'm starting to be able to love unconditionally. I'm not expecting men to take care of me. I used to get into relationships where I would sell out because I didn't think I could take care of myself. I don't need to sell out to anyone today. I have a support system that loves me unconditionally. I'm starting to develop more relationships with women, and I'm starting to trust them. I have a lot of anger toward women because my mother was so unemotionally there for me. I transferred that to my relationships with other women. I'm not being so naive about relationships either. The more I love myself, the more cautious I get in relationships. To jump into a relationship is unhealthy; I may be setting myself up to be hurt. The relationships I'm in I really cherish because they're quality relationships. My friends care about me and I care about them.

How do you protect your own needs today?

H ARRY ▸ There are limits I am formulating as to what I will allow myself to experience from other people. Just recently someone was angry with me, but I was experiencing what he was saying as insulting. I said, "Now our talk is finished and you will need to leave." He did, and I felt good about that. What I did was something I had learned from a very healthy caring friend. Everything I get still comes from relationships and I choose much better ones now than I ever did. The thing that I've learned from these new relationships is that I've got a right to choose and to set limits. I maintain my boundaries in a positive sense. When I come into contact with another person, I'm aware of where I stop and he starts or where I stop and she starts. I get to play there more.

How are you learning how to speak up for yourself?

B ETH ▸ I had a frustrating experience with my last boss. Often I would be on the phone in a business conversation with a client, and she would walk up to me and start talking. It's hard to talk to two people at the same time; but I took all the blame on myself and internalized that I wasn't capable of having two conversations at once. This woman treated me with very little respect. It didn't matter to her I was on the phone talking to someone else. It took me several months to finally get up the courage to say to her, "I'm really sorry, but I don't think it looks good for the business if I get distracted when I'm on the phone. Could you please not talk to me when I'm on the phone?"

I think I'm getting better at being able to voice my discomfort when it needs to be voiced and sticking up for what I want or need. I'm working on it.

Do you give yourself credit for surviving?

D <u>ICK</u> ► I definitely do. I feel like a survivor. I was a hostage to my emotions, my problems, my gambling, and my drinking. These were problems I inherited or genetic problems that I had. I just felt I was hopeless. I was hopeless when I began my recovery, but I don't feel that way today. Damn right I give myself credit for surviving; I give myself a hell of a lot of credit.

Do you feel comfortable giving and receiving love?

A <u>LICE</u> ► I can give love to my daughter and my grandmother. I don't know that I can give love to my husband or anybody else. I give little bits and pieces of it, but it's very much held in check because I'm fearful of the vulnerability it creates. I think it has to do with self-esteem. When I was a young child, my parents, whom I loved, were not able to care for me or treat me in ways that were healthy. Being locked in my room for hours when my mother had a headache was not healthy. Having no one when I cried or was hungry did not demonstrate love. I think I decided way back in infancy that I would learn to shut off love and not accept it, because if I did accept it, then it wouldn't be there for me.

Can you love yourself?

A <u>UDREY</u> ► I'm trying. I'm taking itty-bitty steps. When I bought the red suit, that was trying to love myself. When I went into therapy and joined ACOA, those were acts of love for myself. I see this whole business of recovery as self-love. I understand so much better why I have not been able to give love, and I have come to know that you can't give away what you don't have. I am discovering self-love slowly.

EARNIE LARSEN ▸ In recovery you baby-step your way forward. Along the way, you experience enormous "all of a sudden" breakthroughs. The breakthroughs are all related to self-esteem issues. A man is able to say no to a new job that will pay him more money but requires an eighty-hour workweek. He wants more money, but he is able to say, "I'm not a beast of burden. I don't have to do that to myself." A woman with a weight problem realizes her husband has never known her thin. She really cares about her husband, and what she finally gets in touch with is "I'm afraid if I lose weight, he might not like me anymore." Recognizing her fear of failure by succeeding was a breakthrough for her.

Recovery starts with enough pain that no matter what it takes, you're willing to get out of the hurt. The second step on this recovery journey is the desire to do something based on that pain; there's a need to come to an understanding of what is causing the pain.

The next step is acceptance. You cannot accept what you don't understand. The opposite of acceptance is delusion, denial, or plain ignorance. In this stage of understanding and acceptance of your reality, the grieving process occurs: "Yes, I came from an alcoholic family" or "Yes, my parents were not perfect" or "Yes, I have been an abuse victim." Acceptance helps you make peace with your past; it doesn't mean you have to like it.

The next step is forgiveness. You can't forgive what you have not accepted. The opposite of forgiveness is resentment and revenge. That fixates you at the point of pain. Forgiveness is a gift that you give yourself. It's not about "them." It's about you refusing to punish yourself any longer because of what happened.

After forgiveness comes letting go. Letting go means we get to the point where we are no longer controlled by the past.

The last step is moving on. That's where you start coming out the other side and doing different things. In the recovery process you go from "I hurt like hell" all the way to "I'm doing the things I never thought I could do and they're taking me to the place I want to go." Recovery is understanding the definitions and rules that have been given to you, the patterns that you have acquired, bringing them up to the conscious level and looking at those definitions, rules, and behaviors as healthy or unhealthy. Embrace the ones that are healthy. As to the ones that aren't, change them, act in a different way, and become to some degree a different person.

You can't recover alone. Does it have to be a professional? Not necessarily. But recovery is not one of those things you can do sitting at home with willpower. Your own self-talk always makes sense, no matter how crazy it is. You are too close to yourself to have perspective.

In a real sense, recovery as a process never ends. The payoff of recovery is a sense of serenity based on being in control of your life. It's not control in the sense that there will be no surprises. However, you don't have to say yes to everybody, and you don't have to say someone else is right if his opinion differs from your own. In your life you are calling the shots about what you'll do and who you are. You don't have to surrender to another you nor go to war with him. Those are ways in which people respond from a dysfunctional standpoint. This is positive control over one's life and a real sense of freedom. You are no longer controlled by nameless old demons. The more you recover, the more you become capable in relationships. When you keep out of toxic lose-lose situations, you can maximize the potential of relationships that can work.

There are huge numbers of very motivated, goodwilled adult children working very hard in recovery but not necessarily making much progress. Often a program of recovery is not very focused on specifics. In creating my own body of knowledge on adult children, I asked people in the program, "What are you working on?" I always got the most general kind of responses: "I'm working on me" or "I'm working on codependency."

A program that is not focused is not going to be very effective. It is very important for recovering people to get very specific about what habits and patterns they are trying to change because of the pain in their lives. I don't find enough of that. I really don't.

11

LETTING
GO
OF THE
PAST

Pain, anger, and grief are parts of the process of becoming who we really are. Breaking through the denial that our childhoods were "happy" or "okay" is acknowledging the facts and the reality of what happened—not how we wished it had been or how we tell others it was.

Confronting our past and blaming our parents may bring many resentments and no rewards. In most cases, our parents did love us and did what they were capable of doing. Each of us is an unrepeatable mystery with special gifts and abilities. A large part of our skills, values, and uniqueness also came from our difficult childhoods.

My own abilities to put together this book, give speeches, counsel alcoholics and their families, conduct television interviews, and enjoy my family, friends, and life all come out of the same background as my struggle. My education and values came from the same parents as my confusion and hurt. My capacity for love, friendship, caring, feelings, humor, surviving, and growing have to be weighed in the balance with any negatives. I would rather be me than anybody else I've ever known, and I am grateful to my mother and father for the gift of life and the many good things they passed along to me.

All our lives, we thought we could change the way our parents are, but we can't. We are as powerless over them now as we were back then as children. Most of them will never become what we really want or deserved a long time ago. Some of them will soften or grow, as we are doing. Accept them and love them. They did what they were capable of doing, just as we are doing what we are capable of doing. We have new opportunities for growth that they didn't have.

We can learn a lot about our parents by looking at ourselves. Had they come along thirty or forty or fifty years later, they might be sitting in a support-group meeting alongside of us. If they were dysfunctional, we are dysfunctional. If we are dysfunctional, they were dysfunctional. It works both ways.

John Bradshaw is nationally known as the host of two PBS televison series, "Bradshaw On: The Family" and "Eight Stages of Man." His *Bradshaw On: The Family* has been published as a book and produced on audiotapes and videotapes. Based in Houston, Texas, John at one time studied for the Roman Catholic priesthood and earned three degrees from the University of Toronto. For the past twenty years he has worked as a counselor, management consultant, and public speaker on such subjects as "Incest and Sexual Addiction," "The Nature of Shame," "Co-Dependency," and "Adult Children of Dysfunctional Families."

JOHN BRADSHAW ► When something's functional, it works. I've got a hammer. It's got burn marks on it and it's banged up, but it's still a perfect hammer. It hammers nails. It works. When you say people are functional, they work. They don't have to be subjected to a norm. People can function emotionally but be at very different levels. They can be very different but be functional. They can all work in different ways.

Functional families have lots and lots of problems. The difference between a functional and dysfunctional family is that a functional family will solve its problems. The members have the means to cope, to fight fair, to solve problems. They know how to do that. A dysfunctional family will deny the problems and act as if the problems don't exist or will try to create roles that keep the problems frozen in the center of their lives. "Fully functioning" means you can see and hear what you see and hear, not what you're supposed to see and hear. You can feel what you feel, not what you're supposed to feel. You can want what you want, think what you think, and imagine what you imagine. When you're functional, all those powers work to get your needs met. "Dysfunctional" means that the very basic things about a human being, the power to know, want, love, choose, feel, and imagine, have broken down.

The most obviously dysfunctional homes are those of the chemically addicted family, the incest family, the physically violent family, the emotionally abused families, the eating-disordered family, the religiously addicted family, and the work-addicted family. It can also be a fateful thing such as "Mama's been sick for ten years" or "Dad was wounded in the war." Those can cause dysfunction in a family as well. In a dysfunctional family the common denominator is that there's some stresser that everybody's adapting to. Each person in that system has to give up his or her own feelings, needs, and wants in order to adapt to that stresser.

Adult children of dysfunctional homes are all violated in some way. They're violated because they don't get to be themselves. It's really emotional battering. Anybody from a dysfunctional family has also been abandoned. Either physically or emotionally, the parents were not there for the children. There was nobody emotionally at home to take care of the child's dependency needs, which is why they became adult children. The parents were so into their own adult children issues that the child was raised by children. If you don't have a sense of yourself and a sense that you matter, then you're being emotionally murdered.

Adult children walk away from childhood and their dysfunctional homes with many wrong beliefs about themselves. The core belief is "I'm not okay." The deepest level of that is shame. If I believe you are flawed and defective as a human being, then you can't stay inside yourself; you've got to go to the outside. You must relinquish yourself to the outside, which is exactly what co-dependency is. Co-dependency leads people to make wrong choices because they have the core belief that happiness lies outside of them in another person, a bottle of booze, cocaine, sex, money, or worldly fame and prestige. A person believes if he or she can just get some of those things, "I can patch up this hole in my soul." A wrong belief about ourselves leads us to wrong choices.

Adult children haven't had their developmental dependency needs met, so they're going to pass this on to their children. Either they're going to do to their children what was done to them, or they're going to try to do the exact opposite and relive their childhoods through their children. They become the kind of parents they wish they had had, but that's not necessarily the kind of parents their children need.

An old biblical passage says, "The sins of the fathers are visited on the children to the third and fourth generation." Shame begets shame. A shame-based needy parent cannot possibly teach a child self-love and self-value. So adult children find each other, marry, and have children who become adult children who find each other, marry, and have children who become adult children. What is happening in our families is a great crisis. Adult children have great trouble in relationships because they try to make everyone into a parent.

We also stay loyal to the rules of our parents. One of those rules is that you can't question the rules. How can it go on for hundreds of years? We've had these rules, which are not democratic rules at all. Parents are the masters. Kids don't have emotions. Emotions are weak. Life-affirming instincts must be crushed. How do we know how to be parents? The only way we know how to be parents is by what our parents taught us about how to be parents, so we keep the cycle going for generations. Once you can't be who you are, once you believe that you're flawed intrinsically, then you have to alter your mood. One way to mood-alter is to play a role, the role of parent.

The family is a system, and the system has needs. If one member of the family system is dysfunctional, everyone becomes dysfunctional. As adult children, we adapt to the needs of the system. Almost all parents would have done it differently had they known what to do and been relieved of the unconscious bondage of themselves. Children idealize their parents. A child needs parents for survival. We make them good and us bad in order to survive. Dad's a drunk, so we say, "It must be me."

Today there is a tremendous opportunity to break the chain once we have some awareness. You can leave a functional family: it's open and flexible. But a dysfunctional family has become so frozen and rigid that nobody can get out. You can't have a relationship with your parents until you've left. In a dysfunctional family it's all enmeshed. It's as if you were to take your hands and put your fingers together so that they become entwined. That isn't a relationship. You've got to separate your hands in order to have two distinct people to have a relationship. You've got to leave home before you can go back home. It's difficult. It involves a grieving process, but it can be done and hundreds and thousands and millions of people are doing it.

Once a person is aware of family dysfunctionality, there's the responsibility of doing something about it. To leave these family systems involves grieving, wishing it could have been different and wishing we could have had a normal childhood. Grieving is suffering. The end of the process is acceptance— being born again. From realizing that you've been violated and you're a survivor, you move out into empowerment, choosing your own life. The process is tough because in dysfunctional families there is survivor's guilt. As you start leaving that system you want to run back and get your brother or your sister. Unless they're ready, they're not about to listen.

There's a lot of pain in the early part of recovery, because you're experiencing all the feelings that you had twenty-five years ago but never felt because you got into your ego defenses, roles, and addictions. Those things kept you from having to go through legitimate suffering. Recovery involves finding a new family of affiliation, such as a group or meeting; leaving home and your family of origin; and becoming your own person. You have to be willing to be able to stand extraordinarily alone. In that aloneness, you find yourself. Then there unfolds an incredible discovery process whereby you learn who you are from the inside, not from the outside. You learn that you can engender good feelings from inside of you.

What does the concept of powerlessness mean to you?

B ETH ▸ Powerlessness means that I'm not responsible for everybody else and for what happens to everybody else.

J AN ▸ I can't control other people, and when I try, they become uncomfortable. It also gives me a sense of freedom and makes me realize the only thing I have any power over is my own attitudes.

H ARRY ▸ To be powerless is to let go of a fantasy picture of myself being able to control and therefore be accountable for the external reality around me.

M ICHAEL ▸ I'm unable to alter or interfere with what is God's creation. When I try, I get disastrous results in my life. I'm powerless to swim upstream. Powerless is not weakness. It is letting what's there be, grow, and evolve.

A LICE ▸ The first two lines of the Serenity Prayer say, "God grant me the serenity to accept the things I cannot change; the courage to change the things that I can." The things I can change are inside of me; everything outside of me I'm powerless over.

K AREN ▸ Powerlessness is a sense of relief. It's like somebody's lifted a huge burden from my shoulders and I don't have to carry it anymore. I don't have to fix anybody. The only person I'm responsible for is me, and I'm going to have a lot of help with me.

MARY ▸ I don't have to do it alone. It's okay to get help.

JEFF ▸ Powerless means I don't have to prove that I'm powerful. I don't have to be alone and afraid anymore. I can face life with the help of other people. This problem is bigger than I can face by myself.

AUDREY ▸ It's a sense of becoming aware that I'm not alone any longer and that there are all kinds of resources available to me. The only thing I need to do is to step forward and accept it.

MANOLITO ▸ I do my best, and I leave the rest to God because I've turned my life over to His management. I'm not in control of the exterior world; the only thing I can be in control of is me.

JIM ▸ People do things because they're them, not because of me.

Can you accept this concept of powerlessness over your mother's alcoholism?

MANOLITO ▸ Yes. I'm powerless over that. I didn't cause it and I can't control it. The only thing that I can do about it if I want to help her is be a good example.

Can you accept the sense of powerlessness over your brother's suicide?

BRIAN ▸ That's a hell of a question. I never thought about it before in that context. I guess I still blame myself. I still think if I'd done something different, he would still be here. Yet, I was powerless over the way he chose to live and I was powerless over the family we grew up in. I was powerless over him becoming an alcoholic and powerless over my inability to care about him then. I loved my brother, I miss him, and I wish he were back. I am powerless. It's very hard to accept power-lessness over my brother's suicide.

Can you accept powerlessness over your father's workahol-ism?

B ETH ▸ Yes, definitely. I can be grateful for the fact that he finally changed. I regret the years that were missed, but I accept that he was powerless over himself because of his father's alcoholism.

Can you accept powerlessness over the fact that your folks got a divorce?

M ICHAEL ▸ Intellectually, yes; emotionally, having just discovered recently that I held the belief that I caused it is still confusing—but the answer is yes, in time.

Can you accept powerlessness over your birth, adoption, and your husband's alcoholism?

L YNN ▸ It's total powerlessness. All the way along it has been totally out of my hands. When I was born, someone made certain decisions, and I don't think they were very good ones. I don't think they'd occur now. I don't think they would pull me out of that foster home after five months today. It's all different now.

When I was with my husband, I felt totally helpless that I couldn't get him well. He's well now, and there are days when I wish he could have gotten well while my daughter and I were still around—but things didn't work out that way. I've always felt a sense of powerlessness.

Can you accept the concept of powerlessness over your father's alcoholism?

A UDREY ▸ I now realize there was absolutely nothing that I could have done as a five-year-old to avoid alcoholism in my family. I no longer need to hang on to these feelings I've carried around for so many years. I was totally powerless over what happened. It wasn't my fault.

Can you accept that powerlessness over your mother's abandonment?

A UDREY ▸ I'm still dealing with that, but I haven't come that far. I still have a lot of sorting out to do. That question makes me uneasy.

Do you accept the idea you didn't cause your father's alcoholism?

M ARY ▸ How can a little kid cause her daddy to drink a fifth of Jack Daniel's every night? On a rational level, it's easy to look at it and say, "Of course, it wasn't my fault," but it's been a lot of work in therapy to emotionally believe that. When I did accept it, the obsession to want to overeat and the obsession to want to drink went away. It's living my life today that is my problem. I didn't have any role models. I'm really still an infant, but I'm an adult by society's standards.

Do you think your parents were dysfunctional?

D ICK ▸ My parents were definitely dysfunctional. As far as my father's gambling and my mother's selfishness are concerned, I was powerless. I didn't have any control over them. I had nothing to do with their personalities, but who they were spilled over on me.

Do you accept the reality that there's nothing you could have done to fix your parents?

J EFF ▸ I know intellectually there isn't anything I really could have done; but on a feeling level, I don't know. I haven't gotten to 100 percent yet. My dad is quite ill, and the doctors have given him about a year to live. I want to heal those wounds while he's still here. In spite of it all, I love my dad, and I've seen some heavy-duty changes in him since he's become ill.

Have you come to realize that your folks couldn't show you the love you deserved because of their own dysfunctionality?

KAREN ▸ Only recently. Last week, when I was with my mother, I had a rare opportunity to tell her that I loved her the way she was and she didn't have to change. I no longer blame her for what she did or didn't do to me because she was a product of her upbringing. It helped us to connect on a deeper level than we ever have in thirty years. If I tried to talk about this before, she considered it a direct attack on her mothering. She became very defensive and closed about it. It's only been recently that I've realized that I have to forgive them if I'm ever going to be forgiven myself for all the insane things I have done. They were products of how they were raised.

I need to have the same conversation with my dad. I hope to have it soon. Blaming and hating my parents was only hurting me—certainly not them. I've finally gotten to acceptance. It's taken a long time.

Can you accept your parents as dysfunctional just as you are?

JIM ▸ Yes, they were a product of their environment. They taught us not to trust or show feelings. There wasn't the love there we were looking for. They gave us things, but it wasn't what we needed. Then they expected our reaction to what they gave us, and it wasn't what they wanted. We received it differently, and they gave it for the wrong reasons. I guess my folks did the best they could with what they had.

Did they do the best they should?

JIM ▸ I don't know about "should."

Should a parent hug his kid?

JIM ▸ That they should. As I said before, my parents didn't express love.

Should they have?

J I M ▸ Yes.

Should parents teach children?

J I M ▸ Yes, parents should teach children.

Did they teach you?

J I M ▸ They didn't learn how to teach me.

So they didn't teach you?

J I M ▸ They didn't teach me. My parents should have taught me.

Should they have hugged you, supported you, and played with you?

J I M ▸ Yes.

Did they?

J I M ▸ They didn't.

Should parents do those things?

J I M ▸ Yes.

Do you feel deep down inside that your mother and your father loved you?

A L I C E ▸ I think they loved me in the way they could, but that was very limited and not adequate for my needs as a child. What I'm working on right now is learning to have the feelings of sadness and anger so that I can move on with my life.

Do you feel it's all right to be angry about what you didn't get?

A LICE ▸ I need to so that I can get better. Once I have experienced the emotions, then I won't have to hide from them.

Do you understand that you became a different person in order to survive your dysfunctional background?

H ARRY ▸ I became a whole bunch of different people in order to survive my childhood. My mother's depression, neediness, and seduction, and the omnipotent picture of the surgeon, are encoded deep in my life. They're encoded in every relationship I enter. Because of the years I've been hidden from myself, who I am grew from my beginnings and couldn't change until I became aware of it.

Can you see that you adopted a role within your family to get the attention and love of your parents?

B RIAN ▸ I'm having a lot of trouble knowing what that role was or how that role differs from who I really am. The role was to be bright and precocious, please adults, be successful, make a lot of money, and don't enjoy it. It's my mother's life I've led, not mine.

I am here, but I'd like to run the hell out of this room right now. I'm in touch with so much pain, anger, and sadness right now, I could burst. The longer I sit here, the more I think, "My God, your whole life is still unreal." I have the feeling that I have so many years invested in my unreal life, how the hell do I ever let go of it and say, "Fuck you, you're not me"? I can't do that. It's pain. It's unbelievable. I thought it was anger. I'd like to tear this table to pieces. Now it's anguish. My God, I can't stand being this way anymore. Either I'm using energy to keep it all suppressed, or I come someplace like this and feel overwhelmed with the pain and the sadness. I want to escape. I just want to get out of whatever it is I'm in. I feel like the last best hope is chasing off to the other end of the earth for more work on myself.

The real me is going to get out, and the rest of it be

damned. It's a terrible struggle because there are so many unbelievably strong defenses to preserve the status quo. But I'll get through those. The defenses will break down.

Do you know that who you are today is not really who you are?

K A R E N ▸ Who I thought I was and who I really am are two different things. All those adaptive roles are falling away. The real me is starting to emerge. Who I am today may not even be exactly who I am, but it's much closer to the truth than it ever has been before. Every day I get closer. I was the hero. I was the fixer. I was the emotional candy man who made everything okay. I still slip into that role, but it happens less and less. I'm moving from extreme crazy and insane behavior and more onto the middle ground. That old behavior now feels strange when I slip back into it; before, the healthy behavior felt very strange. It's been very subtle. It's a shifting that's taking place along a continuum, a moving in the right direction.

Is it okay to feel very sad about your childhood?

A U D R E Y ▸ I don't know what happened in the last couple of minutes. When Jim was speaking and you were asking all those questions, something came over me. I started rationalizing immediately. I started thinking that parents don't do a whole lot of hugging and loving when the big question is, "Is there going to be any food today?" When you're trying to survive, a lot of hugging and nurturing is not at the top of the list. It did not occur with me. I'm trying to figure out why this question is upsetting me so much. My only thought was to rationalize why the hugging and nurturing did not happen. Maybe that's why I'm upset. I don't know.

Do you think when you grew up there were poor, starving, black families in the South where kids were getting hugs and kisses?

A U D R E Y ▸ During childhood I'd never thought of that; but since I've been an adult, I have come to realize that evidently there were hungry people who were normal. I asked myself recently, "Why did the problems occur in my own household as an adult when I had done just about everything the American way to make sure that they did not occur?" The answer came to me: it's because I grew up in a dysfunctional home, and the normal things that people experienced, I did not experience. That's why these problems occurred in my household.

Yes, there were poor families around us when I was growing up. There was a father and a mother in those homes. I used to visit a woman, her husband, and family. She had a little baby. I can remember sitting beside her. She was bathing the baby in a wash pan because she didn't have the normal facilities. I'll never forget the smell of the Ivory soap as she bathed her baby. I would have wanted to have had a mother bathe and care and pamper me like that.

Where do you think you'd be today if somebody had bathed you in that wash pan?

M ANOLITO ► I wouldn't be here. I wouldn't be dealing with what I'm dealing with now. I probably would be grown up and be in a relationship where I felt comfortable and in a job I liked. I'd probably be living a rather calmer and happy life. The struggles I would face in my daily life wouldn't be the struggles I face today. It's a wonderful question.

Is it all right to be angry that your parents didn't do those things for you?

B ETH ► Something I'm just learning how to do is be angry at my parents. My therapist says I'm always apologizing or making excuses for them instead of just being angry. Maybe it's not yet "okay."

Is it all right to be angry with your parents?

J AN ► I'm really angry at my mother. It's amazing. It seems like there is a lot more anger directed toward mothers than fathers and many of us had alcoholic fathers. Maybe it's because of my own alcoholism that I'm not very angry at my father,

who's still a practicing alcoholic. I'm angry at my mother—and
she's been dead twenty-two years. It's still sitting here inside
me. I think it's okay to feel angry at her. I just don't know what
the hell to do with the feelings.

**Is it okay to say, "I don't have all the answers and I need
help"?**

HARRY ► The healing has been in asking for help. The
healing started in my life with my alcoholism and when I realized that I would need to ask for help. My mother not only
taught me how to talk but also that if I ever wanted help, it
would never come. I see that picture of an angry father in a
doorway turning away with disgust in his eyes, and I'm sur-
prised that someone I thought was never there inside of me has
been able to ask for help. I'm deeply grateful to the people who
have given it to me; I'm deeply grateful to my own therapist.
I've been screaming all my life, but I never knew what it was I
was screaming about. Now I know. There are no answers;
there's only a process. Even when I say that, I get scared because the only way I've ever felt safe was to have an answer.

I don't mind being powerless. When I'm powerless, I'm
not helpless. I can say, "Help me." As a child, I was not only
powerless but addicted to my parents. You're supposed to be.
They feed you or you die. I was also helpless. I wanted my
mother; but when she began to sexualize our relationship, when
she took me from the bathtub to the bedroom and I liked it,
then it became real scary to want my mom and there was no one
to tell. I blamed me and said it's a fantasy or it was that way
because I wanted it.

I would like to take that bad mom and keep her inside me.
That way I would still have a mother who was this long-suffer-
ing woman who finally died. Even as I say that, I know enough
now that right behind her there's a grandmother, and behind
her, probably another. There were ghosts in my nursery, and
they weren't even dead yet; they were downstairs in the kitchen
bitching. I had to get the help of much saner people than those I
grew up with. I've been able to do that. It's all grace that people
have come into my life when I needed them.

Is there a sense of discovery at getting to know who you really are?

A LICE ▸ I've never known who I was. I dressed exactly like the people I worked with in whatever job situation I had. In three months my clothing, hair, and makeup matched the uniform of the organization. I even have taken on dialectical differences in my speech. Learning who I am is a painful process because as an adult, I'm learning things that children learn. That means I'm learning them in a void because I don't have the information that thirty-five years of living should have provided. I'm learning who I am, but I'm not sure yet because I'm not finished dealing with the "where I came from" issues. I'm not going to know fully who I am until I've completed that process through the program and therapy, and grown up.

Do you accept the idea that what happens in your life is your responsibility?

M ARY ▸ You've got to stop blaming sometime, but you have to feel it before you let it go. I started crying when Audrey talked about the bathwater and the baby. I grew up in a household on Fifth Avenue and I still didn't get what I needed. There was a nanny who gave us anything we wanted, but the missing link was love from my parents. I felt really unloved.

It doesn't matter what side of the tracks you grew up on: a dysfunctional family is a dysfunctional family and the symptoms are the same. Everybody's pain is relevant to the person that's going through it. I, too, wanted my mommy to bathe me. I wanted my daddy to hug me. I had people in my life who were paid to do that. "To thy own self be true"—they've been saying that for a long time and I believe it. That's what I can hold on to as I go through this dance of life, because I've never danced to this orchestra before. It's scary.

Have you accepted responsibility for your life today?

L YNN ▸ I figured out the other day that I have nothing in my life now that I'm ashamed of or not proud of. If there's a person in my life who's not treating me right I talk to that person. I lay it on the line. If I have to, I end relationships because I'm trying to surround myself with people who are supportive and contribute to my life. There's nothing in my life now I feel bad about. I'm much more in control of my life now. I really don't do anything I don't want to do.

Is it scary to accept that responsibility for your own life today?

J A N ▸ It's terribly scary. I don't think I would have been in a disastrous thirty-two-year marriage if I hadn't grown up in the kind of family I had. I don't want to sound like I'm blaming my dysfunctional childhood for what I've done, but it certainly played a big part in how I lived my life. Quite frankly, I'm terrified right now, but I know I can't go on living the way I've been living. I've gotten a lot of help in other areas in my life, and I will this time too. All I can do now is put one foot in front of the other. I'm not going to be living as well, but somehow that doesn't seem as important as it used to. I have freedom. I can think for myself and it's worth giving up some of the material things I had, to have that freedom. But yes—responsibility is scary.

How have you let go of blaming your parents?

H A R R Y ▸ Blaming my parents is something that I do, but they're not here, so it's only me I'm hurting. AA talks about having one foot in the past and one in the future and pissing all over today. That's probably what I'm doing when I'm blaming. There's a difference between feeling anger at being made to suffer for their needs and feeling sad. It's important for me to remember my mother did sit with me and teach me how to talk one word at a time as well as not responding when I screamed for help. It lets me bring the picture of the mom I loved and the mom that I hated together. As they come together and I deal with the pain of that, I feel as if I have a whole me and a whole relationship. That's not blaming her for doing something that she couldn't do. That would be like saying, "I'm angry at my mother because she didn't speak Chinese." The truth is, she grew up in Pittsburgh. The language of life I learned has big pieces that don't work, but I'm capable of learning new languages. Kids need somebody to say, "I love you"—and then not to just say it, but to do it. I hope I never pay somebody to hug my son or daughter. I want to be accountable for my child.

Why is letting go of the past difficult?

MICHAEL ▸ One of the biggest hindrances to growth was an overwhelming sense of loyalty toward my family and a horrible sense of betrayal of them by daring to walk in the door of an ACA meeting. If I addressed the reality that Chinese was not spoken in my house and therefore I learned English, that's just a fact. I learned English because that's what happened where I grew up. That is not a judgment. We all accept that. But if I were to dare address similar facts that in any way could be taken as an attack on my upbringing, my family would reel in horror. I was raised in an environment where many things would result in a mother who, because of her own hurt and pain, would turn away. Result: I'm alone.

It is not blaming parents to reveal the facts of how you learn to deal with the world. When it is taken as blame, it is a tremendous, manipulative device that can be used to control people. The last big wall I couldn't break through turned out to be a wall of loyalty and betrayal. I dared uncover such things, and all they were were facts. Chinese wasn't spoken; English was spoken. Feelings weren't discussed. It's not a judgment. They weren't discussed. They didn't know how. Is that clear?

What's the payoff for letting go of the past?

JIM ▸ Someone asked me once, "In one word, what would you say was the most important thing in AA?" I said, "Honesty." The most important step for recovery in any program is honesty. Then someone else asked me, "What do you credit for your success in the program?" I said in one word, "Maintenance"—maintaining a constant program one day at a time. I recognize that anything which happened in my childhood I have to deal with one day at a time.

There's no such thing as a free lunch. If I did anything in my childhood that was my responsibility, I have to pay for it. If we make a wave in our life, we're going to have to ride that wave. It's not going to go away because we found out we were adult children. The program taught me that I can live with whatever did happen. We have to live with that wave, but we find out in the process, we can live in any waves or any storm that we've created or someone has created for us. We can get through it. Eventually the sun's going to shine and the water's going to smooth out. The day we have that peace and serenity about how we feel about ourselves, that's when the storm quits. How you feel inside takes you into a new day, a new horizon. It's a nice feeling.

ROBERT SUBBY, M.A. ▸ I say to my clients, "What you are finding out about you will tell you a great deal about who your parents really are. Anything you feel as a consequence of that reality is the potential truth about how they're feeling if you could ever get through all their layers of denial. Once you accept that, you can then understand your parents in a balanced way. This is not to excuse what they did wrong that hurt you, but it also recognizes they're human beings. If you're going through a lot of crap, they went through a lot of crap. You're very fortunate in having a place to work some of it out. It's not an excuse for dismissing them from responsibility. They still were people who didn't give you what they should have given you. However, see your parents as people who could be sitting where you're sitting but weren't given that opportunity, and it's not likely that it's going to happen now. That doesn't dismiss you from your need to recognize that there were things you didn't get and that you should have gotten." Often some logical part of the adult child says, "Well, Mom and Dad did the best they could at the time they did it with the skills and tools they had."

That's all well and good, and who's going to argue with that logic, except that it invalidates all the facts about things they didn't do right. "With that kind of thinking," I tell them, "you don't have any right to feel sad or angry because 'they did the best they could.' That way you end up minimizing your own reality and invalidating yourself. What I want to hear from you is what you feel and that what happened to you back there really happened. I want to hear you say that you have a right to those feelings and that those mistakes were not your fault. Don't sit here and pay me good money and defend your mom and dad. They don't need you to defend them." "But I feel guilty," the adult child says. And I tell that adult child, "That's an issue you're going to have to accept. Some part of you makes you feel guilty for having real feelings, and that's not Mom and Dad anymore—that's you."

I see the adult child going, in typical adolescent developmental style, through the crisis of rage and unforgiving postures against the parents as the child recognizes how the parents hurt him or her. Then I help such people to validate that they have a right to be angry and hurt and sad. Then I ask, "What about the fact that your parents also did some things right? You have values and qualities and skills which they gave you, so let's try to move toward a balanced understanding of them." Once we get past that, I ask, "Now enough of them. Who's been responsible for your life since you were twenty?" Ultimately, for adult children, that's the bigger issue.

You must come to embrace personal responsibility. As adults, you have rejected yourself. You have abandoned yourself. Given your history, it's understandable why. That's what you were trained to do. That's what feels comfortable.

12

BECOMING

YOUR

OWN

PARENT

According to psychologist Nathaniel Branden, "Anyone can suffer. It's what human beings do easiest. The hardest, most challenging thing in life is to make yourself happy." For adult children, to be happy requires hard work in recovery, but it happens.

In recovery we confront our pain, find fresh answers, take actions that often go against the grain, and try on unfamiliar attitudes and feelings. Different people come into our lives, and the results, we find, are worth the effort. Something magical and spiritual happens—this time from the inside out. We say, "This is my life and I am very capable of living it in a creative, healthy, and happy way." Becoming your own parent is a necessary part of the healing process.

Webster defines *nurture* as training, upbringing, the sum of influences. Nurture also means to supply with nourishment, to educate. In recovery you learn to nurture yourself. As you become your own parent you learn you are important and worthy of healthy love. You surround yourself with good and healthy people to love and who love you in return. Your new parent encourages you to try a different way. This is a gentle parent who has time and energy for you and who respects and loves you not for what you do but because you are you. In becoming your own parent you learn to appreciate and celebrate your specialness and you learn to love yourself and others unconditionally. You identify your needs, internalize them as rights, advocate for yourself, and take the necessary action to achieve the happiness you deserve.

I have the right to be happy.
I have the right to my feelings.
I have the right to express my feelings.
I have the right to be angry.
I have the right to say no.
I have the right to make mistakes.
I have the right to grow.
I have the right to live my life the way I want to.
I have the right to have fun.
I have the right to love and be loved.
I have the right to be me.

Cathleen Brooks is the founder and executive director of Next Step in San Diego, California. This national center for education, training, and consulting in the alcohol and drug field provides help for children, adolescents, and adults who have been affected by parental chemical dependency. Cathleen is the author of *The Secret Everybody Knows,* a book for children written from her own personal experience. A nationally recognized speaker, trainer, and consultant, she specializes in program development for organizations wishing to provide services on a local level. Cathleen is the president and a founding board member of the National Association for Children of Alcoholics.

CATHLEEN BROOKS ▸ The adult child is taught by most recovery programs to get in touch with the notion of an almost separate spirit being, the little child. I'm comfortable with anything people have to do to get in touch with the fact they once were a child who was very badly hurt and to acknowledge those hurts are still there. Personally, I no longer think of myself as having separate beings inside of me, although I certainly did go through that process in early recovery. Today I think there will always be hurts in me that came from that child. There will also always be the joy and spontaneity that the child never experienced but I'm now getting to experience as an adult. I believe one must become *as* a child.

Adult children in recovery must develop the childlike openness to learning, the childlike acceptance of not knowing, the childlike need to be taken care of, the childlike need to have fun, the childlike need to be wrong and make mistakes, the childlike ability to have spontaneous emotions, and the childlike adventure to try something they've never tried before. I don't see that as a part of a person; I see that in recovery as *the* person. It isn't that there's a child somewhere mystically within whom you have to pull out and give teddy bears to so that you know who you are. I did go through that stage. Now I am *as* a child as I approach things. I'm aware that I have those wonderful childlike qualities and I know it's okay to be that child. It's also okay to be an adult too. If you're going to talk about the child within, also talk about the intelligent, competent adult within.

Everybody lives out his or her childhood issues; everyone is an adult child because every human being still has that child within who has never fully resolved the childhood hurts, fears, disappointments, and survival behaviors developed to deal with them. The child in a severely traumatic environment does not have time to grow up. Adult children need to go back and reexperience the growing-up process.

It looks as if we're broadening the concept of adult children to include everybody whose father didn't make it home for Christmas when they were eight years of age. There is a specificity about what happens to children in alcoholic families that should not be lost. Severe trauma can also include physical abuse, incest, and other sexual abuse. It can include the death of a parent, because we do not do well with death in this society. In many cases, trauma includes other chronic illnesses, especially mental illness. However, there is something very special about children with alcoholic or addicted parents. That specialness usually has to do with the fact that the trauma which was suffered is not acknowledged by any other human being. There is an enormous resistance to even acknowledging that a pain or trauma occurred.

I think we've learned a lot from studying children of alcoholics that can apply to children who have suffered other traumas, but I don't think we should ever lose sight of the denial, the secrecy, and the shame that go with alcoholism. When children from an alcoholic family hear the term "dysfunctional family," they do not think anybody's talking about them. They get very misty-eyed and say, "Oh, those poor kids." They see it as someone else. This is the reason why these children of alcoholism and these adult children of alcoholism have failed in classic psychotherapy. I see people in my practice who have gone to ten different psychotherapists and have spent a fortune with no progress. They come to a therapist who understands the uniqueness of an alcoholic background, and six months later they're on the road to recovery because somebody finally identified it.

With alcoholism, overeating, gambling, sexual abuse, physical abuse, and workaholism, there is an overwhelming attachment to something. The attachment of a parent to work, eating, or having sex is greater than the attachment of the parent to doing what is good for the child. Does that mean there isn't love? No. It means that in each case the parent is disabled from being able to provide an environment in which the child knows he or she comes first. All children need focused attention; they need to know that they are number one. The problem is not a lack of love; it's a lack of the parent's ability to let the child experience the love. There's a really important difference between the two.

In a healthy family system the concern is always the child. If the message the child got is that the parents cared more about booze, money, arguments, or protecting their image, the child never learns that he or she is important. If a child sees Mom and Dad put all those other things first, then the child learns that he or she should put all those other things first too. The child sees that those are the things that are important in life and begins to co-opt to that system. The child begins to put energy into making the fighting stop or making the drinking stop, because those are the things in focus. The problem with the adult child syndrome is that long after the need to co-opt to the system has passed—the need geared toward parents giving a child a sense of self-worth—the child still has the same belief system. An overwhelming compulsivity or an overwhelming attachment to anything other than the child, where the child does not get focused attention, is going to create the adult child syndrome. The adult child syndrome is that set of beliefs which says, "I have absolutely no knowledge that I do come first." When the family energy is focused on the problem of the adult rather than on the needs of the children, the results for the children are the state of not knowing they come first, the state of believing that they have to fix the situation, and the state of believing that life is about surviving instead of enjoying and that the meaning of life is to get through the struggle of life. If a child lives in a world where the focus of life is how to solve the problem, that child doesn't have any orientation on what he or she would like to do today.

Characteristics of the adult child of an alcoholic syndrome are: taking yourself too seriously, feelings of guilt, responsibility for others, a sense of inadequacy and failure despite your achievements, inability to trust others or yourself, procrastination, and a tendency to isolate, and discomfort when life is calm. It also includes feelings of impending disaster, the need to control situations and other people, unsatisfying intimate relationships, overeating or other weight problems, alcohol and drug abuse, compulsive "dedication" to work, and ignoring your personal needs.

There are painful parts of the adult child syndrome that have to do with people believing that nobody will ever love them in a primary way. This is why there are tragic adult child intimate relationships. Either adult children pick people who will not put them first, or by accident they get somebody who does put them first but they do everything they can to push that person away. Human beings have a strong connection to their natures, and they will rebel against anything that doesn't feel natural. If an adult child grew up in a system that does not meet needs, there will be an almost infantile desire to get those needs met, and the way that the child will deal with that is to layer it over with the belief that it's not normal to get those needs met. Adult children go through life desperately seeking to get their needs met. They are seen as very clingy. They don't have boundaries. They say, "Help me; make me feel better." If anybody happens to do it, they rebel and push them away. That's the infant saying, "I need this," and the adult child saying, "Oh, that's not normal; those are irresponsible desires."

The first step to recovery is to acknowledge there's something wrong: "The reason I am the way I am is because things happened to me and I lived in a world where my basic human needs weren't met. I did the best I could. I survived and I developed as a result of that need to survive a set pattern, beliefs, and behaviors that may or may not work very well right now." The second step is finding others who experienced the same thing, to reassure yourself that you're not crazy. That's when you start going to groups or meetings or even reading a book. The third step is a recognition of real feelings. Real feelings are not the storytelling kind of feelings, such as this happened and then that happened. What's happening to you right now is what's important. It's the beginning of the unfreezing process. A lot of adult children say, "I don't want anything that hurts," and they move back to emotional numbness. Step four is the educational process. A good clinician is helpful at this point to say to the adult child, "The pain is part of the process; it won't kill you. We have miserable feelings. They would have killed you when you were five, they would have killed you when you were thirteen, but they won't kill you now. You're safe now."

Unfreezing of feelings is a very painful and dramatic time. It is crucial to get in touch with those very raw things that you may never have experienced when you were little: raw feelings of anger, raw feelings of abandonment, raw feelings of sadness.

You begin to experience the childhood feelings you couldn't afford to experience when your parents were drinking or compulsively acting out. The miracle moment is when you wake up one morning and say, "I don't know how to do this. I don't know how to take care of myself. I don't know what to do with these feelings. I can't fill my briefcase this morning with things that will make me forget. I have a wonderful person in my life, and I don't know what to do about the fact that this person loves me. I don't know how to do my job. I've been faking it for twenty-five years. I have grandchildren, and I never learned how to be a parent." It's a terrifying experience, but it's the miracle experience. The whole survival of the adult child is based on "I know how to do that." We never ask anyone for help because nobody was ever there for us. When you can say, "Please help me," get out of the way. If you can get to that point, you've made it.

The fifth step is when you begin to say, "My sponsor isn't the answer, my husband isn't the answer, nobody's the answer." You can ask them for nurturing and you can ask them for help, but they're not going to do it for you. Healing occurs from within.

You begin to realize that parent voice in your head told you, "It's your fault," "Better watch out," "Don't do that," "Be good," "Keep up the false face." It's a scared voice; it isn't a mean voice. That parent voice probably kept you alive when you were a child. That was the voice that said to you, "Keep your mouth shut," "Don't tell them how you feel," and "Don't express your anger." That's the voice of the person that took care of you when you were little and grew up. That voice is you yelling at yourself.

The key to understanding the recovery process is to know it all makes sense. It's not trying to heal adult children from something that is crazy and dysfunctional. It's trying to heal them from something that made sense back then and did such a good job of helping people survive that it's hard to give up. Adult children hang on to such things as "Don't trust people," "Don't let people get close," "Be good," and "Always do better," because it helped them survive, not because it was crazy.

The first lesson about self-parenting is realizing that you have been parenting yourself all along. You have been parented. You already know how to do it. Don't worry; you're already an expert.

When that inner voice says something negative or critical, say to yourself, "Okay, I'm doing it," and then realize you're safe now. Begin saying, "I'm having some bad feelings and I hate it when I yell at myself. I feel terrible." The next step is to admit, "I don't know how to change that, but I think maybe some other people do." A therapist, good friend, or lover can help. It has to be somebody outside of you at first. You might go to a friend and say, "God, I really screwed up. I was late for work. I'm beating up on myself. Can you give me some feedback?" The helping person can say to you, "When you were late for work this morning, it's because you're so dedicated that you were up last night reading all that new company literature. I think they're incredibly lucky at the office to even have you." The helping person is teaching you how you might want to talk to yourself.

Try to think about people in your life who do talk to you that way. Make a list of those people, and then ask yourself, "How often am I spending time with them?" Many adult children find they're not spending enough time with those people. They're spending time with people who are critical. It feels normal because they've adapted to the negativity. Whenever you feel freaked out, know that there is a teacher or helper there for you to go and sit with, someone who talks to you lovingly. Put the problem on the table and get their help. Becoming your own parent takes a long time.

You've got to find new parents, at least until you can be one for yourself. You cannot grow up an orphan again, trying to do it all by yourself. Listen when people say loving things to you. Then start asking them to do it for you. The next thing you do in self-parenting is begin to say those things to yourself. Since you have been so vigorously critical of yourself all your life, you have to be vigorously supportive of yourself. Most people have a very hard time.

Be a loving or supportive parent for yourself. If you have one "parent" saying, "You are a screwup," and the other "parent" saying, "You're okay," whom is the adult child going to believe? If you're the child of an alcoholic, you'll still believe the parent screaming at you, but you'll at least hear the power of the second message. Adult children should be quite exuberant in their self-praise. They feel like vomiting, of course, because they can't stand praise; they go into an anxiety panic attack. If you ask adult children how sick they are, they can do a twelve-minute monologue.

So we find somebody who talks to us in a positive way. We ask him or her for help. We begin to talk to ourselves that way. Eventually, it becomes normal to talk to yourself that way. It becomes automatic to self-parent in a loving way. If an abused child who's been beaten is taken out of the abusing home and put into foster care, is that child going to start believing in his or her own self-worth because he has a new parent who doesn't beat him? No. Is he going to start believing the foster parent when the foster parent says, "We really love you"? No. However, if the foster parent adopts the child and over a period of twelve years is consistently loving and supportive, eventually the child's going to believe the new parent. That's the process. Recovery is the process of adopting ourselves as children. It's a process of becoming our own new adoptive parent.

J I M ▸ The inner child is still there in me. I talk to myself about the child that's in me today as opposed to how I used to be. It's a pleasant dialogue. I'm aware of choices I have, what I want to do, how important it is I do it, and what the outcome can be. Whatever I do is all right. That's where the parent comes into play. When I get to thinking of what should I do or shouldn't do, it comes around to whatever I do is all right. This gives me the opportunity to be free. Yet there's a sense of responsibility that goes along with it. Being responsible gives me more freedom. The parent in me today lets go of expectations. That's where my real parents made mistakes, expecting me to do what they thought I would do or should do.

A L I C E ▸ My child is very frightened, very insecure, and very needy. The parent that I have within me, that I grew up with, is very critical. Whatever I did was not right, wasn't good enough, or was stupid. It was a unending monologue of criticism. It's been really hard for me to break into those tapes. The first step was to learn that the tapes existed and I was hearing those things. One of the big things I've learned to do is pray for self-acceptance. That's hard for me to do because I've been trained to be so self-critical. I can be very harsh on myself. One of the questions I ask myself when I'm trying to parent myself is "Would I want this for my daughter?" or "What would I do for my child?" I can then turn that around and ask, "What would I want for my little child inside of me?"

By using that question, I've been able to get medical treatment for the daily migraine headaches that I walked around with for years. It took a therapist to say to me, "If your daughter had headaches, would you take her to the doctor?" I became very tearful because the answer was yes. It was very hard to say that I wouldn't do for myself what I would do for my own child. That's the kind of parenting I'm trying to do. It's all pretty much in my head, but it involves action too. The key to it is talking to myself like a good parent.

JAN ▸ When I decided that I had to do something about my alcoholism by going to AA, I didn't get any approval or support from my husband. I heard the same messages from my husband as I did from my mother. The two are very similar. I remember thinking, "God, if he'd just put his arms around me and tell me it's okay." I can really remember realizing, "I'm not going to get it from him, so I have to take care of myself." I remember getting to a point where I had my own approval. The way I've been able to get through this whole thing was finally I was able to be a parent to myself. I felt the loss of parenting as I grew up; and getting married as young as I did, I know I was looking for another parent, and again that parent wasn't there. A lot of things have opened up to me because of finally being able to be my own parent. To have people care about me without being critical and to have them accept me as I am with unconditional love has made my growth come a lot faster. I haven't been struggling for that love I never got. The love has been there. That has made it a lot easier.

MARY ▸ The parent in me is very punitive. Nothing I do is good enough. It's always my father's voice. Today I choose other role models. They are people who are living the type of life I want to live. I also listen to that child part of me. It's not uncommon to see me driving around talking to myself. If I feel frightened about something, I comfort myself. I'm really listening to that inner part of me I have ignored for so many years.

HARRY ▸ I have a whole bunch of different inner parents and inner children. Every time there's an inner parent, there's an inner child in relationship to it. Sometimes there is a child that doesn't expect anyone to meet his needs, a child who expects something horrible to happen, or a child who expects to receive something. They're also my own attempts at creating a parent to make myself normal. The more experience I have in recovery, the less susceptible I am to fragmentation of both my inner parent and my inner child. With increasing insight and emotional experience, I have become more and more able to hear the voices on tape. I can talk back to those voices and say, "That's what you say; that's not what I say" or "That's what you want, but that's not what I want." I've been able to make choices. It's not just the old tapes that will sabotage me. My inner child is not only loving, caring, and wanting; it's also terrified and full of rage at times. Part of my fear is that rage will destroy whoever it is I'm needing at the time. Some parts are very hard to hear as tapes because they're me. It's me talking. It is really hard to argue with myself if it's coming out of my very core.

I made a crummy choice about parents before I was born, but part of playing the hand I was dealt is that I've been able to make better ones. I've been able to choose a therapist with whom to go through some of this experience who is more available and nurturing. Somebody is now there for me, which I never had before. Being able to relive those past experiences with somebody else who's able to confront me when I'm demanding things, who doesn't disappear when I get mad, or who is able to respond in a caring way alters the structure that I call me. That's the difference, I think, between the experience of meetings and the experience of individual therapy.

AUDREY ▸ My inner child is frightened and is always saying, "I'm scared, I'm afraid of abandonment, I need and want love." My inner child is so full of fear that I avoid difficult situations and take few risks. I don't trust that the inner child could really take care of the situation. That inner child would be totally out of control, so I'm always on the lookout for situations that could create problems for that child. Currently I am going through retraining and reprogramming. I'm using individual therapy and my twelve-step programs. On the job I feel like a strong parent. I am a good parent to my students.

Recently I asked myself, "Do you ever stop and listen to your own lessons?" I had been emphasizing to my students that people are responsible for themselves. Driving home that day I said, "You are responsible for yourself just as they are. You have to make choices for yourself." Change is not always easy. The fact that I don't trust is making it more difficult for me to deal with myself. But this inner-child concept is so new to me. I will find myself taking my child, putting that child in my lap, and loving that child. The fact that no one else knows it's happening makes it okay.

B ETH ▸ Accepting myself as being a good person, knowing that there is a part of God inside of me, becoming a little more selfish with my own time, not saying yes to everything that comes up, and doing something I want to do just for myself are all real important. Not always spending Saturdays cleaning house, not taking things so seriously, being less perfectionistic, and not taking what my parents think as rigidly as I used to are helping me a lot. My parents are very intelligent people, but I can disagree with them and I don't have to feel guilty anymore. The therapy I do is a way of becoming my own parent. My therapist says, "That's okay" when I think I've done something wrong. "Don't worry; you're not excommunicated from the church because you had an abortion." I didn't go to communion for six years because I thought I wasn't allowed to. Being able to get "that's okay" from someone else makes it easier for me the next time to say, "That's okay," to myself.

D ICK ▸ The child in me depended upon the people in AA when I first came into the program. I could not identify as a child with parents, even though I had parents. The older members of AA were the father I never had. I went to meetings with these men. I talked to them after meetings, and many of them became like fathers to me. I could talk to them where I could never talk to my father when I was a child. They became my parents. I looked up to them because the advice they were giving me was good advice. They didn't lie to me as my parents had lied to me many times. I wasn't capable of being the parent when I first came into the program; I was a child.

Once I spent some time in AA, I could become a parent to the new members. This morning I was praying for a lot of my kids, a lot of members of the program that are fairly new. It's a good feeling to realize I can be a parent to people who need help. My love for them is totally unconditional. If one of them doesn't follow my advice, I don't stop loving them. That's what I got when I was a kid.

The role modeling in the program taught me about love. It was through the people in AA that I learned how to love and be loved—and how to love myself.

J E F F ▸ What my parents were and what my parent in me is today are quite removed from each other. I need a parent who has a sense of humor and one who will allow me to get a little bit crazy and have a little fun. I give the child in me the nurturing that I want by being with my children. We had a tickle-fest this morning; it was great fun. My six-year-old said, "Daddy, will you pick me up?" I picked him up and I held on to him. He just wanted to be little. Being with my son that way was caring for me.

One of the hardest lessons I've had to learn concerns effort. I have a tendency to work something to death. Some days I just have to do the best job I can, accept it, and move on. My inner parent teaches me that "good is good enough." I do the best job that I can, and if it isn't perfect, that's okay; I can put it down. The parent in me allows the child in me to cry when the child needs to cry. I had been told, "Big boys don't cry." Well, big boys do cry if they need to. I'm not afraid to share my feelings today, as I once was, and I don't have to hide behind my smile all the time either. My parent allows my child to have feelings and to express those feelings. I'm becoming a good parent to myself and a good parent to my children. I'm allowing myself to be a child along with them. We're all benefiting from it.

BRIAN ▸ I do a reasonable job with my inner child, at least in terms of being able to say I love myself. It's getting easier to stay in touch with my inner child, with me really. The parent is another story. There's no question that the parent tape that plays is my mother. I find right now that I'm in a rebellion against any parent, and I indulge my child. However, I sense there needs to be some kind of limit, some kind of guidance for him, and that comes from my nurturing parent that I developed myself to replace my mother. I can make decisions for myself without regard to what parent tape is playing.

KAREN ▸ I'm just starting to get in touch with this whole concept of the inner child. For the last twenty years I've always slept with two pillows—one of them hugged to me. I don't know if subconsciously I was trying to comfort that person, but it's something that goes in and out of my consciousness. As a child, I was programmed with negative crap and I learned negative behaviors. If I learned them, I can unlearn them. I can replace that negative programming with positive programming. I've been listening to a lot of motivational tapes, trying to surround myself with new role models. One thing I've done is make my own tape. It's called a prosperity commercial. You tape twenty affirmations in your own voice; you say nice things to yourself. I listen to that tape and say each one of those affirmations seven times. So it's one hundred and forty times going to work in the morning and the same thing coming home at night. I hear, "I, Karen, am now peaceful and serene" or "I'm allergy-free" or "I'm very well organized" or "I'm more intelligent every day." I hear the affirmations over and over again. I don't even have to really concentrate, because my subconscious picks it up. I've been dealing with the child in me and trying to be kinder to the child. Reprogramming for me has been the key.

MANOLITO ▸ In becoming my own parent, I've learned to accept myself and develop the talents I have. I look at myself as my own father, and I treat myself as a son. With that kind of imaging, I'm able to feel very comfortable and to heal myself. This is a process of healing because I am wounded. I calm myself down when I'm in a hurry, and I verbally build my self-confidence. If I want to start hearing my own voice, I'm going to have to stop hearing the old voices of my parents. I avoid my real parents much of the time. I do have a good relationship with my father, but my mother is still ill with alcoholism. She knows exactly how to hurt me, and she goes directly to my soft spots with strategic precision. I nurture myself. I treat myself to the things that I like—Broadway shows, movies, special suppers. I also try to do things that I didn't do as a kid. When I turned thirty last August, my birthday present to myself was a cat. It was my first pet ever.

MICHAEL ▸ The biggest job for me in the last two years has been finding the child. When I started looking at childhood issues, I was able to openly admit that I had nothing but contempt for the child that I was, and I couldn't understand why.

The only thing I'd had as a kid that I could relate to was a teddy bear. So I went out and I bought a teddy bear that looked like the teddy bear I'd had. This six-foot-one, two-hundred-pound, ex-marine me would lie in my bed at night and curl up with my teddy bear, trying to recapture what that kid was doing with that teddy bear back then. I had such negative feelings for the kid I could remember. I'd spent all my life trying to change myself into something else to get the hell away from him. Gradually I began to see that there was more to the child than this sweet little kid who was always "fine." All these things combined to get me in touch with a part of myself that, I surmise, had pretty much died around the time my folks got divorced. It culminated about a week ago.

I was with a gal and we were watching TV. I had a real good cry and all of a sudden something changed in me. I found myself developing a deep, demonic belly laugh. I had a big grin on my face and that little kid in me was saying to the world, probably to my mother more than anyone else, "You didn't get me. I made it." I'm in ways just beginning to work with this kid. As far as being my own parent, I am learning to take care of myself by doing the simple things, such as eating right, working out, and getting sleep. I began a parent exercise by imaging my Higher Power as a loving father standing behind me with his hand on my shoulder, just letting my imagination create that. I don't know if it's a psychological trick or a spiritual thing; it doesn't matter.

LYNN ▸ I grew up with a really critical mother, so I'm very critical of myself. I really get down on myself. I can spend days damning myself for something that's really trivial. What I've learned to do is literally shut it off. When this little voice in my head starts telling me, "You shouldn't have . . ." or asking, "Why did you do that?" or saying, "You're going to feel bad about yourself," I shut it right off and go do something positive. I take a walk, spend time with my daughter, or play with the kitten. I just don't listen to it anymore. When I do see my mother and she starts in on me, I walk away now; I do not listen to her. It's been a real difficult thing to get over because I ran my life according to that voice in my head. I don't deal with it now because I know that I'm okay. My therapist is helping me enjoy myself, because my childhood was not a good time. I was not a fun-to-be-around-kid. I was fairly depressed. I'm now learning to enjoy myself and have some fun.

CATHLEEN BROOKS ▸ Adult children can tell they're in a healthy meeting when there is no designated guru or leader. COA is a self-help program; there should be no junior psychoanalysis going on. You should really feel safe so that you can share what you have to share without anybody trying to explain it to you. There should be absolutely no advice-giving in the meeting. The topics and the leadership of each meeting should rotate. Certainly there should be no sense of "if you aren't up to this point of recovery, you're not making it."

In some step-study meetings, they've taken all of their childhood belief systems about "you must accomplish" and "you must keep up" and imposed them on a recovery program. This is an evolutionary process, not a structured process. You can walk away from a meeting feeling very emotional, but if you find you've gone to a meeting five times and each time you feel depressed and you have to process it endlessly, then probably what's going on in that meeting is not terribly helpful or healthy. Other yardsticks to judge meetings by are these: Are people talking about how their lives have gotten better since they've come into the program? Is there an okayness about talking about God? Are people talking about the steps? Are people talking about spirituality?

Spirituality is a knowledge that all the power you've ever needed has always been available to you. In fact, you've been calling on it without even knowing it. Spirituality is an acknowledgment of the power of love. Children of alcoholics are inherently spiritual people because they've always believed in the power of love. They believed that if they loved their parents enough, their parents would get well. They believed that if their parents loved them enough, they would get well. Spirituality says the cycle doesn't have to go from one to another. The cycle of love can be completely within you.

If you love yourself enough, you will get well. Spirituality is a state of knowing where you find that love and what to do with it. The spiritual person in recovery exudes love for other people. There's no desire to get a payback; there's no strategy to this love. Spirituality is an incredibly self-centered state, and the goal you're seeking is to become a totally self-centered individual. You want your center to be right inside of you so that others' moods and issues do not shake your center but you have enough in you that you can be there if another person wants to share it with you. Spirituality starts when you begin to say, "Where can I find love, and how can I experience it?" Then you move around the world looking for it.

13

FUN
AND
AFFIRMATION

Adult children have difficulty having fun. We are jealous of others who do, but it's scary for us. Two personal incidents stick out in my mind concerning my own difficulty in this area.

I met a friend who had just returned from a trip to Nassau. "Did you have a good time?" I asked. "Oh, it was great," he grinned as he produced a stack of color snapshots. "Let me show you," he said proudly. "You'll like these." In the first picture he was with a group of tourists. All of them were smiling. Another picture showed him with a harness around his body. "What's that?" I asked. "Hang gliding," he laughed. "It was terrific." The next picture—a long shot—showed him floating three hundred feet in the air over the ocean, his tow rope attached to a speedboat. My friend Joe is sixty-five years old.

I had been to exactly the same area in the Bahamas a few weeks earlier for a vacation and had left the island early. I teamed up with a friend there but made a hasty exit from the island after winning and losing a few dollars in the casino and buying a few souvenirs (for others, of course) at an outdoor market. Joe had a great vacation; I didn't. I wasn't able to relax.

Another time I gave a speech in Lafayette, Louisiana, and spoke to several thousand people—without notes—for an hour. That night a group of twenty of us went to a local club for Cajun food and dancing. Everyone was having fun. For two hours I sat uncomfortably at the table, unable to get out on the dance floor and have a good time. I was asked to dance more than a dozen times. I didn't; I was afraid.

I talked about this incident one night at a meeting of adult children. After the meeting was over, a guy came up to me and said, "Giving a speech is what you do; dancing is who you are."

Those two events happened over a year ago. Lately I have been enjoying life, having fun, and I'm very happy to report my humor is as sharp as ever.

Rokelle Lerner is a cofounder and consultant to Children Are People in St. Paul, Minnesota, a nonprofit agency that creates and implements chemical dependency prevention programs for elementary-school-aged children. Rokelle's pioneering efforts in prevention and intervention programs for young children and her work on behalf of children of alcoholics have led to the development of services for these high-risk children in thirty-eight states, Canada, Sweden, Okinawa, and Germany. A frequent lecturer, Rokelle is the author of the best-selling book *Affirmations for Adult Children of Alcoholics.*

R OKELLE LERNER ▸ Adult children take themselves seriously because they grew up in an environment in
which they weren't allowed to be children. Things like pleasure, joy, and fun were discouraged. They were made to feel
either ashamed for having fun or that they were doing something wrong. Adult children are coached into seriousness.

Recovery demands examination of the all-or-none phenomenon. When working on the core issues of shame, grief, and
inability to trust, adult children feel as though they have to stay
at that end of the feeling spectrum. They invalidate play and
they invalidate joy. Unless they're hurting, they're not alive.
The only way they feel is when they hurt.

Some children of alcoholics become addicted to stress. I
use the term "intensity junkie" for them. They believe they're
not getting better unless they're struggling. A highly functioning whole person does not walk around in a state of tension or
struggle, dealing with issues. The sure indicator of reaching a
state of integration and balance is the ability to exhibit once
again those childlike qualities of spontaneity, flexibility, laughter, and risk-taking. Adult children must learn how to play.

The beauty about play, according to dance therapist Diane
Halperin, is that adults can experience the spontaneous and the
rational at the same time. That means a balance of the adult self
and the child self. It's through play that we get to try on new
behaviors. It's through play that realities become blurred and so
more options become available. That's why play is so therapeutic. It pushes you into new areas, but you're pretending. It's like
shopping for clothes: you try something on and if you like it you
buy it, but if you don't, you hang it back on the rack. Play is a
way of experimenting with new behaviors.

Risk is hard for adult children, but when they start risking,
laughing, and playing, they're reaching stages of wholeness.
There's a tremendous amount of fear, but there can be joy
within grief and happiness within sadness. That's the balance to
seek in recovery. Whole human beings have the ability to play
all eighty-eight keys on the piano. They can go up and down the
keyboard. They don't have to play three safe notes anymore.

What do you do for fun?

J A N ▸ I don't leave myself a lot of time for fun, I really don't. I run very quickly and fill up my life with a lot of stuff. I'm learning to have more fun now. If someone phones and asks me to a movie or a play, my first instinct is to think of something I have to do. Lately I've been able to say, "Sure, I'd love to go."

B R I A N ▸ I run, work out, and do aerobics. Those have some elements of fun, but the reason I do them really isn't for fun: I do them to be able to continue to overeat and keep my weight down. I work out on machines because I feel unhappy with my body, so I do that to look better, and that's not really fun. That's striving. I know for sure that I run as fast as I can to run away from my feelings. So that's not fun either. Once in a while I'll play tennis, racquetball, or squash, but the fun there is ruined by the fact that I'm so terribly self-conscious about being a poor athlete. That was drummed into me as a kid. I looked in my baby book recently, and my mother had written, "Brian is uncoordinated."

Last week I went to a movie for fun.

B E T H ▸ I do all the normal things, such as seeing friends, going to movies, and going out to dinner. One new thing has been a lot of fun for me. I recently moved nearer to my sister, who has two small children. Playing with them is one of the most enjoyable things I've ever done. It's just opened up a whole new world of fun.

D I C K ▸ I enjoy going to meetings and helping people.

K A R E N ▸ For the first thirty-two years of my life, I was too super-responsible to have fun. The last year, I've been so busy recovering that I haven't had time to play. All the things I do are either goal-directed or they're to fulfill some sort of obligation. I love to play tennis and I'm a good tennis player, but I will not play a game with somebody. I'll hit back and forth and that's it. I don't want to get into competition, because sometimes I might win and then I'd have to take on someone else's bad feelings because of their loss. But last week for my birthday

I bought myself a pair of ice skates. I used to ice-skate when I was young. I haven't done it in twenty years, but I'm going to ice-skate this winter.

ALICE ► Fun is practically a foreign word to me. Children know how to have fun, but I don't know that I did when I was a child. My daughter knows how to have fun, and I allow her to talk me into playing. There was snow on the ground today, so she got her boots on and went outside. I was in the house putting junk away when she beat on the door, asking me to come out and look at her footprints. I was looking out saying, "Oh, they're great, they're beautiful." No, she wanted me outside, and she wanted me making footprints with her. So I did and that was fun. But it was real hard for me.

MARY ► I never heard my father laugh. At breakfast my father would sit at the head of the table with a scowl on his face. I would sit there looking at my mother, who would have been wasted the night before. My first experience of the morning was my father yelling at the help. I learned how to read the *Wall Street Journal* by the age of ten. I hope to hell if I am ever blessed with a child, I don't repeat that pattern. I look back over that, and there was no fun.

Today I take my camera and go walking in the woods, and I shoot. That's fun for me. I like to go to movies. I like to dance. I like to go to aerobics. Meetings are fun for me because most of my friends today are program people.

MANOLITO ► I take singing and acting lessons. I make love. I write film treatments and songs. I go to movies. If there is a big Broadway show in town, I go. I have to force myself to have fun and enjoy the things I love.

JEFF ► I didn't know how to have fun before getting into the program. It was either work or get screwed up. Now I tease my cat with a yarn ball, I go for walks with my kids, and I sit on the floor and play cards with my boys; I roughhouse with my kids and I go to movies and plays with my wife. I belong to an amateur theater group and I play volleyball on Sundays. In the volleyball game, I noticed I would get frustrated if I wasn't on the winning team. This past summer I've been learning how to just play for the fun of it. That's been good for me.

LYNN ▸ If I'm tired of work or taking care of my daughter, I'll take a day off. I get sick days, and that's what they're there for. If I need a vacation, somehow I arrange it. I take hot baths and drink a glass of wine at night if I feel like it. I'm reading a lot of good books these days and listening to good music. I play the piano fairly well. I've developed really solid women friends and a few male friends. I see them when I want, have lunch, and go to movies and parties. I'm just finding out now what I enjoy doing, because I didn't enjoy myself for so long. I did not know what it meant to have a good time.

MICHAEL ▸ I am just learning for the first time in my life what fun is. Recently I went to a dance, and I played pool for an hour. I am learning to allow myself to laugh more openly, but I still feel guilty every time if it goes on for more than a few minutes.

AUDREY ▸ I love to sew, but I don't think I do it for fun. Sometimes I do it to escape and be alone. At work I'll get silly sometimes with some of the staff members; but then driving home, I'll admonish myself for having engaged in it. I watch the kids at school who dance across the floor to bring a paper up to the desk. When the moonwalk was popular, they'd do it up to my desk and back. I'd smile and think, "Boy, I wish I could be that free."

I don't do anything for fun. I'm struggling with this thing, fun.

JIM ▸ Everything I do is fun. I enjoy working, I enjoy playing, I enjoy going to church, I enjoy my wife and family.

HARRY ▸ Fun's an important area of my life. When I got into recovery, it was hard work and the fun disappeared. After I ended a relationship with another addictive drug, nicotine, fun appeared spontaneously. I spent a bunch of money on a good bike and began enjoying riding a bicycle. I strapped it on a machine and rode this morning. I got all sweaty and forgot about everything. It's really great to have fun in my life again. I love to get out of hand at chamber music concerts. Sex, coffee, and chamber music—wow!

R OKELLE LERNER ▸ Adult children are adults who have little kids inside who didn't get their needs met or are adults who never balanced the child self and the adult self. Adult children stay in limbo between adulthood and childhood. They are people who never got to experience the wonderful joy and spontaneity of childhood and never quite reached that richness of full maturity.

The adult child concept doesn't necessarily mean a child's emotional makeup in an adult body. Often the opposite is true. Some children were pushed into early ego development and had to learn to organize their world too soon. They didn't have the opportunity or the protection to explore and be kids. Those are the ten-year olds going on forty-four who never learned to connect their head and their heart together. They feel from the neck up. They can intellectualize the world, but they can't feel very much. Their adult self may be intact, but the child self is lost. Then there are others who stay little because they never had the support for growing up at all. Their emotional makeup is infantile. They never learned to think about what they're feeling. If you never learn to intellectualize about your feelings, you never learn to resolve them. Adult children have to go for balance between the two.

Adult children are their own worst critics. There's a phenomenon called "inner-dialogue disorder," and if you were raised with critical parents, you internalize the messages they gave you. You really don't need your parents around today giving you those messages. You give them to yourself, and sometimes adult children literally drown in their own criticism. One way to change these negative messages is by the process of affirmation.

Kids raised with catastrophic stress can come from any kind of emotionally abusing family. Where there's a parent who has some form of compulsive behavior and when the focus is not on the children but on the parent, kids live in a battle zone filled with negative messages. Depending on the age and stage of a child when the catastrophe hits, that child develops a certain view of the world based on parental messages.

If you were born into an alcoholic home, some of the messages that you may have internalized are, "I'm not supposed to be here," "I have to hurry to get what I need," "I was supposed to be a boy instead of a girl," "My needs are not okay," "Pleasure is dangerous," "To say no is disloyal," "I can't think and feel at the same time," and "Setting limits and boundaries is dangerous." Two common messages are obvious: "I'm not lovable" and "I'm not capable." Adult children stay pretty loyal to those messages. Adult children define themselves in terms of the past. Those messages don't go away, and they contaminate adulthood. Some adult children are living with the unmet needs or the perceptions of a scared five- or six-year-old.

Messages from the past rule the lives of adult children from dysfunctional homes today. Part of adult children therapy is making them conscious of that. The question is, "What kinds of dialogue or messages are clouding your perceptions today and what do you do about them?" Recovery is changing those messages and perceptions. Unless you can learn to feed your imagination with different kinds of thoughts, you will continue to see the world in the same way. What you believe, you will become. If you heard it long enough, it begins to be yours. You begin to live life on the perception of that truth. If Dad told you that you're stupid for ten years and Dad loved you, Dad must be right. You conduct your life on the basis of that truth. If you cling to that belief, you self-destruct at some point.

In recovery, you've got to find out what messages exist, which is part of doing a family history and looking at loyalty issues. Adult children are fiercely loyal. Often, when you start to uncover what these messages are and what you were taught and you start to change those messages and therefore your behavior, you feel as if you're going to die. You feel as if you're going to lose the love and affection of a parent who wasn't there for you in the first place. It's a part of grieving and letting go to come to a realistic view of your parents as humans. No one did your past to you on purpose.

After uncovering the messages of the past, the next step is to do affirmations. Start at the very beginning in repairing some of the notions you have of yourself. If you grew up thinking that something's wrong with you and that you're deficient, you might start with the affirmation "I'm a beloved child of God." When you start using that affirmation, pay attention to that little voice inside of you that's going to disagree with what you're saying. That's the little child inside that has to be worked with. When you say, "I'm a beloved child of God," that little voice inside may say, "No, you're not." It can be a parental message, but in adulthood it's hard to discern this.

Take that voice and work with it. That's where the tool of re-parenting comes into play. If that voice says, "You're a miserable kid," say the affirmation again, "I'm a beloved child of God." See what else comes up. Begin a dialogue with those voices that disagree, and gradually you'll learn to become the nurturing parent. Instead of being terrorized by that voice or your dark side, you start to befriend it. You start to embrace yourself and comfort that voice. Sometimes that voice is a parent. Sometimes that voice is a terrorized child. It's hard to know who that voice is, and it doesn't really matter anymore. The war that adult children are waging now is not against their parents: the war they're waging is with themselves. It's an internal civil war. The point is, don't run away from those messages anymore, and even though you don't believe the affirmation yet, it is what you need to believe.

Affirmation is not another way to run away from yourself. It's different from positive thinking. Positive thinking is often putting frosting on a rotten cake. Sometimes people use the notion of positive thinking to layer over what they feel and abandon themselves further.

When your thoughts start to change, very gradually your behavior will follow. The task for adult children is to have feelings, behaviors, and beliefs congruent. That's when your mental world will be aligned with your spiritual world. Adult children grew up in families where people said one thing and did another. In adulthood, adult children act one way, feel another, and believe in ways that are incongruent with both. Affirmations motivate you to behave differently and get that behavior aligned with what you're believing now. Through affirmation over a period of time, an adult child can really end up choosing health and joy and love.

As adult children start to get healthier they seem to attract people to them who are more positive. Mentors or sponsors can be helpful in learning about affirming yourself, but it's still internal work. You can have positive people in sponsorship, but unless you're at a point of readiness and open your heart to take it in, it's like bouncing off a steel wall.

In the past I have been negative, afraid, and self-righteous. My new self is more easygoing, trusting, and forgiving. Recovery is working for me, and doors are opening, leading to new possibilities.

Along with self-parenting, I have been using affirmations. Some of them I read from Rokelle Lerner's wonderful *Daily Affirmations for Adult Children of Alcoholics* and others I make up for myself. I also use the advice of Sharon Wegscheider-Cruse and Cathleen Brooks. I have identified some very good, positive people in my life, some old and some new, and I have been asking them to tell me how well I'm doing when I am struggling.

Recently on a plane trip after meeting Rokelle, I wrote myself an affirmation letter, which I shared with the Group. I asked each of them to write a letter too. Since the Group had spent so many intense hours together, these letters—very personal self-affirmations—brought tears of happiness, smiles, and applause as each person read his or her letter aloud.

Dear Dennis,

I'm really proud of what you have made of yourself. Many people care about you and love you, and many more have been touched by your television work, books, public speaking, counseling, and support. At the very core of you is a deep commitment to sharing what you have learned about yourself with other people. I have watched you mature from a sad and hurt child —through a very painful adolescence and early adulthood—to a sensitive, thoughtful, and caring adult. From the depths of despair of alcoholism you have navigated into the sunlight of your recovery today.

I often think those of us around you love you more than you

do yourself. It's a thought you might consider so that you can smell the flowers of life right now. You certainly deserve to. Put more fun into your life. More play will make your life even more enjoyable.

I love you just the way you are. Your values, passions, feelings, humor, goodness, age, and special gifts are what make you you. As your friend Father Quinn would say, "You are an unrepeatable mystery of God." It's important that I say all this to you now. It's long overdue. Just keep being who you are and growing.

I love you, — Dennis —

Dear Audrey,

It has taken years, but I want you to know today that I love you. It isn't easy for me, but it's going to become easier. Starting today with this letter, you're going to hear over and over until it becomes ingrained that I love you. Let's bury the past and go forward.

I've watched you grow and develop, and I'm so proud of you. You've overcome numerous obstacles, proving that you are strong. Your accomplishments are numerous and you're going on to do bigger and better things. The bitterness is all behind. You speak so often of your fears, but you're going to let those go; you're going forward to victory. Fear is being replaced with unconditional love, love for yourself, love for all others, and love for God.

What's past is past. Enjoy this day today, and tomorrow, tomorrow. You've done very well and I'm proud of you.

Love,

Audrey

P.S.: You're no longer a victim, you're a child of God—courageous, strong, and able to deal with you.

Dear Dick,

I want to tell you how very proud I am of you. You had a pretty rough time as a kid in a home that wasn't very warm and healthy.

The fact that you have enjoyed such a long time in recovery from both alcoholism and gambling is an outstanding accomplishment. Your friends see you as "honest, spiritual, and generous—a kind person with integrity and a willingness to help others." I know this is true because I've asked them about you. I agree with them 100 percent.

You used to be ashamed and filled with guilt over the many things you did while you were gambling and drinking. You believed you had a punishing God. In AA you found a forgiving and loving God. Once you had a secure feeling that God loved you, you became comfortable with Him and with yourself.

Your commitment to your wife, your family, and the AA program has taught many people about the important things in life and unconditionally loving others.

Congratulations.

Love,

Dick

Dear Lynn,

Your father recently said to you, "Look at all you've accomplished since you've been back." He is right; you've done so much since leaving your marriage.

You're doing very well professionally, your daughter is doing well in school and has many friends, you've made new friends and cultivated old ones, and you're dating and dealing with men again.

Most important, you stand up and speak up for yourself—both at work and in your relationships. If you feel uncomfortable, you say so. If you don't want to do things, you don't. You eat well, exercise, and take time out for yourself. You've done all of this on your own with a child. You've demonstrated that you don't need a partner, but you've expressed the feeling that you might be open if the right man comes along.

Remember back when you were debating whether to leave your marriage? You had a nice house, two dogs, a good job, friends, a baby, and a nice life. You were thirty-five and scared—thinking that no one would be interested in you and that life would end. You thought then that you'd raise your child in solitude and misery. The worrying you went through was worse than the reality. Today you don't have to worry about when your husband will take his next drink, not attend to the baby, or get in a car accident. In contrast, your life today is peaceful and consistent. The risk you took was definitely worth it.

Your husband recently entered a hospital and is now sober. Hopefully he'll remain that way and continue to send gifts to your daughter and communicate with her. It may be too late for both of you, but you could never again live your life around whether he'll drink again or not. He does have the opportunity, if sober, to enjoy his daughter; and most important, your daughter will have a father and not a fantasy of him.

"Look at all you've accomplished." I'm very proud of you.

Love,

Lynn

Alice,

I'm so happy that you are getting help, that you are learning to love yourself. It gives me joy to know about your daughter and that you did not deny yourself the fulfillment of parenting. I see you are doing a wonderful job and have a secure, happy child. Know she's loved. I want that for you—to be secure and happy and to know that you're loved.

You have done much to free yourself from your past. You have an education, you are married to a good man, you're able to give love to your students and child. I want for you to learn to give love to yourself, to accept love from others, and to be free from the past that has haunted you. I want you to feel those feelings which you fear so.

It is okay to be angry with people you love and to love people you are angry with. You will not die, and they will not leave you or die. You will become real if you let those feelings through. You will love and be loved, you will not be alone or afraid, you will be secure and happy and loved. I love you enough to let you grow.

I love you,

Alice

Dear Jim,

You have grown up in a dysfunctional home. You became what you learned and did it well. Alcoholic parent, alcoholic child. Having a long childhood, you began to grow up at forty. Upon entering AA, you are now a seventeen-year-old adult emotionally. You had no respect for self or received any from work, play, relationships, or church. Today you have gained self-respect and the respect of all those around you, especially your family. Some do not like you, but they do respect you. I know today if you continue in your program, all areas of your life will be okay.

Love,

Jim

Dear Jeffrey,

I am proud of your efforts and of you. You have really become a good, loving person. You've continued to try to grow and worked hard at becoming an even better person than you already are. I appreciate the fact you don't give up. I know the road hasn't been an easy one. Continue to show what enthusiasm and hope you can give to people. Your compassion and warmth for others have truly given you the dignity that I know you try to give to others. Know that I applaud your efforts. Know that I love and respect you.

Love,

Jeff

Dear Jan,

I'm writing this letter to tell you how very proud I am of where you are today and the person you have become. You grew up

through a dreadful childhood with a very unhappy family. You
entered into and remained for too many years in a disastrous
marriage. You did your best with four children, raising them and
trying to give them a love that you had never experienced. Three
of them, too, became chemically dependent. You nurtured and saw
two of them through treatment and today have a tremendous
bonding with them. You have turned your life around, first, by
accepting and doing something about your alcoholism; second, by
going out and being successful in the world rather late in life; and
third, by having the strength to end your marriage because you
believe a better life lies ahead.

You are trying to help your children with the changes in their
lives by sharing your own strengths and experiences. Your sense
of decency and humor and your love for those dear to you are
shining through.

Love,

Jan

Dear Brian,

I needed to write this letter to you to tell you some things that I
feel you need to remind yourself of more often. First, when I
remember where you've come from in the past two and a half
years—to have the courage to break through the denial of an
incredibly bad childhood; to devote the energy, time, and
resources to personal growth, becoming the real you; to take the
risks associated with healthy change—I admire your strength.
Second, while letting go of the bad from the past, you have kept
the good—your intellect, your ability to succeed in the business
world, and your positive drive and energy. Third, getting in touch
with your physical self—your body—you are taking care of it,
being comfortable with it and enjoying it, as well as your sexuality,
on a real level, not as a mechanical performer. Fourth, your ability
to love and care for your family, your friends, and others, and most
of all for yourself, helps them to grow on a healthy basis.

I know you will feel better and better about yourself and love
yourself even more in the future. I hope you remember each day to

continue taking charge of your life, to first of all please yourself, to
continue to become the real you, to love yourself unconditionally,
and to know God is there to help you to have fun.

Love,

Brian

Dear Harry,

I wanted to let you know that I'm glad you were born and that
I admire your ability to take the care that I was able to offer and
somehow use it to survive. I'm deeply sorry that you carried our
shame. I see you work and work, striving to become something for
me. I wish I could say, "Slow down, that's enough." You already
are. You'll understand it when it's easier for you to play a good
parent and let yourself be a child again. I guess I just want you to
see how much meaning you bring to life even when you're doing
that. I wish you'd be able to brag about your ability to play, even
though there was no one there to help you celebrate having fun.

I'm proud of the way you could put together what was there
and find ways to get what you need and want in the world today. I
think you're capable and strong enough to feel afraid. You've
become courageous in all the things your new brothers and sisters
say you are.

Love,

Harry

Dear Beth,

You have taken the cards that were dealt to you and parlayed
your unique circumstances, talents, and passions into a winning
hand. Luck helped, but so did hard work and skill. Be proud of
yourself for having built a rich life that includes good friends, a
loving family, enjoyable work, and hobbies. Use the good things
that were taught to you as a child—responsibility to God, family,
and country—and throw out the garbage. Be grateful for your luck
and never forget to say, "Thank you"; but realize that none of
what makes you you could happen without you.

Celebrate each day as it comes, though realize that pain is a part of the plan. It's what makes life interesting, so don't be afraid of dealing with old pains and discovering that greater joys and peace can grow out of the struggle. Be good.

Love,

Beth

Dear Manolito,

I'd like to begin by reminding you that from now on, you will be first and foremost on my list of loved ones. To you, I will devote all my attention, affection, and health so that you can continue healing, so that you can experience the joy of life and God's love, and so that you can ultimately accomplish your mission of helping others to heal and find God's love within themselves and in their brothers and sisters. You have understood and accepted that mission, and that makes me very happy and proud.

I also want to congratulate you for your achievements, the first being surviving; the second, succeeding professionally on such an international scale; the third, getting clean and sober, getting into the minute percentage which accomplishes that; and the fourth, being exactly where you are—alive, well, healing, and getting ready to heal others.

I'd like to remind you that as a reward for your dedication to healing, I am here for you to help you in becoming all that God wants you to and everything you ever dreamed of being. I am here to take you to meetings, to play with you, to help you organize and get your projects going, to help you keep in touch with the finest collection of friends and leaders God can give a person, and to help you find God.

I love you,

Manolito

Dear Karen,

I love you, and I wanted you to know that. You've been through hell and back, a lot of it caused by me. I ask your forgiveness for all the things I did or didn't do. I never meant to deprive you of anything. I simply didn't know any better. I'm so proud of what you have accomplished and the obstacles you have overcome to get there. Your strength is a source of strength for me. I know I placed far too many responsibilities on you as a child; in fact, I never let you be a child. I'm so glad that you are now learning what I should have taught you many years ago. Your determination to overcome all that's been dealt you is astounding. You never give up. I'm so proud of your professional accomplishments. It seems I can tell everyone that but you.

Now you've grown into a beautiful, sensitive woman. I know how much you want to help others. You have and you will. I know you'll continue to help yourself too. Thank God, you're able to give yourself what I couldn't give you. Surround yourself with people like you—positive, spiritual, curious. The others are poison. I can't wait to see what you'll accomplish next. I love you unconditionally; I wish it had always been so. You deserve the best and then some. I'm so proud to be your parent; you'll teach us all a thing or two.

Love,

Karen

Michael,

Getting to know you is so exciting. You have so many qualities that can enliven those people around you. You have a right to be angry. It's a healthy sign. It proves that you know that you deserve respect and acceptance and love just as you are. You needn't prove anything to anyone.

I would remind you that your fear is merely excitement that can't find hope. As you emerge and accept God's help, and the love of me and others who will not hurt you, your hope will grow. You have stood courageously alone. Steadfastly clinging to your integrity, strength, determination, and creative perseverance your effort is, as I've come to see it for the first time, an inspiring example of courage. You have no right to forget that or to deny that anymore. To do so is to deny God and His work. I understand your caution. I'm here to help you learn and test your growth.

I love you,   Michael

Dear Mary,

I never told you how much I love you and care for you. I have watched you grow and turn into a beautiful, loving, creative young woman. I remember watching you in your disease, a scared and lonely child so afraid of being you, always trying to be what other people wanted you to be. Now before my eyes I see energy, strength, and hope. You're starting to resolve the pain of your unloving past. The tapes from your past are not playing as loud.

Mary, you are a victim of a war. I'm glad to see that you're cleaning out the dirt and the debris from your past. Finally wounds can be healed. The past is no longer an accurate scale for deciding what you can and cannot do. Your life is your choice. May it be everything that you want.

I love you,

14

A NEW LIFE

Once adult children discover their self-worth, discard the negative influences of the past, and adopt new attitudes and behaviors, recovery delivers the gift of life itself.

The members of the Group have shared themselves with you, hoping you might see yourself on these pages. This adult children business may be new to you. However, if you can identify with the stories, pain, and hope, you can have what we have. Recovery requires honesty, faith, effort, and time. It's worth it all.

From time to time in my own life now, I experience total tranquillity, total calmness. In those minutes or days, I am so internally centered that no person, event, or situation can move me from that place of peacefulness. It's an absolutely wonderful feeling. Those minutes and days will turn into weeks and months as I continue to grow. I know it will get even better than it is today.

In recovery each adult child moves at his or her own pace and life gets easier and happier. Sometimes it's three steps forward and two steps backward, but it's recognizable progress, day after day.

On this journey to freedom we begin to know who we really are and we like it. It feels good, and feeling good is the way we are supposed to feel.

J E F F ► Recovery for me means getting on with it. To hold things against my mother and father won't help my situation. I learned some positive lessons from my father. He taught me to work hard and to persevere. Things have gotten tough on me quite a few times, and it was some of the lessons that I learned from him that kept me going. I take what I need from my past and leave the rest. To move forward and become the kind of person I want to be is my goal. The role models I have now are the key for me. I can ask help from other people and use the benefit of their experiences to help me grow.

J A N ► I was becoming stuck in my recovery from alcoholism when I discovered how to deal with my adult children issues. My childhood happened. I can't go through the rest of my life saying, "Well, because I was brought up in an alcoholic home . . ." I know I feel today that I can get back into the world. I learned tremendous survival skills from my whole early experience. I really credit that for my being able to deal with my alcoholism. One thing sticks in my mind that I learned from my parents: "You get out of life what you put into it."

MICHAEL ▸ The whole recovery process for me boils down to simply growing toward autonomy as an adult human being. It also means learning for myself, and for my own parenting of my children, that it is not blame for my folks to acknowledge strong feelings that my inner child has always had—his anger, his rage, and his pain. To look at it as blame and avoid the feelings is in fact the disease at work.

I'm rather proud of the work I've done. I got one strong lesson from my family, which is fairly religious, and it was that we are all made in God's image and likeness. They had a sense that their family was not normal, and they were all kind of floundering. They were humble enough to acknowledge that maybe they didn't have it all down pat. But they kept telling me that in spite of anything that went on in that house or the way they dealt with me, I was perfect because God made me. I am incredibly grateful to them for having instilled that message in me. Because of that, I keep finding that message throughout my adult life in meaningful places like AA and ACA. I just can't express enough of my gratefulness to my family for that. They gave me the seeds to be able to do what I'm doing.

BETH ▸ Recovery means looking at the past, dealing with it, and learning from it. It's sorting through all of the mess of messages and getting rid of the bad ones. There were things I didn't learn, so I must learn some new things. I know I have to deal with the past before I can move forward. I see a lot of good coming out of that process. I don't blame my parents at all for how they parented me. Getting angry with them is a good, healthy thing for me to do, but then it's important to let it rest. I can be thankful to my parents for a sense of responsibility toward other people. That's a civic responsibility. I also thank them for my sense of integrity; they're very honest people. Also I've developed a sense of loyalty to my family from them. Doing things out of a sense of duty, even though I might not want to, is something that my parents taught me.

AUDREY ▸ Recovery to me means I must reinvent myself. The ideas are already inside of me and the changes I am making are made clear and visible to me almost daily. I'm learning not to blame my parents. I frequently talked to my mother about prayer in certain situations. I thought my mother was being hard and cold when she would ask, "Well, what are you going to do about it?" That would frequently make me angry because I really hadn't planned to do much of anything beyond praying and waiting. That was my style—pray and wait. When nothing happened, I would get angry. One thing I learned from my mother was that after prayer you go into action. That's always been her style. I said frequently my mother made poor choices. She did some things that were wrong, some things that were good. Choices or decisions that she made did not always turn out well. Now I know that at least she did something. I see that as growth for me. So I learned action from her. All of the affirmations weren't there from my parents. Many things were missing.

However, I keep thinking about a little toy sewing machine that is now in our den, up on a shelf. I put it there some years ago because it was a gift from my dad; it's the only thing that I have from him. We ordered it out of a catalog. When it came, it worked for maybe five minutes and never worked again. But I always held onto it. On my seventeenth birthday I came home from school, and there was a brand new Singer electric sewing machine that my mother gave me for my birthday. All of the neighbors were amazed because here was a gift from a woman who made two dollars a day. I'm grateful because from that Singer, there's a Touchtronic completely computerized sewing machine in my home right now, and it grew from that. The hugs weren't there. All of the words of love weren't there, but that was my mother's way of caring and saying, "I love you." She saw something in me, and it's never left me. I've never been without a sewing machine since I was a child. So I'm grateful, I'm growing, letting go of the bitterness and the feelings of deprivation. My parents were limited but not all bad, and I'm appreciative.

In recovery I've learned all I had to do was to look within. For so long I was looking outside and trying to control. I was making darn sure that those things that happened long ago didn't happen again. This is what has created the problem with my kids. I have learned that you start with self. If you change yourself, all of these other things will right themselves. It's so simple and so amazing.

This morning I looked out the kitchen window at an evergreen tree. It had snow on the branches, and on one branch was a cardinal. My heart leapt. I was amazed. I stayed there for several minutes watching this bird, and I thought it was the most beautiful thing. When I was caught up with all of the fear and worry, I missed all of the beauty that's in the world. I didn't see it; I just wasn't there.

B RIAN ▸ Recovery is the most painful thing I've ever done but also the most joyous. It's a relief to know there really was something wrong with my childhood and with my family and that it wasn't my fault. It's very freeing to be myself, to make my own choices, to take risks, and to make mistakes. Just lately I've been able to get in touch with the fact that my parents, like me, were abused adult children of alcoholics, both of them. I've gotten to feel sad that they died ignorant of that, but I suspect that they always knew deep inside, as I did, that there was something wrong, even though they tried so hard to project on the outside that everything was right. Somehow, feeling that sadness, I can begin the process of forgiveness.

A LICE ▸ I see recovery as choices. Today I have the ability to stop living a life of actions and reactions that I was doing without knowing why but was going to do anyway. It was a compulsive life and I'm stopping that cycle. I need to look at my past. I need to feel the feelings that go along with that. To feel those feelings but leave them behind has been the most difficult part. I don't need to drag that around with me for the rest of my life. I see myself still as a farm girl, a kind of rural damsel, if you will. I live in the country still. I got that from my parents. I like caring for others. That gives me pleasure and joy, and that's something I learned really early in life. Maybe it was inappropriate at that time, but it sure is something that I get reward from now.

D ICK ▸ Where my parents came from was their problem. They had problems with their backgrounds, and they carried those problems on into my life. I'm finding out things as I grow older that I never knew as a child about my parents' families.

I feel so good today because I don't feel unique. I always

felt unique when I was a child. Nobody understood how I felt inside. Nobody understood the home that I was brought up in and nobody understood my parents. The discovery I've made is the fact that I am not alone anymore. I am not alone. I'm an alcoholic, but people have many kinds of addictions. We are all trying to escape. I thought my family was different from other families. We weren't really. Prior to coming to a group or prior to seeking therapy, we're alone because we don't think anybody understands. Once we're able to reveal ourselves the answers to our problems come. Those answers have come for me.

H ARRY ▸ Recovery is being able to do the work of loving. If my marriage were based on feelings, my finger would be bloody because the feelings change and I would be ripping my ring off all the time. Recovery is my ability to meet my needs and the needs of those people with whom I enter into relationships. When I think those needs are authentic, I can move to meet them, and when I think they're not authentic, I can frustrate them. Recovery means I don't have to relapse into a frantic round of attempts to create a false self and another addictive relationship with a drug or a woman or a hobby.

There are many identifications I got from my parents that are healthy. My love of words and ideas and of the ability of ideas to generate feelings and action in my life is profound. I'm deeply grateful to my mother for that. My bed's made today because my dad liked to show me how to make a bed when I was little. That's the way I stay in touch. Recovery means I can get back in touch with loving him too. All the mistakes my parents made were worthwhile; look how I turned out. I'm willing to make my own mistakes with my own child. I want to be a father, and if I make mistakes, that will be okay because my child will turn out alright. I've had to guess at what normal was when it came to parenting myself. I've been able to discover the creative ways I survived as a child and break a pattern that's gone on for a long time. Even as I do so, I'm willing to screw up and be accountable. That's something I've never done before. I could never make a mistake, so I could never become a father myself. Now I can.

L Y N N ▸ I really don't blame my parents much for any-thing that occurred. I think that they were victims of their own situation. I love them for who they are today, and we're friends.

I thank my parents for raising me. I could have been in a series of foster homes and never had a real home. Just on a basic level, I thank them for that.

I always cry when it comes to my father; he's always been a friend. He's always stood behind me. He's always said, "What-ever you want to do, I'm behind you." I can see now that's real hard for a parent to say. He's been my base of support my entire life. My mom's given me good common sense. My mother's got a lot of business sense. She's real practical and she's given me that. They're good people.

M A R Y ▸ Recovery for me is choosing what I want for my life today. I know why I do the things I do today; I'm really grateful for that. There are times when I hurt a lot because I'm in the process of recovery; but I know I'm alive, and that's a real gift. As far as parents are concerned, I'm grateful that the pain at home was so bad that it created my disease. I'm breaking the pattern and I'm seeing a light at the end of the tunnel. My mother has a wonderful sense of humor, and I think I've devel-oped some of that. I'm grateful, at twenty-four, to have been around the world twice, and I'm grateful that I've always had education that's been at top level. I'm so grateful to be in this process of recovery. It blows me away that I can talk about all the things I can today; most people my age are talking about what they bought yesterday.

K A R E N ▸ Recovery is freedom. The nightmare's over. The buck stops here. This is one legacy that's not going to be handed down anymore. For thousands of years probably, it has been. I don't know why I have been gifted with the responsibil-ity of stopping it here, but I'm so grateful I have been. I've been given a wonderful gift. I've been given my life back instead of craziness. All my life I took what I didn't need and left the rest. Now I'm learning to take what I need and leave all the other stuff behind because it no longer applies. I have an overwhelm-ing sense of gratitude. I have been saved. God has something very special planned for me, and it's my responsibility to be quiet and let Him work through me and to help as many other people as I possibly can without hurting me. My mom has a tremendous amount of energy. From her I've gotten determination and strength. My dad is a very hard worker, and his sense of responsibility is awesome; he passed a lot of that on to me. Today I love them as they are. They don't have to change; I wish for their own happiness that they could change, but they don't have to. It's not going to affect how I feel about them one way or the other.

MANOLITO ► To me, recovery is understanding and accepting what went on in my childhood and learning how to give and get love in good, healthy, joyous ways today. It's learning to love and care for myself and those I love. To me, recovery is getting in touch with God's unconditional love for me, facing life responsibly, and enjoying life every single minute of life.

JIM ► Recovery is rebirth. When people are told that they're going to die, they go through five stages. The last one is acceptance. When I came into the AA program, the first thing I had to learn was acceptance. It was a reverse of dying. Acceptance was the beginning of learning how to live. Rebirth. I got a chance to relive.

My parents gave me enough for me to want more. That's why I survived. I think my parents tried to play around with human nature and didn't know how. All of us are human, and it's our nature to be unpredictable. The same is true with Mother Nature; she's unpredictable. We do well when things are predictable in a nice, comfortable setting or among friends. It's when we have to get out there and deal with reality we have trouble. We weren't taught how to deal with the reality of life, so we have to learn. Someone wrote in a book, "Tomorrow is sufficient unto itself." Today we're recovered; we're right where we're supposed to be.

JOHN BRADSHAW ► The term "family systems" is only thirty-six years old. We are now discovering a whole new concept of what a family is. We're discovering new laws of emotional life. We're studying intimacy in a way and learning things we've never understood before. The terrible problems in society we've been experiencing—such as massive addictions, divorce, and runaways—signify the tail end of an epoch. A crisis is a time of increased vulnerability but heightened potential.

We're headed for a stronger emotional life. The future will be a time of greater emotional intimacy and inner life. There will be more value and dignity for the individual.

The greatest hope is the recovering community itself. Society, like individuals, has to hit bottom. This dysfunctional tragedy that exists today is the bottom.

In order for alcoholics to get sober, they have to become rigorously honest. They have to quit pretending, develop discipline, and delay gratification. It's the truth at any cost.

I see the recovering community as a great hope for the world. These people have had to get honest, and they've put discipline in their lives in order to be able to live. The attraction of the adult children movement is a phenomenon. What we grew up with, they told us, was love. It wasn't, it was really counterfeit. Recovering adult children are creating new definitions and concepts of family, home, parent, child, and love.

If we can change ourselves, we can change the world.

EPILOGUE

In one of our group meetings, Jeff told the following story:

A man takes his son on an airplane for his first flight. The son's all antsy and nervous. The father goes looking for something to keep his son occupied, and while he's thumbing through a magazine, he sees a picture of the world. He rips out the picture of the world, tears it up into little pieces and hands it to the boy saying, "There, now put that together." The little boy fumbles around with it for a couple of minutes and gets the whole world back together. The father asks, "Well, how did you manage to do that?" And the little boy says, "Well, I didn't really know what the world was supposed to look like so I looked on the other side and there was a picture of a man. I put the man back together, and the world fell into place."

If you are an adult child, you are very special. If you don't know that, you can find out, but you'll need help from others. The opportunity to know yourself and become the person you were meant to be is available for the asking. But you've **got to** ask.

ABOUT
THE
AUTHOR

Dennis Wholey is the author of *The Courage to Change: Personal Conversations About Alcoholism,* and *Are You Happy? Some Answers to the Most Important Question in Your Life* (later published as *Discovering Happiness: How to Get the Most Out of Life*). One of television's most popular interviewers, his PBS series "LateNight America" is broadcast to over 150 stations in the United States and Canada.

BESTSELLING RECOVERY BOOKS
FROM BANTAM

A NEW DAY
365 Meditations for Personal and Spiritual Growth
Anonymous
Offers spiritual and psychological guidance on overcoming
the struggles we face each day, by the author of the bestselling
A Day at a Time.
34591-5   *Paperback* $6.95/$8.95 in Canada

TOXIC PARENTS
Overcoming their Hurtful Legacy and Reclaiming Your Life
Dr. Susan Forward with Craig Buck
The challenging, compassionate and controversial new
guide to recognizing and recovering from the lasting damage
caused by physical or emotional abuse in childhood, by the
bestselling author of *Men Who Hate Women & the Women
Who Love Them*.
05700-6   *Hardcover* $18.95/$23.95 in Canada

800-COCAINE
Mark S. Gold, M.D.
From the leading expert on cocaine abuse and treatment, an
informative, prescriptive manual with hard facts on America's
fastest-growing drug problem.
34388-2   *Large Format Paperback* $3.50/$3.95 in Canada

HOW TO BREAK YOUR ADDICTION TO A PERSON
Howard M. Halpern, Ph.D.
An insightful, step-by-step guide to breaking painful addictive
relationships – and surviving separation.
26005-7   *Paperback* $4.50/$4.95 in Canada

THE ADULT CHILDREN
OF ALCOHOLICS SYNDROME
Wayne Kritsberg
Real help and hope for adult children in a complete self-help
program that shows how to recognize and remedy the effects
of the dysfunctional family.
27279-9   *Paperback* $3.95/$4.95 in Canada

UNDER THE INFLUENCE
A Guide to the Myths and Realities of Alcoholism
James R. Milam, Ph.D. and Katherine Ketcham
This groundbreaking classic emphasizes treating alcoholism as
a physiological disease and offers information on how to tell if
someone is an alcoholic, treatment, and recovery.
27487-2   *Paperback* $4.95/$5.95 in Canada

RECLAIMING OUR LIVES
Hope for Adult Survivors of Incest
Carol Poston and Karen Lison
A comprehensive, inspiring, and supportive guide with
a concrete 14-step program for healing written by an incest
survivor and a therapist.
28497-5   *Paperback* $4.95/$5.95 in Canada

POTATO CHIPS FOR BREAKFAST
The True Story of Growing Up in an Alcoholic Family
Cynthia Scales
The shocking true story of a young girl who grew up with
every material comfort – and two alcoholic parents.
28166-6   *Paperback* $3.50/$4.50 in Canada

BECOMING NATURALLY THERAPEUTIC
A Return to the True Essence of Helping
Jacquelyn Small
The renown workshop leader's inspiring guide for all who
serve as listeners or counselors in the lives of others. Basing
her work on landmark studies, Small helps us "straight-talk"
beyond our co-dependent or controlling ways of helping others
and teaches how to offer clear and loving guidance directly
from the heart.
34800-0   *Large Format Paperback* $7.95/$9.95 in Canada

FAMILY FEELINGS
Daily Meditations for Healthy Relationships
Martha Vanceburg and Sylvia Silverman
Valuable insights on changing destructive family patterns with
one's spouse, children, elderly parents, and grandparents. By
the coauthor of *The Promise of a New Day* and her mother.
34705-5   *Paperback* $6.95/$8.95 in Canada

Prices subject to change.